DEATH'S DECEIVER

LYNN BRIDGERS

Death's Deceiver

THE LIFE OF JOSEPH P. MACHEBEUF

ψ   ψ   ψ

University of New Mexico Press   Albuquerque

Library of Congress Cataloging-in-Publication

Bridgers, Lynn, 1956–

    Death's deceiver : the life of Joseph P. Machebeuf / Lynn Bridgers. — 1st ed.

      p. cm.

    Includes bibliographical references and index.

    ISBN 0-8263-1810-X. (pbk.) — ISBN 0-8263-1803-7

    1. Machebeuf, Joseph Projectus, 1812–1889.   2. Catholic Church — United States — Bishops — Biography.   I. Title.

BX4705.M23B75   1997

282′.092 — dc21   97-4620

                                                       CIP

Contents

Acknowledgments

Perhaps the most pleasant duty in finalizing this manuscript is the opportunity to thank all those who have generously contributed to its completion. My thanks must go first to James Clifton, C.F.X., of the College of Santa Fe, for everything. At the University of San Francisco Lowell Cohn, Ph.D., revived my flagging spirits, taught me everything I know about the verbal critique of writing, and served as mentor, friend and my role model as a successful writer, writing teacher and all round wonderful human being. Peter Carroll, Ph.D., generously contributed not only his perceptive historical perspective and particular knowledge of American religious history, but his incredibly precise editorial eye. Anne Barrows, Ph.D., encouraged me when I first considered writing a biography. Two members of the San Francisco Jesuit Community also deserve special mention. Luis Quihuis, S.J. patiently helped me to explore the Hispanic perspective on Machebeuf's work in New Mexico, Colorado, and Arizona. Cornelius M. Buckley, S.J., kindly graced me with his remarkable scholarship and his extensive knowledge of French ecclesiastical history.

In terms of content, I am indebted to those historians who forged the trail and smoothed my passage. The scholarship and impeccable thoroughness of Paul Horgan, especially in his biography of Jean Baptiste Lamy, cannot be underestimated. W. J. Howlett provided not only his personal insights into Machebeuf's character, but the biography that inspired Willa Cather's *Death Comes for the Archbishop* and first led me to Machebeuf. And Thomas Francis Feely, Ph.D., provided invaluable documentation of Machebeuf's work in Colorado as well as the best understanding of Machebeuf's financial brinkmanship and complex financial ethics. Historian E. A.

Mares offers what I consider the most comprehensive understanding of the role of Padre Martínez in Taos, along with a tremendous breadth of historical knowledge that places Padre Martínez in perspective. Finally, Jesuit historian Thomas J. Steele has been unbelievably generous in sharing his resources, his considerable knowledge of both Martínez and Machebeuf, his sardonic wit, and, most of all, his time. I remain forever indebted to him.

There are many others, too numerous to name, that have contributed. They include the unbelievably patient and helpful staff of Gleeson Library. They also include the archivists of each and every individual archive, but most particularly Sr. Mary Hughes at the Denver Catholic Archives who permitted me to pillage and plunder her Machebeuf files. Unrecognized guardians of historical treasures, I cannot adequately express my gratitude for all the archivists' responses to most peculiar inquiries, their patience in retrieving and sharing materials, their suggestions in following sometimes obscure leads and directing my further inquiries.

I also thank my editors at the University of New Mexico Press: David Holtby, for his patience, direction, and understanding, and Barbara Guth, for seeing me through the perilous path to print.

Behind the academic, historical, and literary contributors stand those who have kept me going on a personal level. At the top of that list are Don Forée, John Carmody, and the late and much-loved Walter E. McCarthy, S.J., who collectively have seen me through waters rougher than the worst of Machebeuf's trans-Atlantic crossings. Behind them stand my many friends, new and old. You know who you are, and the depth of my gratitude to each of you. On the perimeter are my writing students at the University of San Francisco and Scottsdale Community College, who believed in my abilities even when I didn't and taught me more than I ever hoped to know about writing.

The foundation for the structure of my intellectual pursuits has been, and will always be, my family. You know who you are, too, and by now you have learned more than you ever wanted to know about Machebeuf. Finally, my gratitude must begin and end with Joseph Machebeuf, mon cher Père Machebeuf, for his life, his letters, and his courage, but especially, ultimately, for being himself.

Introduction

In the late afternoon, the shadow cast by the statue of Jean Baptiste Lamy stretches long, blanketing the flagstone in front of St. Francis Cathedral in Santa Fe. Growing up in New Mexico meant growing up in Lamy's shadow. As a child I savored apricots, poached from descendants of the trees Lamy planted. Late spring meant lilacs, trips to Tesuque, and luncheon at Bishop's Lodge, down the terraced hill from Lamy's final retreat. On holidays friends brought delicate wines made from Lamy's grapes, practically the only mature vines in the area.

Having grown up in that long shadow, it was easy to recognize the real Archbishop Lamy standing behind Willa's Cather's character Jean Marie Latour. When I first read Willa Cather's *Death Comes for the Archbishop*, I realized Cather had done remarkably little to disguise her protagonist, merely changed his name. But in that novel I also found a mystery. Father Vaillant, the character who provides much of the adventure and excitement, was Latour's best friend. Was there a historical counterpart for the colorful figure of Vaillant, just as there was for Latour?

I turned to Paul Horgan's scholarly biography *Lamy of Santa Fe*. There, I first met the man who would become as well known to me as my closest friends. There, lurking in Lamy's shadow, I first met Joseph Machebeuf, the historical basis for Cather's Father Vaillant.

There is something magical about Machebeuf. Historian Thomas Feely once observed that almost everyone who comes into contact with him is somehow charmed, somehow enchanted by his dynamic, impulsive character. Paul Horgan was no exception. Willa Cather was no exception. Neither was I. A baker's son born in a small village in the Auvergne province of

France, Machebeuf attended seminary with Lamy. After ordination he began his priestly life in a small rural village, while waiting for the younger Lamy to finish his own seminary training. Together the two friends planned a life of adventure in the foreign missions. Together they would cross the American continent in what can be considered the most dramatic period of expansion in American history. Ultimately making nine trans-Atlantic crossings, Machebeuf traversed both the Old World and the New. In Europe he met with three successive popes; he brazenly solicited funds from the French royal family and was at home in the sophisticated urban centers of Paris and Rome. In America he lived ten years on the Ohio frontier witnessing wave after wave of German and Irish immigration. A decade later, in the Southwest, Machebeuf became a reliable guide on the Santa Fe Trail, traveled almost every path ever cut through the Rockies, and rode overland to Guymas, then inland to Alamos, Mexico, deep in the Sierra Madre. He worked with miners and mestizos, with bishops and buffalo hunters, and undertook solitary travels over thousands of miles to minister to scattered families and communities in isolated areas.

Machebeuf's journeys were not for the timid. Dubbed Trompe la Mort, Death's Deceiver, by fellow Auvergnat Amadeus Rappe, Machebeuf repeatedly proved himself deserving of the title. He swam ashore from a midwinter shipwreck in the freezing waters of Lake Ontario. The indomitable Machebeuf survived typhoid, cholera, dysentery, and malaria. He had a run-in with an angry murderer outside of Tucson, fell off a mountain in Colorado, was attacked by Plains tribesmen on the Santa Fe Trail, looked down the rifle barrels of displeased rancheros, and even confronted a pistol-waving priest. Small wonder that in his later years, as the first bishop of Denver, he was relatively unfazed by the displeasure of the Roman Curia when a formal inquiry was made into what historian Thomas Feely termed his "financial brinkmanship."

In view of his remarkable life, it is surprising that Machebeuf is not better known. The only previous biography, written by W. C. Howlett, a Roman Catholic priest who served under Machebeuf in Colorado, was published in 1908. When I pulled a copy off the shelf of the Jesuits' Gleeson Library in San Francisco, it had been untouched for years — bleached into the cover was the outline of the book next to it. Yet it was Howlett's biography that introduced both Lamy and Machebeuf to Willa Cather, and Howlett's biography that served as the unrecognized and unacknowledged foundation for the better-known *Death Comes for the Archbishop*.

Perhaps the most controversial aspect of Machebeuf's life involves his work with New Mexico's Hispanic clergy following the dual shocks of annexation by the United States and the imposition of European clergy. As often as not, Machebeuf served as a lightning rod for Archbishop Lamy, deflecting anger and becoming the bearer of bad tidings. It was Machebeuf who traveled to Taos to deliver the formal excommunication of Padre Martínez, probably the most influential man in the New Mexico Territory. Machebeuf, too, delivered the suspension of the suave Padre Gallegos in Albuquerque when Gallegos's proclivity for long trading trips, grape brandy, and gambling were deemed unseemly.

Machebeuf's life serves as an important reminder that the fourth flag to fly over New Mexico was French. The French influence in New Mexico is often overlooked. Machebeuf's life shows us how divisions between the Spanish and the French in the Old World carried over to the New. A legacy of mutual distrust between the Spanish and the French served as the rocky riverbed over which many Anglo and Hispanic conflicts flowed. With the arrival of Lamy and Machebeuf, the French seemed to have accomplished ecclesiastically what they were unable to do militarily, moving their sphere of influence from the French lands of the Louisiana Purchase into traditionally Spanish-dominated New Mexico. Actually they were closer to the ecclesiastic equivalent of Kearny's quiet capture in 1846, the establishment of Fort Marcy, and the arrival of American U.S. government in Santa Fe. Appointed by the American bishops in Baltimore, and not the bishop of Durango, Lamy and Machebeuf's arrival brought northern Europeans directly into the heart and soul of New Mexican Catholicism. Machebeuf, as historic point man for the small flood of French clergy to follow, had to bear the friction of that position. He bore the brunt of reactions against Lamy in particular and Anglo-Europeans in general. Machebeuf was well chosen for the task, because above all, Machebeuf was a great pastor. Machebeuf had interpersonal abilities that allowed him to flourish in even the most potentially unfavorable situations. They may have come to like him grudgingly, but almost everyone eventually came to like him. He may have been the man chosen to "fouetter les chats," to fight with the cats, but he almost always emerged unscathed.

Machebeuf's personal views of Hispanic culture reflect a long, complex process of maturation. His early work was sometimes darkened by ignorance and misconceptions about New Mexico's Hispanic Catholicism, but by the end of his life he had grown far beyond mere tolerance, to a deep love and respect for the Spanish-speaking people of the American Southwest. One of his primary concerns in the selection of his successor was whether the individual chosen would be a good shepherd for Colorado's Hispanic communities. And while he became fluent in Spanish, he never really achieved the same level of comfort and fluency in English, which somehow failed to speak to his romantic soul.

Machebeuf did not always find success in his endeavors. And if Machebeuf was not able to bring definitive solutions to the issues he faced, it is, most likely, because no solutions were to be found. Many of those issues remain unresolved today. Machebeuf faced questions of democracy versus authoritarianism in Church structure. He struggled with the integration of minorities in a strictly delineated hierarchy. He tried to impose standards of sexual conduct for the clergy, in communities that neither supported nor demanded clerical celibacy. Machebeuf confronted the Irish question in immigrant parishioners' support of the Fenians and felt the bitterness of discrimination himself at the hands of the Know-Nothings, the no-Popery movement. He struggled with the problems created by the rapid growth of urban Denver and the ever-increasing demand for services that growth created. He found himself stretched between the past, the difficulties of transition created by the U.S. annexation of New Mexico, and the future, an increasingly secular society that no longer recognized the church as the sole source of moral authority.

And yet, in spite of the difficulties Machebeuf encountered, in spite of the illnesses and accidents he survived, one of the most integral and admirable parts of his character was his optimism. Regardless of the size of the challenges he faced, the distances of the landscape he traversed, or the weight of the responsibilities he shouldered, Machebeuf never lost his hopeful outlook. In seven decades of life, I found only one point when his determined optimism wavered. His discouragement was certainly understandable; it was prior to his consecration to the episcopacy, when the crippled but still energetic Machebeuf contemplated the added burdens — responsibility for manpower, fund-raising, building and administration of the Colorado Catholic Church — without any prospect of significant help.

Ultimately, it is Machebeuf's indomitable spirit that retains its appeal across time. Even Cather, a visual writer noted for her extensive physical descriptions, was taken more by his great soul than by the body that housed it, describing the same in her portrait of Father Vaillant, the character based on Machebeuf. "There was certainly nothing in his outer case to suggest the fierceness and fortitude and fire of the man," she writes. "If the Bishop returned to find Santa Fe friendly to him, it was because everybody believed in Father Vaillant — homely, real, persistent, with the driving power of a dozen men in his poorly built body."[1]

It is poignant, touching really, that Machebeuf was willing to stand back in the shadows, to allow his close friend Lamy to serve as the focal point for both the Roman Catholic hierarchy and for history. But perhaps the time has finally come when Machebeuf, one of the most intriguing, amusing, and appealing characters in southwest history, can be brought into the forefront and receive just a small portion of the recognition he so richly deserves.

April 1996
Phoenix, Arizona

Part One

Citizen-Priest: France

1812–1839

ONE

The Auvergnat

↓

Spring comes late in the high country. Although it was past Easter, the bright Sunday morning was cold. Cool air swept down off the snows that still blanketed the nearby mountains, swept across the empty plaza, and cut through the tension that filled the small town of Taos in the spring of 1858. Stark branches of stately cottonwoods, not yet fully leafed, cast a pale filigree of shade on the beaten dust of the plaza, but the doors of adobe homes and shops were closed against the threat of trouble. Only a lone mongrel, hungry, with nose close to the ground, wandered unaware across the deserted square.

The men came from the east. They were a mismatched group, Hispanic and Anglo, a mix of dirty denim and leather over dusty boots, of woolen waistcoats and string ties beneath battered hats. On foot, they moved down the east side of the plaza, to a spot near the southeast corner, stopping in front of Carlos Beaubien's house.[1] Beaubien emerged, revolvers snug on his hips. He tipped his hat to Kit Carson, the leader of the group, then nodded solemnly to Carson's in-laws, the men of Don Franciso Jaramillo's family, and to Céran St. Vrain, the French fur-trader. The men arced into a semi-circle around the doorway, waiting for the man who brought them together, whose bodyguard they formed.

Joseph Machebeuf stepped out of the dark doorway and blinked in the clear, wintry sunlight. Although only forty-five, he looked a dozen years older. His face was weathered, his once fair skin a burnished brown, aged by sun and wind. His blue eyes seemed bleached by years of exposure, strangely pale against his sun-browned skin, sharpest when fixed on distant horizons. His hair, once blond, was now the color of land without water, a

9

sandy indistinct color, a rough, dry thatch framing his angular face. His thin frame was lost in his heavy vestments, his Roman collar too big for his thin neck. But most striking about the small man was his smile — a heavenly smile that lit up his plain face — it illuminated the blue eyes, exuded peace and confidence, bringing a welcome sense of surety to the tense group of men surrounding him. Smiling calmly, nodding reassuringly to the members of the group, he set about his grim business. Together they headed down the south side of the plaza.

Passing the closed trading posts, they crossed Camino de la Placita and made their way toward the church just west of the plaza. Here the streets were no longer empty. Small groups of men were scattered around, some armed and menacing, some seemingly just curious. One group slouched against the wall in front of Padre Martínez's house, hats pulled low, hands in pockets. Another stood at the corner of Don Fernando and Camino de la Placita, voices low as they commented on the approaching priest. More huddled beneath the trees that sheltered the church.

The wooden doors to Nuestra Señora de Guadalupe were open, and even from a distance the hum of the voices that filled the church could be clearly heard. On each side of the entryway more men gathered, those who could not find a place inside, now murmuring, now going silent as the priest and his companions passed by them. His companions stopped just inside the open doorway, falling away, but Machebeuf continued up the aisle alone.

The church was filled, teeming with people, flooding into the overflow outside. Here were the missing women, filling the seats on either side of the aisle, dark heads bowed beneath feathered hats, dark mantillas, or humble shawls. The men lined the walls, a rough mix, hats in hands, shifting uncomfortably, as if unconsciously resisting the constraints of the pious environment. The tension was a tangible presence. It hung, like an unwelcome visitor, over the crowd and streamed out the open doors, drifting through the dusty town. Everyone knew. Everyone was there. Everyone expected trouble. Today was the day Padre Martínez was to be excommunicated.

Machebeuf moved slowly up the aisle. Fr. Juan Eulógio Ortiz, the newest resident pastor of the church, fell in step behind the French prelate. The two men stepped up to the altar, then, after bowing, bent and kissed it. Immediately Machebeuf launched into the High Mass, his voice droning in sonorous Latin, the crowd calming and settling, reassured by the familiar ritual.

With the homily the reassurance fled. Burdened by a heavy French accent, Machebeuf began an explanation of the nature of excommunication.

Excommunication, he explained, was the most serious punishment the church could pronounce. One who was excommunicated was separated from the body of the faithful, separated from the life-giving sacraments of the church, and denied a Christian burial. Through this act, the excommunicant lost the general graces of the church.[2] Padre Martínez's faults were grave. He had shown disobedience and insubordination. In taking his disagreements with Bishop Lamy into public, Padre Martínez had shown himself rebellious and contumacious, and it was this last element that predisposed him to his punishment. From this day forward Padre Martínez must be considered vitandi, one to be shunned. He must be avoided in society, lest his articulate nature and rebellious stance further confuse the community and endanger their souls. Machebeuf explained that even excommunication, the most extreme of the church's punishments, was meant to be medicinal. Its purpose was to bring the lost sheep back to the fold, back to contrition and fulfillment of duty, back to a life of grace. It was not Bishop Lamy, he concluded, that denied the life of grace to Padre Martínez, but Martínez himself, whose stubborn nature would not permit him to acquiesce and accept the bishop's instructions, to regain the mercy God so freely dispensed. Dramatically Machebeuf unrolled a sheet of paper and slowly read the decree of excommunication. His work complete, Machebeuf made a final announcement for the benefit of any of Padre Martínez's supporters who had the desire to return to the bishop's good graces. He would remain in Taos for the entire week. He would help Father Ortiz in hearing confessions.[3]

The room was silent. Padre Martínez was the most influential man in Taos, perhaps in the entire New Mexico Territory. He was not just a man of great learning and political acumen, not just a leading citizen, a landowner, Padre Martínez was their priest. Padre Martínez was the man who had baptized most of those present in the church, including the convert Kit Carson. Padre Martínez was the man who had blessed their marriages, heard their confessions, and buried their dead for the last thirty years. Padre Martínez was a native son, born in nearby Santa Rosa de Abiquiú, who had lived in Taos a lifetime, and now grew old beside them. And this stranger, this light-eyed foreigner came to condemn their padre? Besides, the foreigner would soon be on his way. First to Arroyo Hondo to fulminate the excommunication of Martínez's primary supporter, Fr. Mariano de Jesús Lucero, then on to minister to outlying communities. And Padre Martínez would still be among them, still living in the house across from the church.

Who was he? Who was this foreigner sent by the bishop to disgrace their priest? Who was this man? Where did he find the courage and the determination to ride from Santa Fe, to come to Taos, to tell the padre's closest friends and supporters to shun his company? Perhaps from the rocky soil of his homeland.

Joseph Machebeuf was an Auvergnat. He sprang from the craggy landscape of Auvergne, one of the roughest regions of France. The Auvergnats are known to be tough and sharp witted, hard, pugnacious, and obstinate. They are a people of fierce pride and tenderness, and a man from Auvergne "does not give his friendship easily. He is as direct, as bracing and suspicious as his country."[4] Like the tough volcanic stone of Puy-de-Dome, like the granite and basalt of the volcanic mountains of Auvergne, Machebeuf had an unyielding strength of will. His small frame carried a tenacity that left him unfazed when confronting marauding bands of Apaches and Comanches or the shotguns of hostile ranchers. He seemed a man immune to trauma, whose confrontations with death served as a foundation for colorful stories, a source of self-deprecating humor, something to be shared with friends the way others shared a bottle or a meal. And it gave him ample opportunities to put into practice a saying familiar in the patois of the Auvergnats, "Latsin pas — Never give up."

Auvergne remains an ancient mountain province on the massif-central, the mountainous plateau of south-central France. The surrounding mountains are crowned by the Puy-de-Dome, an extinct volcano that lends its name to the political district. Other puys, or volcanic cones, spring up in a jagged fringe. Beneath the cones of gray-and-black volcanic stone, grassy meadows carry the scent of valerian, cow-parsnip, and wild thyme, of rich dark soil and peat bogs. Thick forests meet fields patiently carved from the earth generations before, where lower hills are contoured by massive dry stone walls. Auvergne carries, to this day, an untamed quality, as if the smooth veneer of French civilization had been halted at its borders, prevented from smoothing away its rough edges.

Spending hours alone amid Auvergne's fields and forests bred a fierce independence into Machebeuf, a willingness and ability to endure solitude. It was this independence that enabled him to spend immeasurable time alone, riding through the deserts of the American Southwest, at a time when journeys were measured not in hours, but in weeks or months. And it allowed him to develop the skills necessary for survival on those treks, the self-reliance demanded by the hard life of a frontier missionary.

The rough landscape of Auvergne worked another characteristic into the Celtic blood of Joseph Machebeuf — a deep love for the beauty of nature. A form of reverence, a love for the beauty of the created world, enabled

Machebeuf to see nature not as a hostile force to be conquered, to be civilized and restrained, but as a wonder to be explored and celebrated. It made him prefer the canopy of stars to the most palatial enclosure, prefer a world as big as the American West to the safe confines of his native parish. The wildness and open air of Auvergne would prepare him to face an even more sublime landscape, bring an element of the familiar to the vast distances of the Southwest, to the towering granite of the Rocky Mountains.

Auvergne has never been considered the most sophisticated of the French provinces. Viewed by some of their more sophisticated brethren as backward and provincial, the people of Auvergne are used to hard work and are unimpressed by the pompous. It is a region of farmers and craftsmen, of small tradesmen like Machebeuf's father. Throughout his life Machebeuf would show a preference for the company of simple folk, for the humble and hardworking, and a distinct aversion for the pretentious. It was not a trait that necessarily endeared him to all members of the rigidly hierarchical Roman Catholic Church of the nineteenth century. Still, that preference for the simple life did endear him to thousands of people he came into contact with throughout his life as a missionary. He found himself welcomed and deeply valued by Irish and German immigrants on the Ohio frontier. He received unending hospitality from Hispanic people throughout the Southwest. And he worked comfortably with Native Americans, from the Pueblos of New Mexico to the Papagos of Arizona. He traveled unafraid through lands ruled only by roving bands of Apaches and Comanches. He lived not in a cloister, safe from worldly influences that might test his faith, but with the roughest men and women the American West could produce, with trappers, cowboys, ranchers, and miners, with people least receptive to his apostolic work. Ultimately, he traversed both worlds, meeting with three popes, brazenly soliciting funds from the French royal family, at ease in Paris or in Rome, then returning to the isolated Catholic families of the American Southwest, developing a taste for chile and beans, happy in the company of a good horse or mule. And he did so with consistent charm, with a frank and sincere sense of humor, unafraid to laugh at himself or at the paradoxes presented by the world in which he lived.

Machebeuf's life began in the quiet village of Riom, when a baker's son was born on 11 August 1812. In a small ceremony, the baker's family welcomed their first-born, naming him after his paternal grandfather, Projectus Joseph Machebeuf. They could not have known that the child would never follow his father's trade, would never assume a place in his father's thriving business. He would never become a respected family man and retire complacently amid successive generations. They could not project the very different destiny that awaited him, one which none of his family could foresee, one which defied any logical prediction.

He was baptized within a few days of his birth, in the church of St. Amable, at the west end of Riom's main street. St. Amable's stone Romanesque towers, built seven centuries before, sheltered the small gathering led by Abbé Dalleine. The young priest stood serene in his freshly laundered surplice as the child's mother, Gilberte Plauc Machebeuf, carefully held her new son. Louise and Jeanne Feuillarade, neatly groomed and radiating a sense of feminine proprietorship, whispered nearby. Close friends of the Machebeuf family, the two spinster sisters had arranged the introduction of the child's parents, watched the acquaintance blossom into romance, and now saw the first fruit of their endeavors. The baby's father, Michel Antoine Machebeuf, stood proudly by, confident of the respect due his position as owner of the most flourishing bakery in Riom. Later, in nearby Volvic, he raised a glass with his own father, Projectus Machebeuf. Both of the Machebeuf men would have been pleased that the child, healthy and a boy, would carry on their name.

The infant, wrapped in the family's white baptismal gown, was blissfully unaware of the life that lay ahead of him. Neither he, nor any member of his family, could imagine that he would ever become a bishop, would make nine trans-Atlantic crossings and spend the greater part of his life in distant America. They could not know that he would ride thousands of miles alone across the American Southwest and Mexico, and survive enough mishaps to earn him the title of Trompe la Mort — Death's Deceiver. They could not imagine him becoming a reliable guide on the Santa Fe Trail — the trade route that stretched across the plains from St. Louis to Santa Fe — or that he would be equally at ease with bishops and buffalo hunters, with miners and mestizos. They could not know that he would confront Padre Martínez in Taos or serve as Lamy's vicar general. They could not know that he would become one of the most intriguing, beloved, and infuriating characters in the history of Colorado, a state that did not yet exist, nor that when he died, seventy-seven years later, no building in the burgeoning town of Denver would be large enough to hold the crowds attending his funeral. And they had no way of knowing that when his time came, he would be laid to rest thousands of miles and an ocean away from his birthplace.

TWO

Volvic

✣

Machebeuf's birthplace, Riom, was no longer the capital of Auvergne, but remnants of its history were still scattered along its grass-grown streets and shady boulevards. Stately derelict mansions stood in mute testimony to the town's past glories. The fourteenth-century Palais de Justice had crumbled into ruin, except for the apse, which held the three-hundred-year-old windows of Sainte Chapelle. Sixteenth-century mansions stood empty in the sleepy silence of the surrounding streets. Their owners had followed commerce and government to the new capital at Clermont.

A resting spot for pilgrims traveling to the shrine of Santiago de Compostela in Spain, the nearby city of Clermont had constructed a Gothic cathedral by 1262. The Seminary of Montferrand developed just outside the city and served as an important center of learning for the surrounding areas. Clermont would produce successive generations of scholars and theologians. The city would eventually be home to such intellectuals as Blaise Pascal, who was born in Clermont, and Pierre Teilhard de Chardin, who grew up in the surrounding countryside.

Associated with the parish of Volvic for generations, the Machebeufs were known as *paysans aisés*, comfortable peasants, who had risen to become landowners and had several small parcels of land nearby. In the past, most likely, they made their living farming or herding cattle, for there was a long-established tradition of cattle-breeding in the region. The surname is probably a combination of two words. The French verb *macher* means "to masticate," or to chew, and *beuf* could be a shortened form of *boeuf*, the French word for "beef." In historical records the name is alternately spelled Machebeuf and Macheboeuf. It would have its closest English translation in beefeater. Established as lower bourgeoisie by the early nineteenth century, the Machebeufs' economic situation was at least strong enough to afford some investment in their progeny, whether in the form of education or in securing apprenticeships.

In France of the early nineteenth century, the family was virtually the only source of financial, emotional, and social support, particularly in the years following the Revolution. The country was recovering from sweeping political change, and social mobility, when it existed, was most often in a downward direction. Joseph Machebeuf's vocation to the priesthood was as much his family's decision as his own.

Machebeuf's family was a devout, traditional, French Catholic family. His grandfather, whose name he bore, had once hoped to enter the priesthood. The elder Projectus Machebeuf had been a student in seminary in the years preceding the French Revolution. The cataclysmic events surrounding the Revolution meant the abandonment of his plans; he had returned to Volvic to resume his position as a local landowner. His marriage to a local girl produced four sons and three daughters, the eldest of whom was Machebeuf's father, Michel Antoine.

Projectus Machebeuf must have given some encouragement to religious vocations among his children. Michel Antoine entered an apprenticeship to a master baker in Clermont, but one of his sisters pursued the religious life. Joseph Machebeuf's aunt kept house for his father until he married, then joined the Order of St. Vincent of Paul and became one of the Sisters of Charity. She probably worked at the sisters' hospital in Riom and later became the superior at one of the largest hospitals in Paris.[1]

One of the many saints associated with the episcopal see of Auvergne is St. Projectus, sometimes spelled Praejectus. In the year 666, when he was called by the voice of the people, Projectus became the bishop of Auvergne, a title later changed to the bishop of Clermont.[2] St. Projectus is the patron saint of the parish of Volvic, the ancestral home of the Machebeuf family, where Machebeuf spent his summers visiting with his grandfather and roaming the Volvic Mountains.

In different parts of France, St. Projectus is known as Priest, Prest, Preils, or Prix, and while not entirely uncommon as a name in France, particularly in Auvergne, the name is virtually unheard of in America. After his arrival in America, Machebeuf decided that in English the name Priest Machebeuf encouraged a certain disrespect. He transposed his first two names and was known afterward as Joseph P. Machebeuf.[3]

The marriage of Machebeuf's parents had been arranged by the matchmaking Feuillarade sisters, two maiden ladies who ran a school for small children in the Machebeuf household. Little is known of Mlle. Plauc, Machebeuf's mother, except that she was an appropriately devout and virtuous young woman. Her marriage was considered a happy one. She provided Machebeuf's earliest education, no doubt aided by a series of suggestions contributed by the Feuillarade sisters, who retained a sense of proprietorship toward the child. His sister, Anne, was not born until he was four years old, his brother Marius, two years later. In his earliest years Machebeuf had the benefit of being the sole focus of considerable feminine attention.

Prior to his marriage, Machebeuf's father had established a bakery in Riom. The business flourished and provided a relatively solid source of revenue for the family. Biographer W. J. Howlett described the elder Machebeuf as "a man of strong and firm character whose every wish was law" and as one who imposed "his authority by no undue harshness but in a manner to insure reverential respect and gain [the] fullest filial affection of his children."[4] He managed to instill in his son a healthy respect for authority, one that would aid Machebeuf in his dealings with superiors in the church. But it is safe to assume that Machebeuf did not spend a great deal of time with his father in his early years. Running a business and supervising his family's properties would have occupied much of his father's time. Perhaps it was the abundance of feminine companionship in Machebeuf's early childhood that contributed to the gentleness in his character so often commented on by his contemporaries.

Machebeuf was given the nickname "Blanchet," or "Whitey." He was a towheaded child, with white-blond hair that darkened to brownish-blond in adulthood. Comments from contemporaries have created a portrait of a small, wiry child with pale hair and eyelashes, known for his lively nature and diminutive size. Historian Paul Horgan gives a good description, "Mischief played about in his gaiety; his small, plain, clever face was animated by a venturesome spirit; his little body hated to be still."[5] Although lively by nature, Machebeuf was never considered very strong, and his energetic disposition often taxed his physical health.

When concerned about his health, his family sent him to his grandfather in Volvic, hoping that the stability of the grandfather's home, combined with the fresh mountain air, would restore his health. It was a practice that continued into his early adulthood, and even his studies in seminary would be interrupted by periodic "cures" in the Volvic Mountains. Perhaps it was the chance to hike, to explore the surrounding countryside, as much as anything else, that contributed to his recoveries. Even as a child he demonstrated a propensity to "rest in action," a phrase he would later adopt as his personal philosophy.

The visits also permitted him to spend time with his grandfather, whose character seems closer to Machebeuf's than that of his father. He absorbed some of the old man's deep sense of spirituality and heard stories about the old man's unrequited dreams of entering the priesthood. Finally, the summers spent in Volvic established, early in life, a connection between the physical freedom of roaming the mountains and the sense of spiritual freedom that profound faith can provide.

When Machebeuf was old enough to begin formal education, he was entrusted to the care of the Christian Brothers. A teaching order, founded in 1684 by John Baptist de La Salle, the Christian Brothers are not priests but lay brothers, who live in community, take religious vows, and devote their lives to education. When La Salle founded the Institute of the Brothers of the Christian Schools, he introduced the first popular system of education in France. He also introduced a number of innovations — instruction not in Latin but in French, free schooling, and emphasis on the instruction of each student as an individual. Widely imitated, some consider the methods of the Christian Brothers the origin of modern primary education.[6]

When Napoleon signed his Concordat with Pope Pius VII in 1801, one of the few orders allowed to continue their work without interference was the Christian Brothers. Napoleon pragmatically recognized their value as educators and the importance of stability in primary education. Thus, while a number of schools saw religious instructors removed from office and replaced by government teachers, Napoleon allowed the Christian Brothers to remain in their posts. Impressed by the kindness shown him by the Christian Brothers, years later, Machebeuf would continue to inquire about them in letters sent to his family. He developed a genuine and lasting affection for a number of the brothers.[7]

In addition to the gentle influence of the Christian Brothers, Machebeuf knew a number of the Sisters of Charity, who ran the Hospital for Incurables at Riom. Doubtless through his aunt, who joined the order after his father's marriage, the family maintained a lasting friendship with the sisters. Machebeuf had no shortage of role models in religious life throughout his formative years.[8]

When the time came for Machebeuf to begin his classical studies, his parents enrolled him in the College of Riom. The college had been established by yet another religious order, the Oratorians, but the Oratorians had not been as fortunate as the Christian Brothers in the chaotic period after the French Revolution. They had been removed from their posts at their college in Riom, and the school was being run by government teachers. Family members and friends considered it a dangerous period for the young Machebeuf, worried that he would fall under the worldly influence of his lay professors, that he might be exposed to ideas not in keeping with their carefully constructed Catholic environment. When he completed his studies there, he would enroll, just as they had hoped, in seminary.

When Machebeuf was nine, tragedy struck his family. Without warning his mother was stricken with "brain fever," probably meningitis. She died a few days later. The loss affected Machebeuf profoundly. His sister, Anne, was five years old at the time, and his brother, Marius, was only three. Of the three children, Machebeuf was the one who was closest to his mother. One of his unmarried aunts arrived to keep house for the grieving family and came to be greatly loved by the two younger children, but Machebeuf, attending to his studies, never developed quite the same bond. The loss of his mother severed an important tie to his family, one that would help make future separations easier to bear.

By the early part of 1830, seventeen-year-old Machebeuf felt confined in Riom. His studies in rhetoric almost complete, he was eager for adventure in the outside world. His restlessness brought him very close to abandoning his family's hopes for his future in the priesthood; he almost enlisted in the French army. His nation was also in a period of transition. For fifteen years, the Restoration allowed the reestablishment of the Catholic Church in France. Church and state had been effectively reunited; a spirit of collaboration bloomed between members of the clergy and the government of France. In 1824 the aging Louis XVIII had been replaced by Charles X, and Charles's relationship with the church was conspicuous in the traditional rites of his coronation at Rheims. So close was the collaboration between church and state that by 1825 the Law on Sacrilege was passed, making theft of sacred vessels or profanation of the Sacred Host a capital offense.[9]

Not everyone in France was supportive of the alliance between the temporal and spiritual realms. Gallicans within the church challenged the prerogatives of the papacy, and liberals without saw king and church united in inhibiting their freedom. The spirit of revolution was growing, but Charles X seemed confident in the army's ability to protect his position, a confidence that had been heightened by the army's conquest of Algeria.

French Catholics "celebrated as a crusade" the Algerian victory.[10] Across the country they praised the victorious French army, in parades and celebrations dedicated to the glory of France. One such celebration took place in Clermont, where a grand review of the troops was held. Flags flew, the music played, and pretty young women threw flowers to the passing soldiers. In the crowd, without his family's permission, surrounded by a group of friends from college, stood the restless and naive figure of Joseph Machebeuf. Overcome with patriotism, Machebeuf decided that his future lay with the glorious French army, marching into a life of adventure and prestige. He and his companions boasted to each other of their courage, urged each other to enlist on the spot. No such impetuous move was made, but young Machebeuf left the event convinced that his future lay in the military.

News of his enthusiastic attendance at the event reached his father. Needless to say, Machebeuf's father did not welcome the prospect of his half-educated son becoming cannon fodder in the French army. But he was surprised by the enthusiasm his son had shown and reticent to forbid the enlistment lest he encourage a reactionary rebellious response. He retreated into silence.

After a period of ominous quiet in the Machebeuf home, he summoned his son for a conference. He laid before him the hopes that his family had always entertained, that he would enter the priesthood. He reminded him of the investment his education represented and wisely closed the conference by saying, "After all, you are free, but consider well what you are to do, and then do what you think is the will of God."[11]

Machebeuf, thrown into all the turmoil of adolescent angst, considered his position. He consulted with a number of friends and advisers. He spoke to his spiritual director, Abbé Dalleine, pastor of the church of St. Amable in Riom. The abbé had known him since his birth, had known of his family's hopes for his vocation, and thought young Machebeuf was destined for the priesthood. Machebeuf came away from the interview with a new direction. He returned to his father and announced his determination to enter the Grande Séminaire de Montferrand in Clermont as soon as he had completed his studies at college. He asked his father to present him to the priests of St. Sulpice, the Sulpicians who ran the seminary, so that he might prepare to enter the priesthood.

In July 1830 the streets of Paris were again in chaos. Following a coup d'etat Charles X fled to England, his armies unable to restrain the forces of revolution. The bourgeoisie succeeded in enthroning the Duc d'Orleans, Charles's cousin Louis Philippe.[12] Young Machebeuf would not have much opportunity to evaluate political events around him. He was about to be cut off from the outside world, to enter the strictly protected and controlled environment of a nineteenth-century French seminary. Doubt and uncertainty had marked his years at college in Riom, and he felt terribly unsure as to what direction his life should take, but some form of intuitive gravity pulled him into the priesthood.

On a fine fall day in Auvergne, at the beginning of October 1831, he walked into the great stone enclosure of the Grande Séminaire de Montferrand. At nineteen years of age, Machebeuf stepped into another world.

THREE

Seminary

✧

Dark stone buildings shadow the streets of Clermont. It is an old city, a medieval city, where tiny gardens are wedged between walls of volcanic stone, and small fountains pour endlessly into stone basins. Cobbled streets in the old quarter are crowded by structures laboriously carved from the same dark stone, and cracks between the cobblestones catch the dust of early summer, the first drifting snows of winter. On quiet mornings the sound of bells echo through narrow streets that open into secluded court-yards or little plazas. Abruptly, the Church of Notre Dame du Port rises in twelfth-century grandeur, its Romanesque arches and gleaming clerestory windows watching over the heart of the ancient city.

The Grande Séminaire de Montferrand stood in solemn dignity on the outskirts of the city. A fortress of seventeenth-century buildings, the man-sard roof protected its echoing corridors, their silence broken only by mur-mured conversations, the swish of soutanes, and the swift, silent movement of seminarians and their Sulpician educators. In these dark, institutional, high-ceilinged rooms, Machebeuf was to spend the next five years of his life.

The priests of the Society of St. Sulpice administered the Grande Sémi-naire de Montferrand. Founded by Jean-Jacques Olier de Verneuil, the Sulpicians were a partial answer to the need for a systematic approach to the training of candidates for the priesthood. Olier, the son of an aristocratic family, had been educated at the Jesuit college at Lyon and had studied theology at the Sorbonne. In August 1642 he became the curé of the parish of St. Sulpice, in the Paris Foubourg of St. Germain. Olier established a community of priests and seminarians that came to serve as a central model for French diocesan seminaries. Within Olier's community, students concurrently studied at the university, assisted in liturgical and sacramental activities, and adjusted to life within a religious community.[1] The program flourished and Olier was invited to establish seminaries in other dioceses. By the time of his death in 1657, he had established institutions in Nantes, Viviers, Puy, and Clermont.[2] As the network of French seminaries expanded, graduates of Olier's schools increasingly provided the staff. The Sulpicians came to be recognized as the leaders in the reform of the French clergy.[3] By the nineteenth century, French seminaries were dominated by the traditions associated with the Sulpicians, and the Grande Séminaire de Montferrand was a model Sulpician seminary.

In French seminaries of the nineteenth century, the primary concern in the formation of a candidate for the priesthood was his spiritual orientation. Theological studies, or intellectual disciplines related to the priesthood, were supplementary. The central theme was to encourage the seminarian to live a life in imitation of Christ, to identify each aspect of Christ's teaching, and to incorporate the actions of Christ as much as possible into his outlook, character, and action. Students were trained in the administration of the Sacraments, given preparation for hearing confessions, and learned how to teach the catechism. Those who were particularly gifted intellectually might be given additional academic or intellectual training. But spirituality best guaranteed a highly motivated and appropriately decorous priest in years to come.

One Sulpician superior at the time of Machebeuf's education wrote that his order had never proposed "to make its members into scholars or doctors, but rather useful servants of the clergy, which has a great deal more need of the prayers, example, and guidance of those whose task it is to train them than of the lessons and their teaching." He concluded, "piety is a great deal more necessary than extensive and profound learning."[4] The Sulpicians sought to foster the virtues of "douceur et tendresse," of gentleness and kindness, grounded in a deeply felt Catholic spirituality.

It is not easy to instill piety and tenderness in a group of high-spirited young men, even for those with the best of intentions. A central tenet of Christian thought is humility, but an eagerness to foster humility, if not well implemented, could mean interpreting enthusiasm as a lack of docility, curiosity as impudence, or ability as vanity. Obedience was primary. Candidates were being trained to become members of a strictly ordered hierarchy, where obedience would serve them far better than independence. From the moment a young man entered a seminary in nineteenth-century France, he could be certain that his daily life would be strictly controlled, that he would be constantly observed. One seminary, at Viviers, was constructed so that Sulpician superiors could observe residents not only in the corridors, but in each individual cell.[5] Every aspect of the candidate's life was scrutinized and regulated — every minute of his day was carefully planned. The candidate's life was subject to the règlements, or regulations, of that particular seminary. The règlements were unbending and complex rules, and the best student was considered the one who accepted them without question. Docility was the best evidence of piety.

Awakened by a bell that signaled the beginning of the day's activities, students had prescribed amounts of time set aside for prayer, meals, religious observances, study, assisting older clergy in liturgical services, and supervised interaction with their fellow seminarians. Students were to maintain silence unless specifically instructed otherwise, and always to behave with deportment. Joking, argumentative behavior, or any form of competition were discouraged. Students were to walk at a stately pace, with eyes cast demurely downward, and demonstrate priestly modesty and gravity.

For a young man described as clever and mischievous, for one who hated to be still, the confinement and rigidity of seminary life must have come as quite a shock. Not surprisingly, no records portray young Machebeuf as a model student in the Grand Séminaire de Montferrand. The only virtue that he seemed to come by naturally was gentleness, and it must have taken all the sweetness of his disposition to overcome his superiors' displeasure with his mischievousness and independence.

Still, there were benefits for Machebeuf. The doubts about his future had been overcome, he was committed to a vocation that had been the dearest hope of his family, and he had his loved ones' full support and blessing. The questioning that haunted him throughout his college years had come to an end. The structured life of seminary brought predictability and peace. The day after his entrance he wrote to his father expressing his "gratitude to God, and thanks to his kind and worthy parent for the thousand favors and acts of kindness which he had received from him," commenting particularly on "this last act by which he was enabled to see so clearly the grand vocation of his life." If Machebeuf had any remaining ambivalence about his future in the priesthood, it was not expressed in writing. "From that time on, all his letters had that fixed and settled tone, and never once showed any sign of wavering intention or regret of purpose."[6]

It may be difficult for some modern readers, accustomed to a great amount of personal freedom, to understand how one could find a sense of peace in the restrictive atmosphere of a nineteenth-century Sulpician seminary. But there is a certain kind of liberation that is only born through discipline, through the end of ambivalent questioning and acceptance of the work at hand. It may be harder still, to understand how an environment of endless rules and regulations could foster the gentleness and kindness that were goals of Sulpician formation. The world of complex regulations provided Machebeuf with infinite opportunities for transgression but also provided infinite opportunities for forgiveness, opportunities to see kindness extended at each breach of regulations. Machebeuf learned forgiveness by being forgiven. The règlements of the seminary system, together with the confessional nature of the Catholic faith, ensured Machebeuf's first-hand experience of the mercy that he would soon be dispensing to others.

Still, life in the seminary did not completely agree with young Machebeuf. The close confinement and enforced inactivity soon resulted in a deterioration in his health. Within a few months he was allowed to leave Montferrand in order to rest and recover.[7] It was not exertion but passivity that was toxic to Machebeuf. He could find rest only in action, and he plunged himself into intense physical exercise. It marked the beginning of a pattern that continued throughout the five years he spent at Montferrand. Whenever possible — when superiors were concerned about his health, when students were allowed a break from their studies during summer months — he would return to his grandfather's house in Volvic. Here, he would once again roam the surrounding countryside, pound his energy into the foot trails of the Volvic Mountains, and absorb the strength of the land that had nurtured him. His health and outlook restored, having once again carved into his soul a connection between physical freedom and spiritual peace, he would return to his work at the seminary.

The close confinement of the seminary protected him from emotional isolation, for life there brought him into direct contact with young men who shared his values and goals: his devotion to the Church, his hopes for a successful future in the priesthood, his frustrations with the endless regulations of the institution. And many of his fellow seminarians came from similar social backgrounds. In the years between 1812 and 1837, small French towns contributed over half of the candidates for the priesthood.[8] Many of the ordinands came from families whose occupations were concentrated in those towns, from the class of artisans or shopkeepers, from households headed by butchers, bakers, shoemakers, carpenters, tailors, or small traders.

The sons of the artisan class were so highly represented in the French seminaries of the nineteenth century for a several reasons. Their fathers' urban professions did not require their children's continual efforts in the fields or necessitate the oldest son being groomed to succeed his father in the role of landowner. This allowed greater concentration on education and a higher percentage of literacy among townspeople. The children of the artisan class were also more likely to come to the attention of the parish priest in church or catechism, more likely to be singled out for encouragement and support. Additionally, since the artisan class had already met their basic economic needs, their sons were less likely to be viewed as already contaminated by the vices that often accompany extreme poverty and less likely to be seen as trying to use the church to improve their social standing.[9]

In the seminary Machebeuf met young men of the same social background, who would become his friends for life. Intense personal friendships, while necessary for emotional support and potentially advantageous over the course of a career, were far from encouraged. All seminaries had regulations prohibiting special or long-term friendships. Students were never to be in groups of fewer than three, and entering another student's room or engaging in activities not supervised by superiors was grounds for expulsion. Part of the concern on the part of administrators was doubtless due to the fear of homosexual relationships among the seminarians, but as great a part was purely a spiritual consideration. The arid legacy of Christian asceticism lent credence to the idea that inordinate fondness for one individual interfered with a more universal outpouring of love and charity. Accordingly, one regulation in Marseilles's seminary stated that amitiés particulières, particular friendships, "are based on truly natural inclination and not on charity or on the desire for perfection . . . the least harmful consequences of which are dissipation, waste of time, contempt of others, infraction of rules, and distrust of those who are there to guide us."[10] Seminaries, particularly Sulpician seminaries, hoped to foster the ordinand's rejection of the material world — his contemptus mundi — so that the seminarian could begin the process of divorcing himself from the lives of ordinary men.

Regardless, some friendships develop where every discouragement, every obstacle to be overcome only serves to strengthen the bonds between two people. Such was surely the case when Machebeuf met Jean Baptiste Lamy. Theirs was a friendship that would cross oceans and continents, span decades, and bind the two men together for life. Only death would separate them.

In many ways the two young men were opposites. Machebeuf was diminutive, with fair hair — a source of perpetual motion and mischief. Lamy was tall, dark, grave, and intellectually inclined — a slow-moving, serious young man. Machebeuf was gentle and cheerful, with a kindness and tolerance carefully nurtured by his mother, encouraged by his gentle Christian Brothers' education. Lamy could be brooding, even pedantic, with the intellectual and analytical fierceness of his Jesuit educators. But they were both Auvergnats, and they shared the stubborn, tenacious character associated with the region. They both had a healthy sense of humor that enabled each to overcome the most frustrating situations. And they both had a capacity for hard work, one that sometimes exceeded the limits of their physical endurance. Latsin pas! Never give up!

Jean Baptiste Lamy was born in the village of Lempdes, forty-eight kilometers from Clermont. His parents were also paysans aisés, well-to-do peasants, and like Machebeuf, Lamy was an old, respected surname in the region. Born on 11 October 1814, to Jean Lamy and Marie Die, Lamy was the youngest of eleven children, only four of whom survived to reach adulthood. Lamy's family was, if possible, even more devout than Machebeuf's. Of the four surviving children, Louis and Jean Baptiste entered the priesthood; the daughter, Marguerite, became a Sister of Mercy; and the youngest son, Etienne, had two children—one of whom became a priest; the other, a nun. As a child, the dark-haired Lamy was serious and studious, obedient and considerate. These traits later earned him the description of "innocent as a lamb"; he was called "Innocent" or "Lamb" in seminary. He exhibited a natural inclination for religious life and a natural ability in academics. His family enrolled him in the Jesuit college at Billom, a few miles outside of Clermont-Ferrand, before he was nine.[11]

The Jesuit college at Billom was the oldest school in Clermont, having been inaugurated in 1556 at the request of the bishop of Clermont, Guillaume du Prat. Du Prat had established relations with the Jesuits while attending the Council of Trent and became determined to have the benefit of their educational expertise within his diocese.[12] Founded by the Jesuits in the sixteenth century, the college passed to other hands following the suppression of the Society of Jesus in 1773 and was reopened by the Jesuits around 1816.

Lamy spent nine years under the influence of its Jesuit educators. His Jesuit education honed his intellectual abilities and left a lasting imprint on his developing character. Lamy would retain a strategic, carefully analytical approach to problem solving and a sophisticated, albeit sometimes high-handed, approach to administration. He would also retain an ability to work successfully with the Jesuits who ran the Propaganda Fide, or Sacred Congregation for the Propagation of the Faith, which oversaw and financed much of American missionary work. After his studies in Billom,

Lamy was enrolled in the Petit Séminaire, a preparatory seminary in Clermont, and finally in the Grand Séminaire de Montferrand. It was in the
major seminary that he met Joseph Machebeuf.[13]

Machebeuf could not match Lamy in intellectual prowess — he was never
an outstanding student — but he could outdistance him in other areas. Machebeuf's natural warmth and gaiety countered Lamy's more serious disposition. His solid physical orientation countered Lamy's more high-strung,
nervous outlook. His interpersonal abilities smoothed feathers ruffled by
Lamy's autocratic tendencies. And the two young men shared one important similarity: both were fascinated by the romantic adventures of missionary priests.

Machebeuf's love of adventure, the siren call of distant, unknown lands,
had not been laid to rest when he chose to enroll in the seminary rather
than the army. It was reawakened by his friendship with Lamy. Lamy had
always shown a particular interest in the lives of successful missionaries.[14]
Missionary life combined the spirituality of the priesthood, the adventure
of the explorer, the familiar structure of the Catholic Church, and the
beckoning call of the unknown. The two friends exchanged stories, read-
ings, and hopes for their lives as missionaries. It became their strongest
bond.

In 1833 their appetites for missionary work were further whetted by the
visit of Bishop Benedict Joseph Flaget. The old bishop, too, was an Auvergnat and had attended the same seminary decades before. The leathery
old prelate told them of his consecration as bishop in Bardstown, Kentucky,
his nights in the tents of the Algonquin Indians, his log-cabin church. He
told them of his work in France and Sardinia, inspiring others to undertake
missionary work in distant America, and stood as a living example that one
could indeed embrace such a life and survive, could return to Auvergne to
tell the tale.[15] He planted his seeds of adventure deep in the fertile imagina-
tions of restless young men such as Machebeuf and Lamy.

Flaget was one of several missionary priests and bishops to visit the
seminary during those years. Writing in the third person in his 1889 "Reminiscences," Machebeuf recorded, "during the second year of his seminary
he felt inflamed with the desire to devote himself to the foreign missions,
increased also by the visit of Father Odin, later Provincial of Lazarists in
Missouri, bishop of Galveston, and finally archbishop of New Orleans.
Having himself spent several years in the new settlement of missions
among the Indians, he represented in persuasive language the good that
could be done by zealous missionaries for the salvation of souls." When
four students left the Seminary of Foreign Missions in Paris and went to

Indiana with Bishop Bruté of Vincerine, "The young seminarian Machebeuf asked then to be allowed to go with Mgr. Bruté. But he was ordered by his superiors to finish his ecclesiastical education at MontFerrand, be ordained and then take the first opportunity afforded to go with some other bishop who would apply for missionaries."[16] Disappointed, Machebeuf reapplied himself to his studies.

The years at seminary slowly passed. On the eve of Trinity Sunday, in 1836, Machebeuf was ordained a deacon. On 21 December of the same year, Bishop Feron, the bishop of Clermont, laid his hands on the head of young Machebeuf.[17] Machebeuf received the episcopal blessing and sacerdotal consecration that ordained him a priest in the Catholic Church. He was twenty-four years old; the five years of preparation, training, and education had come to an end. He was ready to begin his life's work.

FOUR

Le Cendre

ᔦ

The years of restrictive restlessness had finally come to an end. In the deeply moving ceremony of his ordination, Machebeuf had given himself completely to God. It was not within his nature to do anything by halves.

After the rigors of seminary, it was customary for newly ordained priests to take a period of rest. It allowed a period of transition before assignment to active ministry. Most used it to spend time with their families, knowing that their first assignment might take them far from home. Machebeuf had enjoyed the advantage of his family living in close proximity to the Grande Séminaire de Montferrand. He had also enjoyed the added time of his periodic cures in the Volvic Mountains. He felt little need to spend additional time with his family. In keeping with one whose philosophy was Rest in Action, he asked to be assigned at once to active ministry. Directly after his ordination he was made assistant pastor to the parish of Le Cendre, seven or eight miles from the town of Cournon.[1]

The parishioners of Le Cendre saw a small, blond, tenacious twenty-four-year-old priest sweep into their community. Machebeuf had spent the last five years of his life preparing for the work that now lay before him, and he dove into his work with abandon. Because Father Le Maistre, the pastor of Le Cendre, was an elderly man, much of the active parish work fell directly on young Machebeuf's shoulders. Within weeks he was giving homilies, starting catechism classes for the children, and making visits to the homes of the sick and the poor. The sight of Machebeuf's blond hair and black cassock soon became so familiar that the parishioners began to suggest they would no longer need the gardes châmpetres, the rural police.[2]

Fifty years later Machebeuf would publish his reminiscences about his early work at Le Cendre. "At the period when Father Machebeuf was appointed assistant, the pastor, Father Le Maistre, was very old, infirm, and entirely deaf. He would not resign, however, as it was his wish to die among his parishioners, having baptised and married most of them. Father Machebeuf was sent to him with the title of assistant, but in reality [was] the pastor, the old priest having left the parish entirely to his direction."[3]

Machebeuf was ministering to simple, country people — French peasants with direct ways and direct needs. He was completely at home: within miles of his birthplace, surrounded by the people he knew best, doing work that he clearly loved. And he brought with him a zeal reserved for the newly ordained and the convert, a conviction born of emotional certainty. No parish could withstand the whirlwind of his leonine energy. The young storm named Machebeuf, however, soon encountered opposition, despite his later claims that everything had been left "entirely to his direction." The opposition came from an area most unexpected — his very devotion.

Father Le Maistre was one of the older priests who had weathered the storms of the French Revolution and survived its devastating effects on the ranks of French religious orders. By virtue of his age, by virtue of his sheer survival, he demanded respect. Machebeuf was too well schooled in obedience to deliberately challenge the old priest's authority. The aging priest must have been pleased to have such an energetic young assistant, one who freed him from some of the physical demands of active ministry. But the warmth with which Machebeuf was received by the community must have brought with it some sense of displacement. Four months after his arrival, two generations of French Catholicism squared off against each other in the tiny church in Le Cendre. A conflict developed over Machebeuf's devotion to the Blessed Virgin.

Machebeuf lost his mother at nine, before the usual age when children transfer their emotions to a source outside the family. He embraced a devotion to the Blessed Mother, a response encouraged by every aspect of his environment. Machebeuf's devotion to Mary went far beyond an attitude popular in his generation. It included a reaction to a profound personal loss. Seventy-five years later, his sister would write of his deep love for his mother. "He had known her too well, and loved her too much, to forget her so easily. Better able to appreciate her love and care, his grief would have been without solace, were it not for his devotion to the divine Mother, to the Comfortress of the Afflicted, which the lost one had endeavored to instill into his heart from his earlier years."[4]

The nineteenth century saw an upsurge in devotion to Mary in France. In 1814, a young shepherdess in Perigod had twice received visitations from the Blessed Virgin. Fourteen-year-old Marie-Jeanne Grave was told by the Virgin that her parents must cease work on Sundays or they would be punished by God. Marie-Jeanne dutifully relayed the message, but her parents ignored her warning. Within a year, as the Virgin had foretold, both her parents were dead. Marie-Jeanne died a year later, and miraculous events were manifested at her funeral. A local cult sprang up in memory of her devotion.[5]

By the 1830s another apparition had become known throughout France. The Virgin had appeared in the chapel of the Sisters of Charity, on rue du Bac, in Paris. Sister Catherine Labouré saw Mary "shedding beams of light on the world," and a second vision told her that a medal should be cast commemorating the event.[6] The medallions began to be produced in 1832. By 1834 the Medal of the Immaculate Conception, or médaille miraculeuse, was being distributed throughout France by the Sisters of Charity. In the same year the Sacred Congregation of Rites granted permission to celebrate Mass in honor of the appearance. Doubtless the medallions would have come to Machebeuf's attention. His aunt was a Sister of Charity, working in their hospital in Riom. In December of 1836, the same month that Machebeuf was ordained, yet another manifestation appeared to the parish priest at the Paris church of Notre-Dame des Victoires. He immediately undertook organization of the Confraternity of the Immaculate Heart of Mary, and within a few days effected the conversion of one of the ministers of Louis XVIII. A surge of conversions followed in the wake of the newly formed confraternity.[7]

From 1831 to 1836, the years Machebeuf had been in seminary, he had been encouraged in his devotion to the Blessed Mother. "He had been trained by the priests of St. Sulpice, and their training had so strengthened his hitherto deep-seated love and reverence for the Mother of God that it was as natural for him to have confidence in her as in his own parents, and he could not well understand how anyone could object to the public expression of so beautiful a sentiment."[8]

It was unthinkable that Machebeuf would not plan special events to celebrate his Marian devotion in the parish of Le Cendre. The month of May is traditionally considered the month of Mary, and as May approached Machebeuf began to plan a special series of May devotions. May devotions were a new practice in France, one that had been encouraged during Machebeuf's years in seminary but not one that was necessarily appreciated by the previous generation of priests. Biographer Howlett attributes the elder priest's reticence to the legacy of Jansenism, which still ran strong in France, perhaps more so among priests of the old curé's generation. Jesuit historian Thomas J. Steele, who edited the 1987 reprint of the Howlett biography, is not so certain. "What Howlett identifies as the older generation's Jansenism seems to be a lingering rationalism from the eighteenth-century Enlightenment, and Machebeuf's (and Lamy's) self-styled anti-Jansenism seems to be just romanticism — a return in the Church to certain medieval devotions such as those to the Blessed Virgin."⁹ Whatever the source, special devotions to the Virgin, spectacular visions, or manifestations, violated LeMaistre's sense of Augustinian austerity. Machebeuf's superior objected to his plans, deeming them unseemly. Machebeuf must have been persuasive. After a period of considerable tension between the two men, the old priest relented and granted permission for the celebrations.

Immediately Machebeuf wrote to his sister, who was studying with the Sisters of the Visitation in Riom. He asked her to create a number of artificial flowers, which he would use to decorate his altar. It was the first of many requests. Over the years she would create dozens of vestments and other articles for her roving brother to use in his missionary work. The May devotions were held, with Anne's flowers on the altar, and considered to be a great success. Increased piety was duly noted throughout the parish.¹⁰

Successful as he may have been in his role as assistant pastor, Machebeuf was not long to be held in the confines of the parish of Le Cendre. He had lost none of his interest in the lives of the missionaries and still had the sporadic reinforcement of contacts with Lamy, who was completing his last two years of seminary. He had his memories of Bishop Odin's visit and periodic visits with Bishop Flaget, who continued to use Clermont as a base for his travels throughout France and Sardinia. Machebeuf soon saw the arrival of yet another American bishop. Bishop John Baptist Purcell, the bishop of Cincinnati, was to play a major role in his life.

Purcell, born in Ireland, was also Sulpician educated. Before becoming the bishop of Cincinnati, he served as the president of the Sulpician Mount St. Mary's Seminary in Baltimore, from 1833 to 1835.¹¹ In 1838 Purcell traveled to Rome and wrote to the superior of the Grande Séminaire de Montferrand, Father Comfé, who had been one of his teachers in Paris, asking him to help recruit young priests for missionary work in America. Machebeuf had spoken to a number of his teachers and directors at seminary about his interest in missionary work, and he had already asked to be assigned to the mission of Bishop Bruté of Vincerine in the wilds of Indiana.¹²

In September of 1838 the annual diocesan retreat was held, and Machebeuf used the time to focus completely on his attraction to missionary life. Spending three days in prayer and meditation, he resolved any lingering doubts. He emerged from the retreat certain of his vocation as a missionary.

"Oh my God," Machebeuf wrote, "grant that during my whole life I may remember the 26th, 27th, and 28th of September, 1838, that all my life I may have present to my mind that it was during these days that I gave myself again to Thee without reserve!"[13]

Purcell's request to Comfé could not have come at a better time. Just as Machebeuf had resolved any ambivalence he may have had about undertaking missionary work, a request for his services came. Inflamed with enthusiasm, he urged others in his group to join him in embracing missionary life. First and foremost, he spoke with Lamy, who was just completing his studies at seminary. Without hesitation, Lamy agreed to volunteer. Machebeuf did not stop there, he began talking with his other friends in the priesthood.

One of them was Father Gaçon, the priest in the neighboring parish of Leché. Writing in his "Reminiscences," Machebeuf reported, "Kind Providence had also permitted that the young priest should find in the parish of Leché a fellow-townsman of his in the person of the zealous and saintly Father C. Gaçon, who, being much older and of great experience, became the confessor and director of the young priest. Not only was he a devoted friend and wise counselor of the future missionary bishop, but he and his young assistant were to be companions in the mission to America."[14]

Father Cheymol, the young assistant to Gaçon, made up the fourth in the party of five missionaries recruited by Purcell. The fifth was Father Navarron, who later established a parish in an Ohio county unsurprisingly named Clermont. Together with Machebeuf and Lamy, these three prepared for their departure, trading stories and encouragement about their prospects as missionaries in America. Soon the band of five had relayed their interest back to Comfé, who was able to tell Purcell of his success.

If Machebeuf had felt no compulsion to spend time with his family immediately after ordination, he now had to attend to family matters. His brother, Marius, was sixteen years old and showed a propensity for business. Marius would be able to succeed their father in handling the affairs of the Machebeuf family's land and business. Arrangements were underway to place him in a position to prepare him for his career. His sister, Anne, had completed her education with the Sisters of the Visitation in Riom the year before, and much to Machebeuf's delight, she had returned to that community as a postulant. Her future would be assured once she completed her probationary period with the sisters.

Anne's return to the convent, combined with Marius's departure to begin his apprenticeship in business, created difficulties in the Machebeuf household. His aunt, who had joined the household after the death of his mother, could hardly continue living with Machebeuf's father once the children had left. It would be most unseemly. Neither could she be summarily dismissed from the household; a spinster would have few options in the world of nineteenth-century France. The three Machebeuf children, disturbed by the prospect of their father having to spend his remaining years alone, came up with a solution. If the proper dispensation were received from the church, what was there to prevent their father and aunt from marrying?

Together the young matchmakers, with a skill that would have made the Feuillarade sisters proud, approached their elders and proposed their plan. It seemed the best solution for all concerned. Their aunt could remain in the household; their father would have an already beloved companion for the remainder of his life; and the children would be free to pursue their various directions in life. The couple agreed, and Machebeuf himself performed the marriage ceremony.[15]

By November of 1838 Anne had completed her probationary period at the convent and was allowed to become a novice. Machebeuf preached the sermon for the mass celebrating the event, and on 7 November she made her first vows as a Sister of the Visitation. She took as her name Sister Marie Philomène. In the years ahead Machebeuf would address dozens of letters to that name.

Only one family problem remained to be solved. Machebeuf had yet to tell his father of his decision to become a missionary. Over the years Machebeuf's father had lost none of his protective, autocratic tendencies. The same man who seven years before had opposed his son's desire to enter the military would hardly be delighted to see him depart for an unknown wilderness — no matter how high the level of altruism that sparked the decision. Gravely concerned, Machebeuf consulted his friends and superiors as to how he could best break the news to his father.

Father Comfé, the superior of the seminary, finally made the decision for him. Anticipating his father's resistance, seeing no benefit from family disputes disturbing the last few months before departure, and predicting any such discussion would be painful for both parties, he forbade Machebeuf to discuss his departure with his father. So Machebeuf began his preparations in secret, planning to steal away without word getting back to his father until the act was a fait accompli.

Lamy was ordained in December 1838, almost exactly two years after Machebeuf's ordination. He was assigned briefly to a parish outside Clermont in order to gain some experience in parish affairs. His family was not opposed to his becoming a missionary, perhaps because in the past they had given so many members to religious orders, and Lamy was able to make his goodbyes before his departure.

Machebeuf continued his work in Le Cendre, did his best to attend to his family's needs, organized his affairs, and prepared for the next part of his life to begin. Thirty years later, when Machebeuf returned to Clermont after having been made a bishop, the *Semaine Religieuse de Clermont* described his departure from Riom:

> On the morning of the 21st of May, 1839, two young priests of the Diocese of Clermont, dressed as civilians, passed hurriedly along the streets of Riom before sunrise, and went out of the city by the main road leading toward Paris. Upon reaching the open country they stopped to await the coming of the diligence [carriage] which was to take them over the first stage of their journey to the Seminary of Foreign Missions in that distant capital. Their departure resembled rather a flight, yet in spite of the secrecy the young ecclesiastics were seen, and one of them was recognized by a brother priest and former fellow-student. A few words explained all, and, as this friend grasped the hand of the young traveler in an affectionate farewell, he saw the emotion which shook the delicate frame of the voluntary exile as he cast a last tearful look back on his native city. He realized that a terrible struggle was taking place in that heart whose tender sensibilities were so well known to him. In fact, a great and sublime sacrifice was being accomplished there at that moment. The young priest, in order to spare his family the heart-rending pain of a farewell, and likewise to escape their determined resistance to what he considered his vocation, had passed before the door of his father's house without stopping to enter. His young companion, whose own heart was still throbbing with the emotions of a similar sacrifice, made only the day before, was scarcely less disturbed, but, drawing near to his sobbing friend, he lightly laid his hand upon his shoulder and pointed towards heaven. Silently they turned and continued on their way. The young fugitives were the Abbé Lamy and the Abbé Machebeuf.[16]

The unidentified writer for the religious weekly may have exaggerated slightly, in order to add a touch more drama to his piece, but Machebeuf's own memories did not differ much from this account. William Howlett, who knew Machebeuf in his later years, reported, "His own account was that he passed his father's door in the diligence, and that he lay down on the floor of it in order to escape observation. This precaution was successful, and none of his immediate relatives knew of his departure until it was too late to make any attempt to dissuade him from the step. He had ridden rough-shod over the last obstacle, but he was yet to know the pain of it. Years afterwards he used to speak of his leaving home as more of an escape, and smile at the recollection."[17]

Part Two

Frontier Missionary: Ohio

1839–1851

FIVE

Voyage to Ohio

✦

Machebeuf and Lamy, the two errant priests, arrived in Paris and presented themselves at 120 rue de Bac, the Seminary of Foreign Missions. Here they awaited three companions from Auvergne, Fathers Gaçon, Cheymol, and Navarron, and their new superior, Bishop Purcell.[1] John Purcell, the bishop of Cincinnati, would lead the contingent of clergy headed for missionary work on the American frontier.

The Seminary of Foreign Missions was an exciting place for the two young Auvergnats. They were surrounded by other young missionaries, and a mood of enthusiasm and anticipation prevailed. Machebeuf and Lamy found eight young priests preparing for departure to the Orient — for China, Cochinchina, and Tong-King in Siam.[2] Stories of the hardships and strange customs that these missionaries would meet made their work in America seem less daunting, made the wilds of America seem much closer to home.

Neither Lamy nor Machebeuf were particularly strong physically, and Lamy was still recovering from an illness he had suffered in his last days in Clermont. For Lamy the time in Paris would provide an opportunity to gather his strength for the Atlantic crossing. Lamy's period of recuperation left Machebeuf free to pursue other activities.

Machebeuf's first priority, having left without pardon or goodbyes, was to mend his relationship with his family. Two days after he reached Paris, a letter from his sister arrived, informing him that their father was furious. Accusing his eldest son of base ingratitude, the elder Machebeuf considered his son's departure a repetition of his earlier decision to join the French army, another impulsive and ill-considered move. Sorely wounded that

Machebeuf had left without saying goodbye and angry that he had not sought his counsel before making such an important commitment, Machebeuf's father was making his displeasure known.

"Without being wanting in my duty," Machebeuf wrote to his father in an attempt to soothe his feelings, "I could no longer resist the inclination which I have so long felt for the missions. But, what has, perhaps, caused you the most pain, is that I left without telling you, and without going to bid you a last farewell. Let me assure you that this was not through indifference or lack of consideration for you, but in reality through obedience to the Superior of the Seminary, who enjoined upon me the most inviolable secrecy. . . . He insisted that the interview would be too painful for both of us." Eager to obtain his father's blessing for his undertaking, Machebeuf even considered traveling back to Riom, but, as he explained, "the Superior of the Foreign Missions where we are staying prevented me, telling me that the parting after such a visit would be more painful than what we are now suffering, and that we would be obliged to part in any case." In a final attempt to return to his father's good graces, he closed, "I sincerely hope that you have already forgiven me for all the pain I have caused you, and that you will kindly grant me the favor I now ask of you, and that is, to write me one word assuring me of the pardon which I urgently implore."[3]

Purcell arrived in Paris two days later. Afraid his own words would not be sufficient to quiet his father's anger, Machebeuf asked the bishop to write to him as well. "Forgive this dear son if in leaving you his fears were too great to allow him to bid you farewell," Purcell wrote on 26 May. "It was in this manner that the great Apostle of the Indias, St. Francis Xavier, passed the house of his parents without saluting them, to go to a barbarous land much farther away than ours." Softening his tone, Purcell closed by writing, "Adieu, good Father. I bid you farewell for your dear son, who is now not only yours but mine also, that is, of two fathers instead of one. I shall love him for you; he will pray for you on earth and in heaven by the numerous souls whom God proposes to save through his ministry."[4]

The letters had their intended effect. Within a few days Machebeuf's father wrote to both Purcell and his son, granting them forgiveness and assuring them of his resignation to the will of God.

Purcell seems to have been quite honest in his promise to love Machebeuf, or at least to have already grown fond of the young man. He proposed that Machebeuf become his traveling companion as he completed his business in France before their departure. Perhaps he feared the young man would grow restless while his friend recuperated, perhaps he wished to provide him with a distraction from his family concerns, or perhaps he just wanted an opportunity to better acquaint himself with the young priest who would serve under him for the next ten years. So attentive was Purcell that Machebeuf found himself "quite confused by the attachment which he constantly shows me. . . . It is as he told you in his letter," Machebeuf assured his father, "that I have two fathers instead of one."[5]

Purcell and Machebeuf departed on a series of short visits around France. By July the two were in Le Havre, finalizing travel arrangements and inspecting the *Silvie de Grasse*, the ship that would carry them across the Atlantic. Machebeuf was unprepared for the luxurious accommodations of the vessel. The cabins, dining room and ladies' salon were all paneled in mahogany, with gilt columns imbedded in the wood. The cabins were designed for two passengers, with narrow berths, "not much more than a foot wide," stacked on the wall of the cabin. Machebeuf explored every corner of the ship, even the stalls for the livestock and the storerooms for provisions. He also toured other ships in the harbor, so that he might have a basis for comparison. The country boy from Auvergne confidently assured his father that "these vessels are veritable hotels, only that the rooms are but six feet square."[6]

After settling travel arrangements in Le Havre, Purcell and Machebeuf returned to Paris, where they met the rest of the group that would accompany them to America. The party consisted of fifteen people. In addition to Machebeuf and Lamy, there were now five other Auvergnats, for Fathers Rappe and Goesbriand had joined Gaçon, Cheymol, and Navarron. The seasoned missionary Bishop Flaget and his vicar general, John McGill, also joined the group, along with two nuns and three priests from other dioceses.[7]

Machebeuf's travels with Purcell had been clouded by his concern for Lamy's health, his worry that Lamy might not be strong enough to accompany him on the grandest of their adventures. But on his return to Paris, he found his friend "promenading after supper" and talking to Fathers Rappe and Goesbriand. Clearly Lamy was well enough to make the crossing. Their departure was set for 8 July 1839. The morning of Monday, the eighth, proved stormy, and the water rough and choppy, so the sailing was postponed until the following day. The *Sylvie de Grasse*, like other ships running the north Atlantic at the time, was probably three-masted, about two hundred feet in length, and carried about a thousand tons gross weight.[8] At eight the next morning she set sail under fine skies, the sailors singing their capstan song and a blessing being offered from the pier, while a crowd of well-wishers waved and shouted final farewells. There was so little wind a steam-powered tug was needed to clear the narrow harbor entrance, and the *Silvie de Grasse* headed slowly for open sea. It was evening before the passengers lost sight of land.

Machebeuf lost no time in beginning a long letter to his family, describing the ship and the voyage, reassuring them of his well-being. He estimated about sixty other passengers in the first-class section, most of whom, he duly noted, were Protestants. But he was more interested in the conditions of those who traveled in steerage. The steerage passengers, about two hundred in all, were mostly German peasant-farming families and a few from the merchant class. The immigrants paid 150 francs for the voyage and brought along their own provisions — the ship supplied them with only wood and water. They were crowded into one large room, separated only by a partition from the quarters of the sailors. The accommodations of the missionaries, although crowded, were far superior to those of the Germans in steerage. The members of his party slept six to a room, and Machebeuf bunked with a Franciscan father from Bavaria and four of the other Auvergnats. The provisions were excellent. Machebeuf happily reported plenty of fresh mutton, fowl, foreign wines, oranges, fresh-baked bread, milk, and butter, "in fact everything of the best that one might find at a hotel in Paris."[9]

The abundance of provisions may have reflected a lack of demand, for within a few hours of sailing, the majority of the group was seasick. Cheymol pronounced himself close to death, until Machebeuf forced him to leave his "box" and take some fresh air on deck. Purcell and Gaçon were sick "only three or four days." Lamy seemed to have had the worst of it, for "he was sick nearly three weeks." Machebeuf cheerfully reported, "while my companions were merely picking at a few dainties, I was managing things about the same as on land. Thus, you see that I would have made a good member of the navy."[10]

He reserved special praises for Bishop Flaget, in what would prove to be the old missionary's last trans-Atlantic crossing. Each morning he was the first one up, saying his morning prayers in the deckhouse. Even when a piece of loose timber injured his leg, the old prelate never complained of the pain. He was continually calm and cheerful. Machebeuf credited Flaget with sustaining the spirits of the rest of the group, attributing even the safety of the vessel to Flaget's serene presence and the power of his daily prayers.

The crossing to America brought Machebeuf the first of his close brushes with death. Despite his boast that he would have made a good sailor, the young priest was obviously not completely at home aboard ship. On the second Sunday of their voyage, as he sat reading on deck with

Father Cheymol, a huge block, bound with iron, fell within three or four feet of the two priests. Seconds later a massive rope, falling more than forty feet, landed on Machebeuf's leg. He was bruised, but not badly. One passenger who witnessed the accident quipped, "a few feet closer, and Machebeuf's mission would have ended."[11]

On 21 August 1839, forty-three days after their departure, the passengers sighted land as the spires of New York City came into view. Machebeuf considered the bay "magnificent," and wrote of the superb forest of masts crowding the harbor.[12] On the docks of South Street, Machebeuf first set foot on the continent that would claim the rest of his life. Awaiting the group were two gentlemen from Cincinnati, friends of Purcell who would accompany them on the remainder of their journey. They escorted the priests across New York to pay their respects to the bishop of New York, Bishop DuBois, a fellow Frenchman and one of Purcell's former teachers.[13] The group left the following morning for Ohio. The journey would take nineteen days.

The first stop was Baltimore, where the missionaries could pay their respects to Bishop Eccleston, and Purcell could renew his contacts at Mount St. Mary's Seminary. As Purcell did not have wagons at his disposal, the group traveled by barge. The most rapid means of transportation were the slow-moving flatboats, drawn by horses or mules that walked on the path beside the canal. The fields, forests, and occasional houses that lined the canals running between New York and Baltimore made up Machebeuf's first view of rural America. Between hills and valleys, the passengers looked out on forests of American elm, river birch, sycamore, and cottonwood, occasionally spotting white-tailed deer or red fox. Traveling at two to three miles per hour, they had plenty of time for conversation. The young priests discussed the work ahead and questioned Purcell on conditions in Ohio. The passengers slept on narrow bunks in small wooden structures built at one end of the barge, the remainder of the space being allotted to cargo. So narrow were the bunks that Charles Dickens, traveling in a similar barge two years later, mistook them for bookshelves. "I decried on each shelf a sort of microscopic sheet and blanket; then I began dimly to comprehend that the passengers were the library, and that they were to be arranged, edge-wise, on these shelves, till morning." As for meals, whatever fare the captain failed to provide could be purchased at canal basins, or from enterprising lockkeepers. When the weather was fair, passengers and crew gathered on the roof of the living quarters, escaping the cramped space within.[14]

Once they reached Baltimore, the travelers transferred to stage coaches pulled by teams of four horses. The coaches, slung on leather straps rather than resting on springs, created an incessant rocking motion and considerable discomfort for some. The windows were open to the elements, with oiled leather curtains that could be buttoned down in case of rain. The coaches took them through continuous forest across the Allegheny Mountains to Wheeling, West Virginia. Frances Trollope, the mother of the novelist, recorded impressions of her ride on the same stretch ten years earlier. "The whole of this mountain region, through ninety miles of which the road passes, is a garden. The almost incredible variety of plants, and the lavish profusion of their growth, produce an effect perfectly enchanting. . . . Oak and beech, with innumerable roses and wild vines, hanging in beautiful confusion among their branches, were in many places scattered among the evergreens."[15]

At Wheeling the party boarded a steam packet that carried them down the Ohio River to Cincinnati. Traveling by steam packet on the same stretch of the river, Dickens recorded his impressions. The packets, "unlike anything we are in the habit of seeing on water," were long, low-slung boats with two paddle-boxes, iron chimneys, and a glass steerage-house jutting up from a smoke-stained roof. The staterooms faced each other across a central corridor "as though they formed a small street." The engine driving the paddle wheels was exposed, "doing its work in the midst of the crowd of idlers and emigrants and children." For three days the packet moved slowly down the Ohio, "a fine broad river," and mile after mile of untouched forest unfolded on either side. Occasionally passengers sighted a log cabin in the midst of a little space of cleared land planted with wheat or still crosshatched by newly felled trees. Often the settlers paused in their work, leaning on ax or hammer, watching silently as the packet passed slowly downstream.[16]

Machebeuf and company reached their destination about the tenth of September. Built on a hill on the curving bank of the Ohio River, Cincinnati was predominantly a city of wooden structures with a few of brick or masonry. In the 1840s it was still a young city, the majority of its streets unpaved. Given the rains of the region they were muddy for much of the year. Still, Dickens called it "a beautiful city; cheerful, thriving and animated." He praised the broad, airy streets, the good shops, and "the private residences remarkable for their elegance and neatness." Modeled after Philadelphia, its broad streets lined by the homes of traders and merchants, the city saw a continuous stream of immigrants. The rapid growth of the city was largely the result of the growth in river traffic on the Ohio. Along the river's edge steamers tied up in front of shops, warehouses, and river emporiums. Farmers all over Ohio used the city's wharves and shipping facilities, and barges and steamboats plied the trade between Cincinnati and New Orleans, taking fresh produce to the Gulf and bringing back sugar, cotton, and molasses.[17] Steamers arrived daily bringing passengers and goods, and the city competed with St. Louis and Pittsburgh to become the preeminent western city.

For a bishopric, Cincinnati was exceedingly modest by European standards. The Catholic church was a big barnlike log structure. American nativism and the No-Popery Movement, sometimes called the Know Nothings, were flourishing, and anti-Catholic sentiment ran high. A local ordinance had been passed prohibiting the building of a Catholic church within the town limits. As a result, the church had been constructed outside of town, then moved into Cincinnati on rollers after the ordinance was repealed. Cincinnati was originally part of the see of Bishop Flaget, the bishop of Bardstown, Kentucky. Flaget consecrated the city's first bishop, Edward Fenwick, in 1822, and Purcell succeeded Fenwick eleven years later.[18]

Prejudice against Catholicism kept Purcell busy in Cincinnati. In addition to overseeing the work of frontier missionaries like Machebeuf and Lamy, he countered attacks by the nativist movement. Anti-Catholic sentiment was on the rise in America throughout the 1830s and 1840s. Publications such as *The Anti-Romanist, The Protestant Vindicator,* and *Priestcraft Exposed* warned citizens of Catholic priests intent on "worming themselves into the confidence and affections of their unsuspecting victims." Protestant ministers headed anti-Catholic associations in cities throughout the United States, fueled by resistance to the assimilation of increasingly large numbers of Irish and other Catholic European immigrants. Nativists viewed the Catholic hierarchy, particularly the pope, as the sworn enemy of America's democratic institutions. On 11 August 1834 tensions exploded in Massachusetts when a group of forty or fifty men stormed the Ursuline convent and school at Mount Benedict and burned it to the ground. Not all Ohioans would welcome the efforts of Machebeuf and his fellow missionaries.[19]

Less than three years before Machebeuf's arrival, the Ohio College of Teachers met in Cincinnati. A Baptist clergyman, Rev. Alexander Campbell, of Bethany, Virginia, devoted his remarks solely to an attack on Catholicism. Bishop Purcell, seated in the audience, objected and was challenged to a debate by Campbell. The minister and the bishop agreed to participate in a series of seven debates, covering seven subjects on seven consecutive days. Purcell fared poorly in the debates, and many citizens of

Cincinnati expressed satisfaction with the way in which Campbell had dev-
astated the arguments of the young bishop. Widely published accounts of
this controversy sparked a number of similar debates around the country.
With the founding of the Cincinnati Protestant Association in 1842, Purcell would be kept busy defending the church against waves of propaganda
launched against Catholicism in the Cincinnati area.[20]

Purcell wasted little time sending Machebeuf and company into the field.
Within three weeks the young priests had been assigned to their various
posts. Machebeuf showed no regrets about the shortness of his stay in
Cincinnati. "I was there but three weeks, and was sick nearly fifteen days of
that time. . . . The Bishop himself was overwhelmed with business and
visitors all day long," he wrote to his family, "and it often happened that his
room was filled with callers while he was taking his meals. You see, then,
that left to ourselves, without anything special to do, and not knowing the
language of the country, our stay in Cincinnati was in danger of growing
very tiresome, and I can assure you that it was with great satisfaction that we
received the news of our early appointments to the missions."[21]

Of the original group, Lamy, appointed to Danville, in Knox County, was
the closest to Machebeuf, about eighty miles away. Lamy ministered to the
Catholics who had followed the same route out of Maryland and to the few
German families that had settled in the area. He and Machebeuf stayed in
touch through letters and saw each other on annual diocesan retreats. Machebeuf was assigned to Tiffin, in northern Ohio, as assistant to Rev. Joseph
McNamee, "a very pious Irish priest, but very sickly."[22] Bishop Purcell assigned McNamee to tending the immediate vicinity. While based in Tiffin
to assist the infirm Irishman, the younger, energetic Machebeuf served as a
roving minister, having sole responsibility for the scattered families in the
hills and forests of the surrounding area. Machebeuf began traveling about
180 miles a month, saying mass in the seats of eight or nine surrounding
counties.

The black soutanes and three-pointed hats that priests wore in France
were hardly appropriate for work on the Ohio frontier. In colder weather,
Machebeuf and Lamy wore matching black cloaks. "Before leaving Clermont we bought some heavy cloth, such as the mountaineers there use, and
at Paris we had it dyed black and made into cloaks, lined again with black
cashmere," he wrote his family. "Then we have knit jackets, woolen under-
wear, stockings, etc., and fur overshoes. When thus equipped we do not fear
either the cold, the snow or the wind."[23] For their work in town, the priests
wore a frock coat, waistcoat, and trousers, with a black cravat, keeping up

respectable appearances. For the missions Machebeuf had a special saddle-bag for his vestments, chalice, and the other accoutrements of the Mass. Although he often rode, within a few months he purchased a buggy, in which he could travel up to forty miles a day and be "less tired than I would be in France after a couple of leagues."[24]

The efficacy of Machebeuf's ministry was somewhat slowed by his questionable command of the English language. Although Father McNamee tutored him, Machebeuf spoke the language poorly. Nonetheless, he began hearing confessions in English within a few days of his arrival. Some of his penitents may have been surprised by his leniency, never realizing that Machebeuf understood only a portion of their nervous confessions.

By February 1840 he was brave enough to attempt his first homily in English, and he duly recorded the auspicious event for his sister in Riom. "The 1st of February, a Saturday, I spent part of the day trying to prepare an instruction in English for the feast of Purification." Machebeuf "pillaged" all of the English books he could find, "and as I was about to put some closing touches on this masterpiece of English literature, I was interrupted by the arrival of a young Lutheran, who came to be instructed in the Catholic religion." Delivering the sermon the following morning, Machebeuf relied upon a tactic learned from Abbé Fauré at seminary. When Fauré lost "himself in the middle of his sermon, he ended by saying: 'My brethren, to shorten your miseries and my own, I will now close by wishing you everlasting life.' "[25]

Nor did Machebeuf's sense of humor fail when it came to his difficulties with another language, German. "On Sunday morning I heard confessions in English, and also in German by means of an interpreter, for I have not yet the gift of tongues." Teasing, he laid the blame on his sister, chastising her by suggesting, "Perhaps you did not pray hard for me, as I asked you to do when I wrote to you."[26]

Through his letters to his family, it is easy to see why Machebeuf was successful in missionary work. He was not a severe, judgmental priest, unfamiliar with the hardships that his pioneering parishioners faced. He was a pioneer himself, and an inexperienced one at that. He described one of his shorter journeys, to a town about ten miles from Tiffin. Riding alone on a snow-covered track he dismounted from his horse and walked for a stretch to warm his feet. When he opened his umbrella against the snow, the horse "took a notion to warm his own feet. . . . He kicked up his heels and started off at a gallop. I could not hold him, and there I was, then, running after my horse, and he disappearing over a hill." Fortunately a young man captured his stray mount and returned him to Machebeuf, who closed the account by saying, "I continued my journey with my body and feet thoroughly warmed up."[27]

Machebeuf's duties generally consisted of visiting isolated Catholic families, singing the mass, and attending to whatever sacramental business was needed — blessing marriages, baptizing children, or providing last rites for the dying. Occasionally, in their eagerness to secure the services of a priest, immigrants would misrepresent a situation. Machebeuf recalled one such occasion in November 1839 when some Irish workmen on the National Road recognized him as a priest. "They called me to a large log cabin to attend a sick man; but there was no sick man! It was a pious fraud to keep me for the next day, which was Sunday."[28]

Machebeuf accepted changes in schedules and lodging with his usual good cheer. His flexibility was remarkable, particularly considering the physical exertion his itinerant lifestyle required. He often held mass in stores or in homes, with calico-covered boxes serving as the altar. For lodging he took whatever was available — private homes, boarding houses, hotels, even taverns. But the true ease with which he adapted to the Ohio frontier is perhaps best represented in a story he later told to amuse fellow clerics in Paris. In the town of Napoleon, Machebeuf had rented a room. After visiting the nearby workers' camps, he returned to find a number of wagons and horses hitched in front of the building. The landlord informed him that Napoleon was the county seat, his house was the largest in town, and Machebeuf's room was the most convenient place for holding court. Machebeuf discovered, "his honor, the judge, was occupying my chair, and the lawyers and jurymen, some rough benches and soap boxes; in fact that court was being held in my room." Accepting the situation Machebeuf left to eat his dinner and say his office. Then, "as I was tired and the court still in session I passed through the crowd of men into my room. I found my bed occupied by three men sitting cross-ways. I whispered to them that having engaged that room and slept a few nights in that bed I had a right to it. They rather hesitated, but as I insisted they got out and as fortunately it had curtains I closed them carefully and, to the amusement of those who were nearby, undressed, [and] went to bed."[29]

For all Machebeuf's lightness, there were real hardships involved. On one of his missionary trips, he had an attack of "shaking fever," malaria. Shortly thereafter, cholera struck the area and rumors of his death spread through the Catholic community. One newspaper even printed his name among the official lists of the dead. Lamy was hit particularly hard by the news. Sadly packing his bags in Danville, he set out to find his dear departed friend, to make sure Machebeuf received a proper burial. To his surprise he found his friend weak, but alive, and well on the road to recovery. The story was relayed to Amadeus Rappe, later the bishop of Cleveland, and Rappe promptly dubbed Machebeuf Trompe la Mort, Death's Deceiver. In the years ahead, the irrepressible Father Machebeuf repeatedly proved himself deserving of the title.[30]

SIX

The Two Sanduskys

✴

In the middle of November 1840, Machebeuf set out to visit his dearest friend at Lamy's parish in the small frontier community of Danville. His "second father," Bishop Purcell, was also visiting Danville, and Machebeuf had the opportunity to present a report of his recent work to his superior. He updated Purcell on the parishioners in Tiffin and the conditions of the more isolated families and settlers. He also reviewed his ministry to the camps, the men working on the construction of canals and railroads, and wove the information into his stories of more colorful adventures. In the course of giving his report, Machebeuf mentioned that a Protestant had donated a site for a church in the town of Lower Sandusky, eighteen miles north of Tiffin. Purcell advised him to pay particular attention to the community and to prepare to oversee the construction of the church. When Machebeuf expressed concern that the additional duties would make it difficult to continue his ministries to the camps, particularly among the Irish laborers building the canal west of Tiffin, Purcell offered a solution. He would send another priest to Maumee, the town nearest the construction of the canal, and Father McNamee would remain in Tiffin. Machebeuf, with his much-improved English, would be transferred to Lower Sandusky to shepherd the two growing towns of Upper and Lower Sandusky. On 1 January 1841 Machebeuf assumed his position as pastor of the two Sanduskys.

In January the snow gleamed white against the dark forests that blanketed the hills around Lower Sandusky. Bluffs of eroded limestone flanked the Sandusky River's icy banks, the surface of the slow-moving river was rough with broken ice. Lower Sandusky, renamed Fremont in 1849, lies in a protected hollow created by low hills. One hill on either side of the river forms the narrow valley just south of Sandusky Bay.

Landlocked by the protective arms of Cedar Point and Marblehead peninsulas, Sandusky Bay is one of the finest natural harbors on Lake Erie. As early as 1720, a map published in Amsterdam identified the eighteen-mile-long bay as "Lac Sandouske." The French adapted the name from the language of the Wyandotte Indians. Referring to the cold water springs flowing nearby, "San-doos-tee" means "at the cold water." For decades tribes of the Iroquois dominated the region, fishing and hunting along the southern shore of Lake Erie.[1]

Europeans had traveled and settled this area for centuries. The French were the first. The great explorer La Salle sailed across Lake Erie in 1679. His annalist, Louis Hennepin, recorded his impressions of the lake's shoreline and the nearby Bass Islands. "We discovered a pretty large island toward the South-West, about seven or eight Leagues from the Northern Coast," Hennepin wrote in his journal. The French priest saw a shoreline filled with "vast Meadows," surrounded by "Hills covered with Vineyards, Trees bearing good Fruit, Groves, and Forests." Those forests "are chiefly made up of Walnut-trees, Chestnut-trees, Plum-trees, and Pear-trees," and the countryside "flock'd" with stags, wild goats, bears, turkey cocks, swans, and "several other Beasts and Birds, whose Names are unknown to us, but they are extraordinary."[2]

In 1760 English trader George Croghan explored the area, reporting that Ottawas and Wyandottes camped around the perimeter of the cool, foggy bay.[3] By the early nineteenth century, white settlers forced most of the indigenous peoples out of the region. Traveling through the area in 1842, Charles Dickens encountered a group of Wyandottes a few miles outside of Sandusky. "We met some of these poor Indians afterwards, riding on shaggy ponies," he wrote in his *American Notes.* "They were so like the meaner sort of gipsies, that if I could have seen any of them in England, I should have concluded, as a matter of course, that they belonged to that wandering and restless people." Ironically, Dickens's sentiment was prophetic. A government agent later told him of treaties already underway that would result in removal of the tribe from their traditional lands and their transfer to a reservation west of St. Louis. The government agent "gave me a moving account of their strong attachment to the familiar scenes of their infancy," Dickens wrote sympathetically, "in particular to the burial-places of their kindred; and of their great reluctance to leave them." The agent, he added, "had witnessed many such removals, and always with pain."[4]

At the time of Machebeuf's arrival, Lower Sandusky was well established, with wooden houses built up to the base of the limestone bluffs and a newly paved main street running east to west through the middle of the town. A trunk line of the Mad River Railroad, still under construction, would soon connect Lower Sandusky to Upper Sandusky, and a magnificent wooden trestle bridge, fifty feet high and a thousand feet long, would carry the trains across the crevice between the two hills that nestled the town. Several newly constructed public buildings, a growing number of houses, and a riverfront lined with steamboats and assorted vessels conveyed the promise of the growing community. But the same riverside location that brought commerce to the town brought disease. From August to October each year, Lower Sandusky was hit with outbreaks of fever. Later, because of his close brush with cholera, Machebeuf would relocate his base of operations to Upper Sandusky, where the climate seemed healthier, the air scoured by the winds off the lake. But initially Machebeuf secured temporary lodgings in Lower Sandusky and rented a large storefront to serve as an interim church. He hired carpenters to build an altar, a confessional, and rough wooden pews. He then rented the pews to neighboring families, a common practice in the period, to raise money for his initial expenses. Soon his storefront church was filled with a mixture of Protestants and Catholics, citizens eager to attend church in a community not yet able to afford denominational scruples.[5]

Eight miles upriver, in Port Clinton, was a settlement of about twenty French Canadian families. They lived on the "borders of lakes, rivers, and swamps" and supported themselves by "hunting and fishing somewhat like the Indians." The head of the group donated sixty acres of land to the church and built a small chapel for services. The unpainted wooden chapel was Machebeuf's first real church in the area, and he visited it whenever possible. In addition to raising money and supervising the construction of churches in the two Sanduskys, he continued to serve as roving minister to more isolated settlements in the surrounding countryside.[6]

Four miles south of the town was another settlement made up of a dozen German families. The patriarch of this group, "whose long and ample coat with its immense buttons," according to Machebeuf, "must date from the time of Henry IV," volunteered to take on the responsibility of teaching Machebeuf German. But with German, as with English, Machebeuf proved a less-than-apt student; he never really mastered either language.[7]

By March 1841 Machebeuf's congregation consisted of fifty to sixty families — mostly Irish, the remainder German. Machebeuf was warmly welcomed and he showed his usual enthusiasm for his work. "There are many evils to reform, and I am glad to say that I have already noticed quite a change, and particularly among the drinkers." Machebeuf had no problem disseminating information to his parishioners. "The women," he wrote, "are the same all over the world. If you want to publish anything you have only to tell it to one of them in a secret."[8]

Perhaps most surprising to Machebeuf was the extent of courtesy he encountered in the frontier settlement. "Everybody shows good will and has respect for the priest," he wrote to his family. "One thing that will astonish you is that the very Protestants have more respect for us than one-half, I should rather say three-fourths, of the Catholics in France."[9] The evils that accompanied the bloody triumph of the French Revolution left a legacy of distrust toward the Catholic Church in nineteenth-century France. The common people associated the church with the monarchy and considered the clergy members of an elite hierarchy. French citizens knew that the church would go to any extreme to reverse the democratic innovations introduced by the revolution.

Many nineteenth-century American Protestants held similar views, particularly in urban areas, crowded by impoverished immigrants, and in New England. The establishment of religious freedom by reformers like Thomas Jefferson in Virginia, however, set a pattern of tolerance for the newer states. On the frontier, settlers "were so engrossed in the task of developing their country . . . that they had no time to reflect on the danger of Popery."[10] Men of God, regardless of affiliation, brought a welcome moral influence, and their churches provided a much-needed social forum for growing towns and settlements.

Machebeuf liked the convenience of his new location, close to the shipping lines of Lake Erie. With his usual optimism, he wrote his father that "From New York, no sailing vessel, but a steamer would take me to Liverpool in fourteen days. . . . Then from Paris to Riom is but a hop-step-and-a-jump for an American." But any trip back to Europe would have to wait until he and Lamy had each built two churches. If his father wished to see him soon, he could simply send money. "If, then, you can find some generous Catholic who will send us 80,000 francs for each church," Machebeuf blithely suggested, "we will both start within a year."[11]

In May 1841 Machebeuf had an opportunity to demonstrate his skill at mediation. The nearby towns of Peru and Norwalk were having problems with their priests. The German Redemptorist, F. X. Tschenhens, who usually served the parish, had been called away suddenly to Pittsburgh. Another German priest, brought in from Detroit during his absence, soon created problems in the parish. "Now, in America, as in Europe, Catholics are not angels," observed Machebeuf. The situation deteriorated quickly, and before long, "trouble broke out, divisions arose, and lawsuits were threatened." Machebeuf, with his genial character and his willingness to work under the most adverse conditions, was asked to take over the parish until Bishop Purcell could investigate and settle the affair. "I came immediately," Machebeuf reported, "and am pleased to see that the turbulent spirits are beginning to quiet down."[12]

This temporary assignment marked the first of Machebeuf's official errands as peacemaker. In the years ahead Machebeuf would take possession of other churches, unify other divided congregations, run interference for anxious bishops, and earn the curious reputation of an ecclesiastical troubleshooter.

In May Machebeuf moved to Upper Sandusky, or Sandusky City, which hugs the ragged shore of Lake Erie midway between Cleveland and Toledo. Even today old shade trees grace brick and limestone buildings, and in the summer season, pleasure craft tie up to the wooden trestles along the waterfront. By the 1820s Upper Sandusky had become a port of entry and a stopping place for vessels on the Great Lakes. It evolved into a shipping center for wheat and corn grown in northern Ohio and destined for markets in Canada and the East. By 1838 Upper Sandusky became the seat of Erie County; two years later it had fifteen hundred residents. When Dickens visited Sandusky in 1841, he described his overnight stay at Colt's Exchange Hotel in something less than enthusiastic prose. "We put up at a comfortable little hotel on the brink of Lake Erie, lay there that night, and had no choice but to wait there next day," he wrote. "The town, which was sluggish and uninteresting enough, was something like the back of an English watering-place, out of the season."[13]

Regardless, Machebeuf was pleased with his new quarters in Upper Sandusky and dutifully reported the improvement in his domestic arrangements to his sister. "If I simply were to tell you that it is a frame house you would likely have but a poor idea of it," he boasted modestly. "I can assure [you] that very few of the country pastors in Auvergne are as well housed as I am." Machebeuf's residence included a parlor, dining room, kitchen, offices and study on the ground floor. The second floor held "two nice bedrooms, with dressing rooms," as well as rooms for the domestic staff below an attic. The house was painted white, "and there is a large garden at the back of it, and a wooden stable." In fact, Machebeuf was a little embarrassed by the relative opulence of his new surroundings, but since the house was the only one for rent in Upper Sandusky, he had no choice but to take it. He closed the letter to his sister with his usual optimism. "When you see our good father and dear aunt, tell them how often I think of them. They need not worry about me — I have never been in need of anything except money."[14]

Two of Machebeuf's most enduring traits surfaced during his years at Sandusky. One was his complete lack of restraint in asking anyone for money. He would shamelessly solicit funds from anyone who would listen — even from those who would not. He had absolute conviction in his mission and an unwavering confidence that anyone aiding him would receive sufficient blessings in return. The second trait was his rather improvident attitude toward debt. His faith was a simple one; Deus providebit — God will provide. His creditors were not always so certain. Machebeuf viewed indebtedness as part of his indoctrination to the American way of life. "When I gather money by dint of scouring through forests and woods to pay my present debts, then I contract more, for, to be a true American, one must have many debts, and in that regard I am the genuine article." With his usual honesty, he described the source of the problem to his sister in Riom. "The principal personage of my household is the most troublesome one. He is always flying around on some business or another and cannot keep quiet. His business is of such importance that my purse is constantly a sufferer by it. This person is none other than your humble servant."[15]

For the most part, Machebeuf's plans were not unreasonable, nor were his investments ill considered. He put his money in land or in buildings, and his judgment was solid enough to assure that most of the property appreciated over time. But his day-to-day finances were far from stable. He raised the money for his two churches largely by subscription. He would press local families to commit themselves to regular contributions, then tally up the potential revenue and borrow against it. His initial subscription at Upper Sandusky raised less than fifteen hundred dollars, which would be paid in installments over the course of a year.[16] He continued to beg shamelessly from friends, relatives, and fellow clergy in France and America, asking for money, sacred vessels, artwork, or anything else his churches could use, and he kept his sister and her companions in the convent busy sewing vestments and altar cloths.

In June 1841 Bishop Purcell came to inspect his work in Sandusky City. Machebeuf's congregation had grown to 110 communicants, another twenty were attending confirmation classes, and the subscription begun earlier in the year had reached $1,600. Machebeuf encouraged a bidding war between two local property owners eager to outdo each other in donations to the church. One, Oran Follette, offered five lots, $530, and all the stone and timber required for the building, and Machebeuf's bidding war came to an end. Purcell hastily accepted the offer. Follette could easily afford it. His colonial house on Wayne Street, built in 1837, was one of the city's most distinctive limestone dwellings, complete with Doric columns, twelve-paned windows, hand-tooled woodwork, and an open fireplace. Follette made his fortune serving as president of the Mad River Railroad and later edited the *Ohio State Journal*.[17]

Following their success in Sandusky City, Machebeuf and Purcell traveled together to Lower Sandusky, where a lot for the church had already been donated. During the visit they stayed at the home of Rudolph Dickinson, who was prepared to donate all the brick needed for the construction of a church.[18] In October Machebeuf laid the cornerstone of the church in Lower Sandusky. Throughout the following year he kept busy constructing the two churches, dividing his time between various disciplines. Machebeuf served as architect, superintendent, mason, laborer, fund-raiser, and occasionally, even as priest.

The young priest could hardly have picked a less auspicious time to undertake his construction projects. Beginning in 1837 the economy of the United States steadily declined. The Specie Circular, issued on 16 July 1836, required that payment for public land be made in gold or silver. This requirement resulted in a drain on the cash reserves of the eastern financial centers. The following year, a fall in cotton prices triggered the failure of several of New Orleans's leading cotton houses and the subsequent failure of their New York financiers. The Panic of 1837 resulted. Still, confidence in American securities persisted, and economic conditions slowly improved from 1837 to 1839. But the recovery could not be maintained, and in 1839 credit tightened again. Demand for currency continued to outstrip supply, and when the Bank of the United States, heavily involved in cotton speculation, suspended specie payments on 9 October 1839, a second crisis followed. This time investor confidence was badly shaken. As one economic historian remarked, "The depression of 1839–1843 proved to be one of the most severe in U.S. history."[19] Numerous banks failed, particularly in the West, and many businesses could not pay their employees—they were simply unable to obtain the cash to do so.

Writing to his brother, Marius, in June 1842, Machebeuf summarized the bleak situation. "I can answer in all truth that [business] could not be in a worse condition. . . . Last spring most of the banks failed, to the great loss of a host of merchants. . . . in consequence every enterprise is at a standstill." The effects of the depression were not limited to eastern financial centers but were striking very close to home. "The company that was building the famous railroad bridge I spoke of has thrown up everything,"

Machebeuf continued, "and now they are talking of tearing the bridge down and selling it piecemeal to pay the debts." As his brother expressed an interest in coming to America to take up a business career, Machebeuf added, "Fortune is more fickle here than anywhere else. Europeans are still coming in great numbers, but it is to buy and improve land." While small businesses were among the hardest hit, western farmers continued to be relatively prosperous. Food prices held up better throughout the depression than those of imported or domestic goods, and Machebeuf closed by offering sound advice to his younger brother. "These tillers of the soil are getting along very well and make a better living here than in Europe, but as you do not intend to take up the spade or the plow I advise you to stay in France."[20]

Machebeuf found his parishioners unable to underwrite the construction of his churches, but he continued working, begging, borrowing, and cajoling his way toward their completion. By October 1842 he was able to report the church at Sandusky City almost complete. Made entirely of stone and measuring forty feet by seventy feet, it had windows, fronts, and corners trimmed in cut stone. Machebeuf described it as "pure gothic style" with a belfry forty feet high. The church in Lower Sandusky, a more modest frame building, had been completed up to the roof. Apparently Mr. Dickinson's promised bricks never materialized.[21]

Machebeuf's churches may have shown considerable progress, but his financial situation continued to deteriorate. The approach of winter and the dearth of funds meant building came to a standstill, while his creditors became increasingly restive. He began to cast around for new ways to finance his venture. He appealed to Bishop Purcell for permission to travel to Canada, certain of the generosity of fellow Frenchmen. Purcell granted him a leave of absence and gave him letters of recommendation to various bishops and priests.

Travel from northern Ohio to Montreal in midwinter proved no easy task. There were no direct railroads and few passable wagon roads. He could travel by water through the Great Lakes, but had no way of knowing how long the waterways would remain navigable. The approach of the Canadian winter meant that certain passages could freeze up at any time. Once he made it across the Great Lakes, he would still have to confront winter on the St. Lawrence River. Above Quebec, the St. Lawrence is icebound from December to April. Below Quebec, where it doesn't freeze solid, navigation is still almost impossible. The tributaries of the St. Lawrence freeze, then break up at different times in different locations. The ice crowds down the channel of the river in piles, creating ice-shoves, or icebergs. If Machebeuf succeeded in reaching his destination without incident, he could still be certain that his travels in Canada, as well as his return home, would be made during the coldest months of the year.

In November 1842 Machebeuf booked passage to Montreal. He crossed Lake Erie without incident. On the crossing of Lake Ontario, he was not so lucky. His vessel encountered a winter storm. In high winds and freezing rain, the ship ran onto the rocks. The passengers and crew abandoned the crippled ship, swimming through the icy, choppy waters to an island in the lake. Together the survivors huddled on the beach, soaked from the unexpected swim, shaken from the experience. When a count was taken, no lives had been lost in the water, but another danger still confronted them. Near-freezing temperatures would bring death in a matter of hours.

Wearily, the shipwreck survivors trudged to a farmhouse, asking for shelter for the night. The farmer agreed to help them, making impromptu arrangements for his unexpected guests. They were kindly received until their host realized that one of his visitors, Machebeuf, was a "Popish priest." The farmer ordered Machebeuf from his house, effectively sentencing him to death by exposure to the frigid night air.[22]

The incident reveals the strength of emotions that found voice in the No-Popery movement. Irish immigrants often took cheap passage across the Atlantic on lumber ships bound for Canada. Once in Canada, they would help load the ship for the return voyage and earn a few dollars. The immigrants then traveled overland to the United States, or bargained with the owners of gypsum vessels for passage to New England ports. Thousands of Irish peasants took advantage of this opportunity, and a constant stream of impoverished settlers found their way into the New England states from Canada.[23] The northeastern seaboard and those areas closest to the shipping lines, inundated by impoverished immigrants, were precisely the areas where anti-Catholic sentiment ran the highest.

The reaction of the farmer was likely a common one in the area. Fortunately the other survivors of the shipwreck, horrified by the farmer's response, objected strenuously. They continued to press the man to allow Machebeuf to remain in the house overnight. Eventually, the farmer relented — on one condition. Machebeuf would be allowed to remain in the house, but only if he slept on the floor.[24] Machebeuf may not have met with the best in American hospitality, but he proved himself, once again, death's deceiver.

SEVEN

Return to Europe

✤

After weeks of travel through the frozen Canadian landscape, Machebeuf rested in "the Paris of the New World," Montreal. At home in the civilized French community, surrounded by Parisian-style architecture and familiar French customs, he took time to update his family on his travels. In January 1843 Machebeuf wrote his father from the Ecclesiastical Seminary, reporting on the success of his journey. "The Bishop of Montreal is himself collecting for a hospital, so I went sixty leagues farther to Quebec," he wrote; "I found there six hundred families poor and without work, and I could expect nothing from them, but the Bishop of Quebec recommended me to the wealthy families, to the priests of the city, and to the Ursuline Nuns." In addition to contributions from the wealthier families, Machebeuf increased his profits by reducing his expenses. He was guaranteed hospitality traveling by "clerical post, that is, from parish to parish." Whatever money he collected could be used solely for the debts on his churches.[1]

In Montreal he stayed with one of his former teachers from Clermont-Ferrand, one familiar with the less-conventional aspects of Machebeuf's character. "Mr. Billaudele, under who[m] I made my studies in the Seminary, is here as Superior of the Ecclesiastical Seminary," Machebeuf told his father, "He desired me to remember him most kindly to you, and you can see that he has not forgotten the old epithet of 'Little Rogue.' "[2]

The "Little Rogue's" trip to Canada lasted four and half months. By his own estimate, Machebeuf traveled about eight hundred leagues, almost twenty-five hundred miles, preaching, begging, and collecting anything that might be of use in his missionary efforts. Returning to Sandusky in the spring of 1843, he immersed himself in the neglected work of his parish. He led catechism for children in communion classes everyday. He gave instructions to adults three nights a week and prepared two sermons every Sunday, "all in bad English," he confessed, "but that mattered little — I was understood, and that was sufficient for me." He also began the construction of his own residence in Sandusky City and completed construction of his two churches.[3]

By April 1843 the church in Lower Sandusky was opened, and by the first of August the church in Sandusky City would be complete except for the plaster. "I do not know when it will be finished, as our present means are exhausted, but I have an immense treasure in Divine Providence," he wrote to his sister in July. Machebeuf's finances were, as usual, largely nonexistent, although in the course of his Canadian trip he had collected money to pay about half his debts. He summarized his progress on the Sandusky church. "I began it with two dollars, and in less than two years I have expended on it nearly $4,000 in money, work, and material, and besides this the walls of my house are finished and the frame of the roof is ready to go up." For all his efforts, Machebeuf's collections never quite caught up with his expenditures. "It is true that I am again at the bottom of the sack and have a number of little debts," he continued, "but I am not discouraged. . . . Every time that I see Father Lamy we say, as the people of Aubieres: 'Latsin pas!' — Never give up!"[4]

Machebeuf carried on with his work through the summer and early fall that same year, but in October, news arrived that undermined his cheerful outlook. His father, gravely ill, was not expected to recover. "Until now your letters have always been for me a source of great pleasure," he wrote to his sister on October twenty-third, "but when your last came . . . a secret dread seized me, and the reading of your letter proved it to be well founded." Machebeuf was seized with a fear that his father would die before he could return to France. His fear was compounded by the guilt he felt about his sudden departure to the missions. He had not said goodbye to his father before leaving for America. Now he realized he might never see him alive again. With his sister's letter he included a letter to his father. If his father was too weak to read, she could read it aloud. Concluding the letter, he wrote, "Adieu, dear Papa; we shall meet in this world, I hope, but if not, then in heaven."[5]

Immediately Machebeuf applied for permission to visit his family in France, but Bishop Purcell was the only one who could grant such permission, and the bishop was out of the country. Purcell's vicar general, acting in his stead, reviewed the situation and concluded that Machebeuf could not be spared; there was no one available to care for his parish in his absence. In addition, neither his Sandusky church nor his presbytery were yet complete, and he was the only one familiar with the contracts that had been let. Even if permission were granted, Machebeuf did not have the money to undertake the voyage.

In November he wrote his sister explaining his failure to return to France. "I am almost ashamed to acknowledge," he said with uncharacteristic diffidence, "that my greatest difficulty would be to find the $200 necessary to pay my way. . . . I have not five dollars in my possession . . . . Oh, how helpless I feel myself! and it almost looks as if I were excusing myself for a lack of affection, but I am forced to make this last sacrifice of ever again seeing our good father." Restless and anxious, Machebeuf continued his work on the parish and his building projects through the winter of 1843.[6]

In the spring Machebeuf received news of his father's death from both his brother and his sister. Bishop Purcell returned from abroad and granted permission for Machebeuf to make the trip home. Machebeuf's brother sent him $223 to cover his fare across the Atlantic, and Lamy agreed to check in on his parishioners when he could. In May he went to the small town of Chillicothe to meet Purcell, who gave him a commission: Machebeuf was to recruit more French religious men and women for the missions while he was in Europe. By June he had put his Ohio affairs in reasonable order, and on 26 June he sailed from New York. Seventeen days later he arrived in Le Havre, the site of his departure almost five years before.

His father dead and buried, Machebeuf no longer felt the same sense of urgency to return home, so rather than travel immediately to Riom, he first went to Boulogne-sur-Mer. There, he met with the Ursulines, hoping to convince them to release enough nuns to establish a school in Brown County, Ohio. The Order of St. Ursula was founded by Angela Merici in 1535. In addition to the vows of poverty, chastity, and obedience, the Ursulines take a fourth vow devoting themselves to the work of education. Along with the Brothers of the Christian Schools, they were one of the few orders permitted to continue their educational work in the years following the French Revolution. With an established history of missionary activity, they would be ideal for the establishment of the Ohio school.[7]

Machebeuf outlined his plans to the Superior of the convent at Boulogne-Sur-Mer, then moved on to Riom, staying long enough to offer what consolation he could to his sister and his aunt and to make legal arrangements for the settlement of his father's estate.

His first attempt at recruitment in Boulogne was not a great success. The nuns were allied to a common order, and permission to leave was subject to hierarchical approval. Unsure whether approval would be granted in Boulogne, Machebeuf began corresponding with M. L'Abbe Graviche, the spiritual director of the Ursuline nuns at Beaulieu. Graviche was encouraging, but there was strong secular resistance to the convent being relocated. Whether the townspeople were reluctant to see their daughters or sisters removed to distant America or afraid the transfer might result in the complete closure of the convent and school is unclear. What is clear is that the community strongly opposed Machebeuf's recruitment efforts. He made little progress. Since he was also commissioned to recruit additional priests for the missions, he turned his attention to Grande Séminaire d'Avignon. He traveled to Lyon, spent a day with his brother, Marius, who was pursuing his business career there, and then traveled through the mountains of the lower Loire valley to Le Puy. Finding no direct means to go further south from Le Puy, he returned to Lyon, and took passage on a Rhone steamer.

Machebeuf arrived in Avignon in the fall and was greeted by "the broken bridge of Avignon, and all the city baking in the sun; yet with an under-done-pie-crust, battlemented wall, that will never be brown though it bake for centuries." The Avignon of 1844 had streets "old and very narrow, but tolerably clean, and shaded by awnings stretched from house to house" alongside "quiet sleepy courtyards, having stately old houses within, as silent as tombs."[8] Machebeuf interviewed faculty and seminarians, remembering the tough, craggy missionaries who had recruited him nearly ten years before. Now he was the seasoned missionary, he was the man with tales of adventure and hardship, trying to convince younger men to undertake work in distant America. Having made the initial contacts, knowing that it would take time before the needed decisions could be made, Machebeuf was free to pursue his own interests. He set out for Rome.

It was his first trip to Rome, and Machebeuf embraced the city with the ardor of a lovesick teenager. He was thirty-two-years-old and had been a priest for eight years. He had read about Rome since his childhood. He was determined to visit every church and holy site possible, given his limited time and even more limited budget. He found a room that cost fifteen cents a day, breakfast for four cents, dinner for twenty-five cents, and took his supper "by heart," forgoing any additional expense.[9] Day after day he traveled around the city, wide-eyed, like the impoverished tourist he was.

His first visit was to St. Maria Sopra Minerva, the church of St. Mary on Minerva. Machebeuf had dedicated his missionary work to Mary's service. The only Gothic church in Rome at the time, St. Mary on Minerva stands on the site of an ancient temple, its vast vaulting interior hidden behind a plain exterior.[10] There he renewed his devotion to his second mother.

Descending with typical energy upon the Vatican, he made five visits to

St. Peter's. Dickens conveyed the majesty of the entrance to the church in the eyes of a nineteenth-century visitor. "The beauty of the Piazza in which it stands, with its clusters of exquisite columns, and its gushing fountains — so fresh, so broad, and free, and beautiful — nothing can exaggerate." Awed, Machebeuf walked from the narrow Borgo Nuova between Bernini's two colonnades, which George Eliot described as giving "always a sense of having entered some millennial view of Jerusalem, where all things small and shabby were unknown." With a sense of reverence Machebeuf walked for the first time into the most famous of all Catholic churches. Wrote Dickens, "The first burst of the interior, in all its expansive majesty and glory: and, most of all, the looking up into the Dome: is a sensation never to be forgotten." Machebeuf climbed to Michelangelo's dome and even to the ball at the foot of the cross. He descended into the tomb of St. Peter, in the subterranean remains of the original basilica, and on the anniversary of the dedication of St. Peter's, said a private mass on the altar over the grave of the first pope.[11]

Next Machebeuf visited the Gesu, the sixteenth-century Jesuit church with its profusion of bronze, gilding, and frescoes, its walls encrusted with marble, its altars covered by priceless statues and bronzes. He said mass at the altars of St. Stanislaus and St. Francis Xavier, the legendary Jesuit missionary to Asia. He said another private mass in the rooms where St. Ignatius of Loyola had lived, perhaps seeking a special blessing from the founder of the missionary order. Machebeuf also made a trip to the church of St. John Lateran, the cathedral of the bishop of Rome, walking beneath the stone facade that proclaims it to be "The Mother and Head of all the churches in the city and the world" and recorded seeing the baldachin, or canopy, that contained the martyred heads of St. Peter and Paul.[12]

Twice he ventured down into the Mamertime prison to see where St. Peter had been imprisoned. This was a frightening chamber. "It is very small and low-roofed," Dickens recorded, "and the dread and gloom of the ponderous obdurate old prison are on it, as if they had come up in a dark mist through the floor. Hanging on the walls, among the clustered votive offerings, are objects . . . rusty daggers, knives, pistols, clubs, divers instruments of violence and murder. . . . It is all so silent and so close, and tomb-like; and the dungeons below are so black and stealth, and stagnant, and naked; that this little dark spot becomes a dream within a dream."[13] Machebeuf was mesmerized. He drank from the spring that is said to have burst forth when St. Peter baptized his jailer and gathered some of the dust from the ground as a keepsake. His own missionary hardships seemed light by comparison to the struggles and persecutions of the earliest Christians.

Not satisfied with seeing only the religious monuments of the city, he visited the Coliseum, the Pantheon, the arches of Titus, of Septimus Severus, and of Constantine, and took in every corner of the city he could manage. He wandered through the world Dickens described as a "field of ruin. Broken aqueducts, left in the most picturesque and beautiful clusters of arches; broken temples; broken tombs. A desert of decay, sombre and desolate beyond all expression; and with a history in every stone that strews the ground." Machebeuf's mood was far from sombre. He was delighted and filled with renewed enthusiasm for his missionary work. He felt, on a deeper level, a sense of spiritual exaltation, a deeply felt confirmation of the belief system that structured his world, that gave moral certainty to his life and his work.[14]

After he had been in the city almost three weeks, his greatest moment came. He received news that he had been granted a papal audience. On 17 November he met with Pope Gregory XVI. At seventy-nine, the pope had weathered decades of battles between church and state. An engraving by Henriquel-Dupont portrays a kindly man with a prominent nose and gentle, drooping eyes whose tired expression is countered by the firm set of his chin. Pope Gregory XVI had known the chaos that the French Revolution brought to the church in France. He had long shown a particular interest in the missions and recognizing that the missions could no longer depend on Catholic governments for material needs, in 1843 he afforded papal protection to the work of the Society for the Propagation of the Faith. This society, established in 1622 to underwrite missionary expenses, was given new impetus in the 1840s.[15] The society would prove an invaluable financial ally to Machebeuf in the years ahead.

Papal audiences were usually formal and often rushed, but Machebeuf was a born storyteller, and he put on one of his greatest performances. As papal aides nervously checked appointment times, Machebeuf regaled the pontiff with stories of his adventures in America, of hardship and suspense, of frontier life and travel, of poverty and near-despair followed by triumph and new horizons. It was customary to ask the pope to bless a small religious article, but Machebeuf showed no such moderation. He brought with him two valises, filled to the brim with Roman trinkets that he could disburse on his travels. Pope Gregory blessed them all and gave the Apostolic Blessing to Machebeuf and all the Ohioans. As aides ushered Machebeuf out of the chamber, the pope's voice rang out, in words the young priest would never forget, "Courage, American!"[16]

Machebeuf's Roman holiday had exceeded his wildest expectations, and he left Rome newly inspired. But before he returned to his mission, he made a final voyage, he traveled to the small village of Loreto, overlooking the Adriatic. Loreto was famous for its shrine of the Holy House of the Blessed Virgin. Legend has it that it was the original home of Christ, converted into a church by the Apostles. After the fall of the Latin Kingdom of Jerusalem, in 1291, angels transported the church to Tersatto in Yugoslavia. When the people of Tersatto failed to properly venerate the church, the angels reappeared and moved the structure again, first to a wood, then to a hill near Recanati. When the people still failed to venerate the structure, the angels brought it to Loreto in December 1295. It has remained there ever since. For centuries Loreto has been recognized as a pilgrimage site; more than fifty popes have made pilgrimages there, and numerous miraculous cures have been recorded.[17]

In Loreto Machebeuf mused on scenes memorized from passages in the Gospel, seeing what was believed to be the scene of the Annunciation and the house of Christ's childhood. Twice he said mass on the altar that previous pilgrims had covered with gold and precious stones. He had more of his beads and medals blessed, and collected another bit of dust as his personal memento.[18] Then, reluctantly, he returned to France, traveling by way of Venice.

Once back in France Machebeuf headed immediately for Beaulieu to check with Graviche on the status of his recruitment efforts. On 20 January 1845 the two of them met with Bishop Bertaud of Tulle and requested the letters of obedience that would free the Ursulines for missionary work in America. The bishop gave his consent. Four nuns from Boulogne and eight from Beaulieu would accompany Machebeuf on his return voyage. But just as he was scheduling their departure for the first of March, complications arose. Questions developed about who within the Ursuline order had the authority to release the nuns. While letters flew back and forth between Beaulieu and Boulogne, the gens d'armes in Beaulieu, pressured by local resistance against the departure of any of the nuns, arrested Machebeuf for violation of an obscure government regulation about religious foundations. Machebeuf stayed in jail overnight, until a brother of one of the nuns interceded. Through his efforts, Machebeuf was released.[19] Recovering from the shock of being a convict, and waiting for the gossip to die down, Machebeuf saw an opportunity for a final round of begging before leaving for America.

He had previously written to the French royal family asking for financial aid to pay the party's travel expenses. In April he traveled to Paris, where he was presented to Queen Marie Amelie. She promised him a contribution and another from King Louis Philippe. By letter he had already received assurances of contributions from the king's sister, Princess Adelaide, the king's son, the Duc d'Aumale, and a royal daughter-in-law. After receiving no further word, Machebeuf approached the pastor of St. Roch, the regal parish, and reminded him of the royal promises. Two weeks later he sarcastically reported, "Madame Adelaide gave me — Guess how much. About 2,000 francs, you say? Just cut off one zero!"[20]

From Paris he directed the final arrangements for his contingent of future missionaries. The situation was still unresolved in Beaulieu, some of the local people still fighting the nuns' departure to America. To avoid further interference from the gens d'armes or the locals, the nuns would be smuggled out of town at night.

The eight nuns split into two groups, one made up of the newly designated superior of the mission and an assistant, another of the remaining six. Disguising themselves as peasant women or servants, they wrapped their habits into bundles and stole away from the convent. Machebeuf met the larger group at Brive la Gaillarde and conducted them to Paris. The superior and her assistant had a more anxious escape. Terrified by tollgate keepers, having run into difficulty securing lodgings, finally, they, too, arrived in Paris.

Machebeuf booked passage for May 4, then he and the eight Beaulieu nuns set out for Le Havre to meet the four Boulogne nuns. In all, Machebeuf had collected a party of sixteen people: the four nuns from Boulogne, the eight from Beaulieu, Father Pendeprat, a priest recruited to serve as his assistant in Sandusky, and three other seminarians, who had already left for America. On May 4 the two Mother Superiors who had traveled to Le Havre to see off their charges blessed the party before they boarded the steam packet *Zurich* and set sail.

Machebeuf's first return to Europe had been a resounding success. He had taken care of necessary family business, journeyed to Rome and Loreto, successfully recruited sixteen individuals for Purcell's missions, and was now shepherding his twelve Ursuline nuns across the Atlantic. On their arrival in Ohio, one of the sisters wrote to her Mother Superior, "During all this long voyage Father Machebeuf was our guide, our provider, our servant, our messenger, our guardian angel, our spiritual father, in fact he was everything to us and we were like helpless children in his hands."[21] Did the naive Ursulines have any concept just how precarious that situation might be?

EIGHT

South to the Southwest

✥

Machebeuf arrived at the South Street docks in New York on 2 June 1845, his contingent of Ursulines in tow. He lodged the ladies near the French church of St. Vincent de Paul, at a boarding house owned by a French Catholic woman, Madame Pilet.[1] For eight days he busied himself with the arrangements needed to transport his fellow travelers to Ohio.

The trip followed the same path he had taken five years earlier. Some rail lines had been completed between New York and Philadelphia, so the group traveled by rail part of the way, the rest by steamboat. At Philadelphia they transferred to canal boats for the journey to Baltimore. Another rail link had been completed from Baltimore to Cumberland. Then, as he had five years earlier, they traveled over the Allegheny Mountains to Wheeling by stage. There they boarded the steamer *Independence*, which took them down the Ohio River on the final portion of their journey. On 19 June the party reached Cincinnati.

Machebeuf stayed on in Cincinnati for a month, still watching over his Ursulines, updating Purcell on his trip, and visiting with clergy in the area. On 21 July, he escorted the Ursulines to Fayetteville in Brown County.[2] Feeling a paternal affection and responsibility for the group, Machebeuf stayed on with them until they were comfortably settled. He left for Sandusky in the middle of August.

Machebeuf had recruited Peter Pendeprat to serve as his assistant in Sandusky. The towns in northern Ohio were growing much faster than those in other parts of the state, and even the energetic Machebeuf was unable to meet the demands of his growing congregation, especially after his fourteen-month absence. Pendeprat accompanied Machebeuf to Sandusky in August of 1845 but was unable to provide much help. He spoke neither English nor German. Accordingly, he could be of immediate use only in the small French settlements, which were the least pressing of Machebeuf's concerns.

Bishop Purcell had added the parish of Norwalk to Machebeuf's duties. Writing to his sister, Machebeuf complained of the added work: keeping accounts, assembling materials for building, and raising money to prevent the Norwalk church from being sold. A "Protestant fanatic," who had furnished materials for the church and not been paid, was threatening to sell the church on demand. Still, Machebeuf was grateful for Pendeprat's help and set about teaching him English. His lessons proved to no avail. In the fall Purcell proposed Father Rappe of Toledo as the bishop-designate for a newly formed diocese, and appointed Father DeGoesbriand, who was serving in Louisville, as Rappe's assistant. By the end of the year Pendeprat was sent to replace DeGoesbriand in Louisville.[3]

In the spring of 1846 the situation seemed to improve. Lamy had completed his presbytery in Danville and suggested to Purcell that a permanent pastor be stationed at nearby Newark. This would leave Lamy free to help Machebeuf in the north, and the two friends could be reunited. Purcell agreed to this proposal. Eager to see his old friend again and knowing that help was finally on the way, Machebeuf dug into the work at hand. There was plenty to do.

Sandusky was still a frontier town. Public drunkenness was common and street fights a daily occurrence. Machebeuf was often called on to separate fighters, sometimes at the front door of the church. Lamy's quiet, authoritative presence would help establish a more civilized atmosphere. As immigrants continued to arrive, the numbers of Catholics requiring Machebeuf's attention also increased. "My own church, supposed when built to be large enough for ten years," Machebeuf wrote at the time, "will not accommodate two thirds of my people now. Six years ago I had thirty families, now I have two hundred."[4]

In June 1846 Purcell came to inspect Machebeuf's work in Sandusky and to bless his churches. The bishop was pleased by what he found. There were now three churches completed, the finest being the one in Upper Sandusky. Built of stone in gothic style, with a 117-foot spire, it was impressive. The cross on top of the church, was, according to Machebeuf, "made by an English Anabaptist, gilded by an American infidel, and placed on a Catholic church to be seen shining by mariners far out upon the lake."[5]

Machebeuf's ambitious plans for Sandusky were far from realized. Writing to France, hoping to recruit more priests for the Ohio missions, he confidently reported, "Today we have a beautiful church, of stone, a presbytery of twelve rooms, a cemetery of two acres, and a school for boys beside the church—all to the value of $7,000 and not a cent of debt on any of it." He outlined his plans for the parish, "I have bought a large two-story house with spacious grounds and all outside conveniences, such as barns, out-houses, trees and fences. In this we intend to install an orphan asylum and a free school under the Sisters of Charity. Still another is a three-story stone building . . . intended as a boarding and day school for young ladies."[6] In spite of the assurances about his financial situation, he was, as usual, in debt. The two new houses cost $1,900 and $2,250, respectively. Machebeuf had put down a deposit on each, intending to pay the balance in five install-ments. When the payments came due, he was unable to meet them, and his parish was unable to provide any additional funds. Strapped, he sold his inheritance in France and used the proceeds to tide him over. He continued to solicit donations from friends and relatives, and never stopped solicit-ing vestments, chalices, artwork, or anything that could help equip his churches.

Purcell finally sent someone out to assist the overworked Machebeuf. First it was a much older man, causing Machebeuf some discomfort; he knew no delicate way to give orders to someone so much older than him-self. Later, Purcell sent a young, newly ordained priest who spoke both German and English. But in many ways the help received was too little, too late. In the beginning of 1849 the potato famine in Ireland brought added difficulties to Machebeuf. The Irish were one of the largest immigrant populations in Sandusky. Writing to his sister he sounded tired: "My work grows heavier every day. Now it is caused by the immigration of the poor Irish who are driven from their country by famine. . . . The number of our poor and sick has so increased that I shall commence a school for the poor and an asylum for the orphans if I can get the Sisters of Charity, or Mercy, to whom I have written." The flood of Irish immigrants brought an in-creased need for services, but they were the least able to contribute to the church. Machebeuf's financial situation continued to deteriorate. He asked his sister to "urge my agents to send me what money they can to pay off part of my loans."[7]

All of Machebeuf's hard work and endless energy had not gone un-noticed. Several years earlier, in Tiffin, he had been visited by Jesuit mis-sionary Peter J. De Smet, already celebrated as the Apostle to the Indians. De Smet had made expeditions into the Rocky Mountain region, across the vast lands west of the Mississippi, and would later become best known for his extensive work in the Pacific Northwest. Recognizing a kindred spirit,

De Smet urged Machebeuf to join him, telling dazzling tales of hardship
and adventure in the American West. The picture of the missionary life that
De Smet painted held a great attraction for Machebeuf. This was the kind
of life he had envisioned when he had first decided to become a missionary.
His thirst for adventure was one of his most consistent traits, and De Smet
was offering a chance to move beyond the frontier, into the unknown
wilderness of the West. Machebeuf agreed to accompany him. When Purcell heard of his plans, he sent Lamy to dissuade Machebeuf. Machebeuf
listened to Lamy's and the bishop's objections, then asked Lamy, "'Eh bien!
mon cher, what would you do in my place?" Before they left Clermont the
two friends made a vow not to part unless absolutely necessary, and now
Lamy's words reminded him of his vow. Lamy responded, "What would I
do? All right. If you go, I shall follow you."[8]

Purcell was wise to send Lamy as his emissary, for Lamy had the greatest
understanding of Machebeuf's nature. Lamy knew that Machebeuf's hun-
ger for adventure was matched only by his loyalty. Strategically, Lamy
played Machebeuf's sense of loyalty against the lure of De Smet's invitation.
Both Machebeuf's loyalty to Lamy and his word of honor stood between
him and the distant missions. Although Machebeuf would relish working
with De Smet in the West, he knew his friend Lamy was not meant for a life
of obscure hardship in one of the Indian missions. He also knew Lamy had
all the prerequisites for ecclesiastic advancement: a sanguine temperament,
a shrewd intellectual perspective, an excellent Jesuit education, political
sophistication, and a calm, authoritative presence. Lamy would be sacrificing a bishopric, perhaps even more, in order to accompany Machebeuf. De
Smet's offer would alter not only Machebeuf's own life but also his best
friend's. With some regret, Machebeuf declined De Smet's offer. Although
the two friends did not know it, their roles were about to be reversed.

On 11 May 1849 three American Catholic archbishops and twenty-three
bishops met in synod in Baltimore. Together they outlined their plans for
the expansion of the church in America. At the conclusion of their meeting,
the bishops wrote to Pius IX, asking for the establishment of three new
archbishoprics — in New York, Cincinnati and New Orleans. They also
asked for four new episcopal sees, in Savannah, Georgia, Wheeling, West
Virginia, St. Paul, Minnesota, and Monterey, California, and requested the
establishment of a vicariate apostolic, for the territory called the Rocky
Mountains.

In the seventeenth century, the nomination of bishops in non-Christian
countries had been left up to the sovereigns of the colonial power control-
ling them — the kings of Spain, Portugal, or France. Too often this resulted

in the positions being left vacant for long periods of time. To remedy this problem and remove the suspicion of political indebtedness from such bishops, the Congregation for the Propagation of the Faith resurrected the title of "vicar apostolic," a term dating back to the fourth century. The vicar apostolic, a bishop nominated by the Holy See, would enjoy the same rights as a resident bishop in his diocese, make a visit to Rome every ten years to report on the state of his vicariate, and have an obligation to see to the development of native clergy in the area. All missionary activity within the vicariate would be subject to the vicar apostolic, who would remain in power until such time as the vicariate was elevated to a diocese.[9]

Concluding their requests to Pope Pius IX, the American bishops recommended that "there be elected a Vicar Apostolic, dignified with episcopal consecration, for the Territory of New Mexico, and its see established in the city of Santa Fe."[10] The New Mexico Territory had become part of the United States following Stephen Kearny's capture of Santa Fe in 1846. With the civil transfer of land from Mexican to U.S. authorities, responsibility for the church in the area had shifted from Durango, Mexico, to the American bishops who determined it should become a vicariate apostolic. Completing their discussions in Baltimore, the bishops scattered back to cities across the country. A few among them began assembling lists of promising individuals to fill the new posts they had requested.

Unknown to Machebeuf and Lamy, Pope Pius acted on the final request of the American bishops in July 1849. On the nineteenth he established by decree the vicariate apostolic of New Mexico, and on the twenty-third he issued a papal bull naming its first vicar apostolic. Father Jean Baptiste Lamy would become the vicar apostolic of New Mexico bearing the title of bishop of Agathonica.[11]

As soon as Lamy received news of his appointment, he wrote to Machebeuf in Sandusky, reminding him of their vow, asking him to join him as his primary aide. He would be needing someone who could accompany him, "not only as a missionary, but as an intimate friend on whom he could count and upon whom he could lay a part of his burden — in short, as his Vicar General." Come to New Mexico with me, Lamy wrote, because "they want me to be a Vicar Apostolic, very well, I will make you my Vicar General, and from these two Vicars we'll try to make one good pastor."[12]

There was a great deal of truth behind the humor in Lamy's comment. In many ways the two friends complemented each other, creating a whole greater than the sum of the parts. Lamy was stronger in intellectual and political pursuits. His grave, dark demeanor, his intellectual fierceness, and his calm aura of command gave him a sense of authority that Machebeuf could never hope to match. But at times Lamy's authoritarian directives were brusque. He could easily ruffle the feathers of those serving under him and be seen as unyielding or rigid. The social arena was Machebeuf's forte. With his slight blond frame, his ready smile, his energy, and his knack for storytelling, Machebeuf could charm away discontent. He could heal the feelings hurt in Lamy's more imperious moments, and he could quickly develop a bond of genuine affection with those around him. Machebeuf could provide the social lubricant that smoothed Lamy's interactions, and Lamy could provide the necessary political finesse when Machebeuf's impulsive actions proved less than judicious.

The decision was not easy for Machebeuf. He had put ten years into Ohio. He had finally begun to reap some of the benefits of his years of work — churches established, schools opened, assistance finally secured. In Sandusky he was independent, his activities were not subject to anyone's direct supervision. As Lamy's vicar general he would be sacrificing his autonomy. Still, given his tendency toward impulsive decisions, he had a far better chance at ecclesiastical advancement with Lamy than without him. As vicar general he would participate on a day-to-day basis in Lamy's jurisdiction over the temporal and spiritual matters of the vicariate. He would be able to exercise nearly all the administrative powers of a bishop and even serve as acting bishop when Lamy traveled abroad.[13] And he would answer only to Lamy, his oldest and dearest friend.

"At first I did not know what kind of answer to give to such a proposition," he later wrote to his family. "I waited ten days before giving any answer to the proposal . . . went to Cleveland to confer with Bishop Rappe and the priests of the Cathedral." It was only when he went to Cincinnati to see Lamy that Machebeuf finally came to a decision. "As soon as he saw me he grasped my hand and summoned me to keep my part of the agreement which we had made never to separate, and he spoke of the time when he was willing to go with me to the West."[14] Machebeuf could bear neither to break his vow nor to disappoint his dearest friend.

Before he could undertake the work with Lamy in New Mexico, Machebeuf first had to part with his parishioners in Sandusky. They did not want him to go. They circulated two petitions, one for Bishop Rappe and another for Bishop Lamy, protesting the loss of their pastor. Two men traveled to Cincinnati to present the petition to Lamy, but missed him, as he was making his retreat at Fayetteville. Two others traveled to Cleveland, but were just as unsuccessful in presenting their petition. "I have left my dear Sandusky," Machebeuf later wrote, "I can hardly think of it without tears. . . . The separation was too painful that I should so soon forget it, or be able to think of it without emotion."[15]

Leave Sandusky he did, and so he wrote his family while traveling down the Mississippi, en route to New Mexico. The usual route to Santa Fe was through St. Louis, then overland on the Santa Fe Trail across the plains, but Lamy had decided that a recent series of Indian raids made that route too dangerous. They would travel downriver to New Orleans, then across the Gulf of Mexico to Galveston, overland to San Antonio and El Paso, and up the Rio Grande valley to Santa Fe. This route would allow Lamy to settle his niece, Marie, and his sister, Marguerite, in New Orleans. They had come to witness his consecration as a bishop and needed to be settled in school and convent, respectively. Lamy went first; Machebeuf followed a few weeks later.

Machebeuf wrote his family, telling them of his move. "But first, I hear you ask: 'What is the *Peytona?* and where is he going?' The *Peytona* is one of the largest and most beautiful steamboats on the river between Cincinnati and New Orleans. . . . It is a miniature world." The boat carried 350 people, plus the crew, an assemblage made up of "Catholics and Protestants, believers and infidels, priests and laics, freemen and slaves, Germans, French, English, Irish, Poles, Americans, [and] Africans." Additionally it carried "160 horses and mules, 100 fat beeves, 400 sheep and 75 gamecocks," along with "400 bales of cotton, 200 or 300 tons of flour, and various other kinds of produce."[16]

The journals of Mrs. Eliza Steele record the Mississippi that Machebeuf saw when he looked up from his studies. "Sometimes it is lined with bluffs from one hundred to four hundred feet high, or a soft green prairie, sloping banks, impenetrable marshes, large cities and pretty villages. The clay which the Missouri brings with it is heaped upon the shores, or in a pile at the bottom of the river, upon which a snag, a long trunk of a tree is flung." The *Peytona* steamed downriver, headed for New Orleans. Machebeuf spent his time on the voyage studying Spanish, which he found "resembles French and Latin a great deal, and has a certain affinity with the 'patois' of Auvergne."[17]

As rich southern landscapes rolled slowly by, Machebeuf found himself entranced by a world he would never have the time to truly know. He recorded glimpses of the final years of the southern aristocracy. "While I am writing we are passing magnificent plantations of cotton and sugar," he wrote. "Each resembles a little village. First there is the house of the master, generally of brick, two stories high and very large. Then, at one side are the little cabins of the slaves, from 25 to 40 feet apart, and each negro family has its little house and garden." Machebeuf was fascinated, and yet horrified, by the conditions of the slaves. He had rarely encountered slavery. "The slaves are always working for their masters," he continued, "without receiving anything but their food and clothing, and these are coarse enough in most instances." The worst moment came when the boat passed through Memphis. "I cannot pass over in silence a revolting scene which took place at Memphis where we stopped for a few hours. We had a slave dealer on the boat and he sold two poor young negro girls to a merchant of that town. The buyer examined them, had them walk back and forth before him, made them talk, and asked them what they could do, and why their master had sold them." The incident upset Machebeuf. Growing up in the aftermath of the French Revolution, he had been surrounded by the French values of liberty and equality. Nor had he witnessed slavery in Ohio. The few blacks he saw in the northern states were freemen or family servants. He wrote about the incident at some length. "Finally, after assuring himself that he was getting the worth of his money, he bought them for $650 each. It was truly pitiful to see these young girls following their new master away, clad in little more than absolute rags."18

After nine days on the river, Machebeuf arrived in New Orleans on 21 January 1851. The *Peytona* steamed its way alongside the levee, described by one traveler as "an area of many acres, covered with all the grotesque variety of flat boats, keel boats, and watercraft of every description." All around him Machebeuf saw "steamboats rounding to, or sweeping away, cast[ing] their long horizontal streams of smoke behind them. Sloops, schooners, brigs, and ships occupy the wharfs, arranged below each other in the order of their size, showing a forest of masts." Disembarking, he made his way into the New Orleans of 1851. An English geologist, Charles Lyell, who described his entrance to the city two years before, wrote that "cypress, hung with Spanish moss, was flourishing, and below it numerous shrubs just bursting into leaf. . . . There were also many houses with porte-cocheres, high roofs, and volets, and many lamps suspended from ropes attached to tall posts on each side of the road, as in the French capital. We might have fancied that we were approaching Paris, but for the negroes and mulattoes, and the large verandahs reminding us that the windows required protection from the sun's heat."19

Machebeuf spent a few days in New Orleans, happy to once again hear French spoken in city streets. He visited with clergy and prepared for the next leg of his journey. Lamy, who had left two weeks before for Galveston and San Antonio, had his own close brush with death. Writing from New

Orleans, Machebeuf gave a casual description of Lamy's trip across the gulf. "The boat was so old and worn out that it was unable to withstand the storms, and it was wrecked near Galveston. It was broken into a thousand pieces and went to the bottom of the sea. Fortunately, the passengers saved their lives, but nearly all of their baggage was lost. Bishop Lamy succeeded in saving his vestments and one box of books." Unconcerned by Lamy's brush with death, as he so often was by his own, he closed his letter in true Machebeuf style, showing no sign of doubt or hesitation. "Onward, then," he wrote, "into the keeping of Providence!"[20]

Part Three

Vicar General: New Mexico

1851–1860

NINE

Santa Fe

✣

After arriving in New Orleans, Machebeuf booked passage to Matagorda Bay on 30 January. In a letter to his sister on 25 January he noted that he would travel under the protection of Mary; the thirtieth was Saturday, and Saturdays are traditionally consecrated to the Blessed Virgin.[1] From Galveston he traveled overland to San Antonio. He might have expected to find Lamy shaken.

When Lamy left New Orleans he had left his niece, Marie, in a convent school. He had also left his sister, Marguerite, who was ill, in the Sisters of Charity hospital. The day after his departure from New Orleans, his sister Marguerite, Soeur Marie, died. Lamy's misfortunes multiplied. In the shipwreck he had lost all his baggage, except his vestments and one box of books, including the wagon he'd bought in New Orleans for use on the trip to Santa Fe. On his way to visit one of the cavalry posts, the mules pulling his wagon shied and bolted. Lamy leapt from the cart, but landed badly, severely spraining his ankle. He would be unable to travel for at least six weeks. Machebeuf arrived in time to bolster his friend's sagging spirits.[2]

Constitutionally incapable of inactivity, Machebeuf found that as he had not yet mastered the Spanish language, he could not take on any active ministry. Before the 1846 war, Texas had been annexed to the United States. Only five years later, by far the largest percentage of the population around San Antonio was made up of Hispanic Catholics, some recent immigrants from Mexico, most long-settled in the area. In 1851, with a population of thirty-five hundred, San Antonio was the largest U.S. military outpost in Texas. The battered walls of the Alamo stood in mute testimony to recent tensions between the Texans and the Mexicans, and the two-story

eastern-style houses built by newly arrived Americans blended badly with
the flat-roofed adobes patiently constructed by generations of Hispanic
residents. Machebeuf began studying Spanish in earnest with Lamy, taking
every opportunity to practice the language with the residents of San Antonio. But studying was not enough to satisfy Machebeuf's restlessness.

Bishop Jean-Marie Odin of Galveston was one of the missionaries Machebeuf heard as a young man in seminary, when he was first thinking of
becoming a missionary. From Bishop Odin, Machebeuf obtained permission to make diocesan visits, including visits to the U.S. cavalry forts constructed along the border of Texas and Mexico. Traveling as far as Eagle
Pass on the Rio Grande, he tended to the needs of Catholic soldiers at the
forts, collecting information and soliciting funds whenever possible. It
marked the beginning of Machebeuf's association with cavalry officers, an
association that would continue throughout his years in New Mexico and
beyond.

By the middle of May, Lamy was strong enough to undertake the next leg
of their journey, from San Antonio to El Paso. He and Machebeuf pooled
their funds and purchased a wagon to replace the one lost in the shipwreck.
It would serve to carry baggage and provisions. They also managed to
obtain a smaller buggy for riding and two saddle horses. Still, these con-
veyances would not be sufficient for their needs.[3] In New Orleans Lamy
had already recruited at least two more priests to accompany them. Most
likely, one was Father Grzelachowski, a Polish priest called Father Polaco.
The probable second, a Spaniard named Antonio Severo Borrajo, did not
remain in New Mexico.[4] Between them they had more baggage than one
wagon could carry, so Machebeuf left the bulk of his own belongings behind, to be shipped to him in Santa Fe on a later supply train.

Whether through Machebeuf's trips to the forts or through connections
of Lamy's, the group secured permission to make the six-hundred-mile trip
to El Paso with a train of government wagons. The caravan was made up of
two hundred wagons, drawn by six mules each and loaded with government
supplies; twenty-five wagons belonging to various merchants or other civil-
ians; and a full company of U.S. cavalry. This would be the most difficult
part of the journey, traveling across Texas, through an arid, barren landscape. Outside of San Antonio rich soil gave way to black earth, supporting
only mesquite and a few small trees. "With the exception of a few fertile
valleys along the rivers," Machebeuf later wrote, "nearly the whole country
from 100 miles west of San Antonio was nothing but a desert or a succession of high hills. The journey was a trial upon patience and human
endurance."[5]

Machebeuf and company nevertheless had advantages not afforded all their fellow travelers. One of the priests befriended the wife of Gen. William Selby Harney. A devout Catholic, she arranged for the group to have permission to draw rations from the government supplies and pay for them at government prices. "This was about half the price we would have paid if we [had] bought our provisions at San Antonio and carried them with us," Machebeuf recorded. "By this arrangement we were never in need of anything, except water, which at times, was very scarce." The scarcity of water forced them to carry barrels of fresh water for themselves and their animals on the journey. Occasionally their Canadian driver would supplement their diet with game — antelope, rabbits, ducks and grouse — and when they passed through the river valleys they secured fresh fish. "On many occasions," Machebeuf wrote, "we actually had the pleasure of catching them with our hands."[6]

What Machebeuf enjoyed most about the journey was the opportunity to sleep under the stars each night, sous la belle etoile, a practice both he and Lamy would continue for years to come. "We had a good tent, loaned us by the General, but the nights were so calm and beautiful that we almost always slept in the open air. And, oh, how well one does sleep under a blanket with his saddle for a pillow after a day's ride on horseback!"[7]

The group first sighted the Guadalupe foothills, a hundred miles outside of El Paso del Norte, a month after they left San Antonio. By the last week of June 1851, they arrived at the Rio Grande towns of San Elizario, Socorro, and Ysleta, founded in the early 1680s.

The year 1680 brought the retribution of New Mexico's Pueblo peoples against the Spanish for Juan de Oñate's savage retaliation against Acoma and for the thousands of unreported hardships suffered by Native Americans under Spanish rule. Led by a medicine man from San Juan Pueblo, Popé, the Pueblos successfully planned and executed an overthrow of the Spanish in New Mexico. Although by today's standards the losses could be considered modest, with twenty-one Franciscan friars and four hundred Spanish colonists losing their lives, there was nothing modest about the impact on Spain. For the first time, Spain had lost an entire province to a revolt of indigenous peoples, a precedent they could not afford to see repeated. Inspired by the reconquest of Spanish lands from Moors in the Middle Ages, Don Diego de Vargas led two hundred Spanish soldiers back to Santa Fe in 1692. The Spanish, together with their language and culture, returned to New Mexico for good.

Following the Pueblo Revolt a number of Native American and Hispanic communities were displaced. Some of the inhabitants, like those of Socorro and Ysleta del Sur, relocated as refugees in the south and named their new villages for the towns they had lived in before the revolt — towns midway up the Rio Grande valley. This duplication of names would cause ongoing problems for Lamy in the years ahead. Back in Galveston, Bishop Odin had decided that these areas would be better served if they were transferred to Lamy's jurisdiction, even though the 1848 Treaty of Guadalupe Hidalgo held that being north of the Rio Grande, they were part of Texas. Technically Odin was acting outside the limits of his authority. For all practical purposes, however, they had been transferred from Durango to the diocese of Galveston.[8] Now Odin placed them under Lamy.

Lamy later wrote to Purcell in Cincinnati of his entry into Socorro saying, "they gave me a grand reception." The villagers, he continued, had built a "triumphal arch under which I had to pass," and the assembled dignitaries included the mayor, the local pastor, and the national guard. "This little spot," wrote Lamy, "is truly beautiful; particularly so to me, arriving from a journey of six weeks over barren plains, and mountains without a tree to conceal their rock precipices."[9]

After six weeks of desert days and six weeks of nights under the stars, the group finally reached El Paso, stopping to rest before beginning the final stage of their journey to Santa Fe. Lamy later described it as "a scattered village, of at least eight thousand souls. Though it seldom rains . . . by a system of irrigation, they have managed to make their country like a garden. The wine is excellent. . . . The houses are low and remarkably clean, and well arranged for commerce, and to suit the climate." Machebeuf remembered, "the Bishop and myself were very cordially received by the pastor, Father Ortiz, who proffered us every hospitality in his power."[10] Father Ramón Ortiz, a handsome and charming man well known to many traders and soldiers, offered his new prelate every consideration. In addition to his hospitality, he supplied much needed information about the journey to Santa Fe. He advised Lamy to write ahead, informing the New Mexican clergy that he was on his way. Lamy accepted the suggestion and wrote to José Antonio Otero, the pastor at the northern town of Socorro, just south of Albuquerque. That letter was relayed to the smaller towns between there and Santa Fe. At the same time, Lamy wrote officially to the Very Reverend Monsignor Juan Felipe Ortiz. Serving in Santa Fe, Ortiz was the vicar forane, or rural dean, to Bishop Zubiría of Durango, Mexico. As vicario foraneo, given powers by special mandate of the bishop, Ortiz oversaw the conduct of priests, administered upkeep of the churches in the district, and served as local representative of the bishop.[11] He reported to Zubiría annually on affairs of the church in the area.

The military escort Machebeuf and Lamy accompanied from San Antonio now split into two groups; one would remain at a military post near El Paso, the other would travel upriver to northern New Mexico. Machebeuf and Lamy left with the second group in early July 1851, beginning their journey up the Camino Real, the trading trail established since the seventeenth century between Santa Fe and Mexico City.

In 1851 the New Mexico Territory was larger than all of France, a vast area that stretched far beyond the current boundaries of the state. It included what are now the states of New Mexico and Arizona, except the southernmost portion added by the Gadsden Purchase, part of Nevada and Wyoming, and the areas of Colorado south of the Arkansas River and east of the Continental Divide. It also included some portions of Utah and additional lands ceded in the Mexican Cession of 1848, under the Treaty of Guadalupe Hidalgo. Since the Spanish expeditions of the sixteenth century, New Mexico was the northernmost territory of New Spain, and generations of Spanish settlers had made their way north and settled along the Rio Grande valley. In 1821, when the people of Mexico rejected Spanish rule, New Mexico came under Mexican control. It remained a part of Mexico until Gen. Stephen Watts Kearny's quiet conquest in 1846, when he established Fort Marcy in the hills overlooking Santa Fe Plaza.

At the time of Machebeuf's arrival the area was a melange of distinct cultures. Native American cultures included the stable pueblos, which dotted the landscape, as well as the nomadic tribes: Comanches and Apaches in the south and east, and Navajos, Utes, and Shoshones in the north. With the arrival of the Spanish, the Spanish language became the lingua franca of the area, allowing different tribes to communicate among one another and allowing Spanish culture to filter into many of the tribal customs. Into this mix, in the nineteenth century, came the newer American immigrants, usually Americans from eastern cities, Texans, or recent arrivals from Europe. They found agricultural communities long established, trading routes that had been in use for centuries, and developed towns, scattered throughout the territory but concentrated in the Rio Grande valley. Machebeuf now passed through these communities on his way northward to Santa Fe.

Once Machebeuf and company crossed the barren desert of the Jornada del Muerto, the legendary "journey of death" between Las Cruces and Socorro, the rest of their journey followed the welcoming banks of the Rio Grande. Moving slowly up the bosque, the flat wooded areas that line the banks of the river, the party traveled on roads established and maintained for centuries, roads shaded by towering cottonwoods and edged by the red of salt cedar. Carefully cultivated fields, deep green against the golden hills behind them, their rich earth dark against the pale blues and lavenders of distant mountains, surrounded the slow-moving party.

This was New Mexico, the Land of Enchantment. A far cry from the rough American frontier of Ohio, this was the land one young traveler and author, Albert Pike, succinctly described in 1833 as "a different world . . . the Siberia of the Mexican Republic."[12] New Mexico had been settled for thousands of years by the Pueblo peoples, for centuries by the Spanish. Here the carefully preserved civilization of Spain mingled with the developed agricultural communities of the pueblos, creating a unique blend of Native American and Hispanic cultures. Spanish culture and the Catholic faith were deeply etched into the landscape, and Machebeuf found himself in another world. Nothing in his previous experience could have prepared him for New Mexico.

The vicar forane of Santa Fe, Don Juan Felipe Ortiz, was described as a heavy-set man with reddish hair. He had a proprietary interest in the church in New Mexico. As personal vicar to the bishop of Durango, Ortiz held the highest ecclesiastical position of the New Mexican clergy, and he was accustomed to acting with almost complete autonomy. Born to a wealthy family in Santa Fe, he had trained for the priesthood and been ordained in Durango, and he had a long-standing relationship with Bishop Zubiría. The Ortiz family had lived in Galisteo and Santa Fe for generations, had long been immersed in the politics of the area, and had long supported the church — building or restoring a number of chapels in Santa Fe and endowing them with costly imported silk vestments and silver chalices from Chihuahua.[13]

Lamy's letter from El Paso had been forwarded to Ortiz by Padre José Antonio Otero of Socorro. On 14, July Ortiz sent out circulars advising the resident priests to receive Lamy with all the honors due his position.[14] News of the impending arrival of a new American bishop echoed down the Rio Grande valley, and in each of the little towns the people of New Mexico did their best to show their new bishop a grand reception. "Everywhere I had to go," Lamy later recalled, "they erected triumphal arches across the road, in village after village."[15] Often the entire village would be waiting to greet the party, to escort them in procession to their local church. In some towns the women laid their shawls on the ground to serve as a carpet, and the children, dressed in their best clothes, came shyly forward to kiss Lamy's ring and receive his blessing. The names of the villages mark another legacy of the Spanish. The party moved northward through Socorro, Lemitar, Belen, Tomé, through the pueblo of Isleta, through the larger towns of Albuquerque and Bernalillo, and the pueblos of San Felipe and

Santo Domingo. At Cochití they finally left the protective shade of the cottonwoods that lined the banks of the Rio Grande and made their way across the open sage mesa to the village of La Bajada. Passing the aging church of San Miguel in La Bajada, they cut through the basalt canyon carved deep into the mesa, then up to La Cienega. They emerged on a stretch of golden plain, on the outskirts of Santa Fe. Nestled in the foothills of the Santa Fe Mountains, the southernmost range of the Sangre de Cristo, the ancient city of Santa Fe lay quietly at the base of the towering blue peaks. The end of their journey was in sight.

On 9 August 1851 the party finally reached Santa Fe. Based on the receptions at the smaller towns, they thought it possible that some of the faithful might come to greet them, but they were not ready for the welcome Vicar Ortiz arranged. About six miles out from the first houses, Lamy saw what he thought was the local garrison, coming to greet the troop detachment they accompanied. Leading the procession, in a "magnificent carriage" was U.S. Territorial Governor James Calhoun. The governor greeted Lamy, presented Ortiz, and swept the two of them into his carriage. The procession into Santa Fe began.[16]

"We arrived at Santa Fe," Machebeuf wrote, "and the entry of Bishop Lamy into the Capital was truly a triumphal one . . . all the civil and military authorities, and thousands of people . . . with the finest carriages and coaches of the city, and vehicles of all sorts for thirty miles around." Machebeuf, overwhelmed by the event, almost gushed in his report. "Some eight or nine thousand Catholic Indians came also, in the fashions of their numerous tribes, and their . . . costumes were a sight to behold." As the procession neared the city, the soldiers at Fort Marcy fired their cannons in salute.[17] The procession continued, probably up San Franciso street, which had been transformed, lined by "beautiful cedar trees, which the day before had been brought in and planted for the occasion."[18] The houses along the route were strung with banners of brightly colored fabric, with silks and carpets hanging from windows and balconies. No bishop could ask for a warmer welcome.

Arriving at the parish church of St. Francis, Lamy entered, still dusty from his long journey. Hundreds of Hispanic women, dark shawls demurely covering their heads, knelt on either side while the men, their hats in their hands, stood at the back. Followed by Machebeuf, the new bishop of Santa Fe moved slowly across the dirt-packed floor, between walls lined by the life-size wax figures of saints, to the altar covered with mirrors, paintings, and hangings. Robed in a purple cassock, draped with a heavy white stole embroidered in gold, Lamy stood and listened as a Mexican

string orchestra played the first few notes of the Te Deum and the voices of
the city of Santa Fe rose to formally greet their new bishop.

"After the Te Deum," Machebeuf wrote, "which was chanted to the
accompaniment of Mexican music, the Vicar of the Bishop of Durango
received Bishop Lamy into his own house, which he had profusely decorated and converted into a real episcopal palace." To further accommodate
Lamy and Machebeuf, Ortiz moved out of the house himself, staying at his
mother's home nearby. But the grand festivities were not over, for "all the
authorities were invited there to a grand dinner, which made us forget our
long trip across the arid plains of Texas." While Lamy and Machebeuf were
greeted by all the local dignitaries — native Hispanics and immigrant Americans, Protestants and Catholics, military and civic leaders — a final touch
sweetened the day's events. Billowing dark clouds built up over the mountains, and, after months of drought, torrents of sweet welcome rain poured
down on the city, filling the streets with rivulets of rushing brown water. In
one day, the new bishop had arrived, the drought was over, and a new era of
Catholicism had begun in New Mexico.[19]

No sooner had the glow of their reception worn off, than Lamy and
Machebeuf found themselves in the first of the many confrontations that
would mark the next ten years. One of Lamy's first actions had been to take
custody of the churches, chapels, and other properties in New Mexico,
beginning with the churches in Santa Fe. One, Our Lady of Light, was a
small chapel on the eastern side of Santa Fe Plaza. The people of Santa Fe
called the chapel the Castrense, referring to its long-standing use by the
military. It had been the military chapel for the Spanish and Mexican gar-
risons in Santa Fe, and accordingly, was taken over by the territorial government after the 1846 war. When Lamy arrived it was being used as a
storehouse by the U.S. authorities. Lamy, disturbed by the thought of a
Catholic chapel being put to such utilitarian use, took the initial steps to
recover it for the church.

One of the territorial officials, Chief Justice Grafton Baker, the presiding
judge for the Supreme Court of New Mexico, strongly objected to Lamy's
efforts. One Saturday night an inebriated Baker declared he would never
relinquish the church. In fact, he boasted, he would see both Lamy and
Machebeuf hung from the same gallows first. Baker's threats traveled like
lightning. By Monday morning a petition was circulated, demanding the
return of the chapel to the church. More than a thousand citizens signed it,
Catholic and Protestant, military and civilian. A surly crowd gathered outside the chapel turned storehouse, where a terrified Baker had taken refuge.

Baker demanded protection from the military authorities, but instead, one of the officers approached Lamy, putting the entire garrison at the bishop's disposal. Concerned that the citizenry might take justice into its own hands, Machebeuf and another of the officers took up positions outside the church, vowing to protect Baker until he yielded to the bishop. Machebeuf later wrote his sister, "the poor judge, wholly humiliated and abashed, went to make reparation to the bishop, and proposed to return the church to him with all possible solemnity." By Tuesday morning, with the governor, as well as civil and military authorities in attendance, the little chapel was formally turned over to Lamy. "I said a few words in Spanish and English," Lamy later wrote Purcell, "and right on the spot I got up a subscription to repair the church in a decent manner. The governor and the chief justice liberally subscribed the first ones and in a short time, we had upwards of a thousand dollars."[20]

Historians disagree about what happened in the days that followed, as the New Mexican Hispanic clergy responded to Lamy's arrival. Some, like Paul Horgan and William Howlett, report that the resident clergy refused to accept Lamy's credentials. "Having paid all proper respect to mitre and crozier," writes Horgan in his biography of Lamy, "Ortiz, and the local clergy over whom he presided, suddenly maintained that Lamy was not the bishop for Santa Fe, and refused to recognize him as such." Howlett implies the problem was in Durango. "The cutting off of the territory of New Mexico from the jurisdiction of the Bishop of Durango appears to have been done without asking his consent," Howlett comments, "and he made some objection to the yielding up of his authority to another without the usual formalities." This hesitation, Howlett maintains, "gave to some of the New Mexican priests the color of an excuse to refuse to acknowledge the authority of Bishop Lamy." Other historians, such as Fray Angelico Chavez, disagree. "Nothing could be farther from the truth, as a careful study of all the documentation shows," writes Chavez, suggesting that previous historians "got this from a very general statement made fifty years later by Archbishop Salpointe, when he wrote that the native priests and people were suspicious of all strangers . . . an innocent observation by a good man who was neither a historian nor a master of English." Whether Lamy's subsequent trip to Durango was to ease the concerns of the bishop of Durango, more firmly establish his authority with the New Mexican clergy, or simply to formally transfer responsibility for the area, is unclear, but within a few weeks of his arrival, Lamy determined it was necessary for both Vicar Ortiz and himself to travel to Durango and meet with Bishop

Zubiría. In the interim, Machebeuf would attend to the business of establishing the vicariate. In the third week of September 1851, Lamy and Ortiz started on the long road to Durango.[21]

Durango, Mexico, is almost 1,500 miles from Santa Fe. Lamy traveled 130 miles down the old Camino Real, through the towns of Placeres, Peralta, Valencia, and Tomé, through villages made up of only one or two families, happy to share whatever they had. He and Ortiz rode back across the forbidding wastes of the Jornada del Muerto, the dry, deadly stretch of desert south of Socorro. Crossing through the villages of Doñana, the ranchos of Mesilla and Las Cruces, he crossed into the Mexican state of Chihuahua. From Robledo he headed south, past empty villages, abandoned in the wake of relentless Apache raids, through the shifting dunes of Los Medanos, and finally to the relative reassurance of the solitary packed dirt road leading into the city of Chihuahua. Next came 500 miles across open country, crossing mountain, desert, and valley, passing huge strangely shaped cacti to the chorus of distant coyotes. Finally passing through the town of Camargo, through Hidalgo del Parral, he came to the hacienda of El Chorro. Resting briefly, he struck out for the final 28 miles to the old city of Durango, the flat horizon broken only by the ragged fringe of cornfields and the outlines of gangly sandhill cranes.[22]

The bishop of Durango, Don Antonio de Zubiría, welcomed Lamy warmly. Portraits of Zubiría indicate a man of strong character.[23] His nose was long and slender, his mouth wide and somewhat downturned. His strong cheekbones, black hair, and almond eyes hinted at a trace of Indian blood. Born in Sonora in July 1781, Zubiría was seventy years old when Lamy met him. His age showed only in the fleshiness of his face, in the heaviness of his frame. He had served as bishop of Durango for twenty years, during which time he had made three tours of New Mexico, the first in 1833, the second in 1845, and most recently in 1850. He knew the land and the people well.[24]

Following the U.S. victory in 1846, Zubiría and the other bishops of northern Mexico had been expressly ordered by Rome to continue their jurisdiction over their original diocesan boundaries. As such, he was not fully prepared for the documents Lamy presented to him. It was the first notice he had received of Lamy's mission. Zubiría had not yet received word from Rome. But Lamy's documents spoke for themselves. Pope Pius IX had granted the requests of the Baltimore Council of 1849. The papal bulls had been issued, and Zubiría acceded to the transfer.

"I knew nothing about it officially," he said, "but this document is sufficient authority for me and I submit to it."[25] As the two bishops settled down to further discussions, attempting to clarify boundaries and jurisdiction, Machebeuf began his work in the new vicariate back in Santa Fe.

Machebeuf's personal debut as Lamy's vicar general was less than auspicious. Father Lujan, assistant to Vicar Ortiz and the pastor of one of Santa Fe's four chapels, introduced him to his congregation. Machebeuf gave the homily, optimistically deciding to give it in Spanish. No one understood a word. After the mass, one of those attending speculated that the preacher "must be a Jew or a Protestant." Another responded with a shrug, "Who knows?" Fortunately a more practical woman took charge of the discussion. How could they doubt "the religion of this man? Did he not give proof that he is a Catholic by the way he made the sign of the cross before giving his sermon?"[26] Machebeuf's reputation as a homilist and a linguist, if not his religion, was firmly established.

The last months of 1851 passed quickly for Machebeuf. He started work on the restoration of the Castrense, hoping Lamy might sing the mass in it on his return. He acquainted himself with the people of Santa Fe so that he could give Lamy a better picture of the political situation on his return. And he began, in effect, an inventory of the resources available to the church in New Mexico, a listing of the churches, other properties, and manpower throughout the territory. Last but not least he continued his spiritual inventory of the area, doing the best he could, with his fractured Spanish, to determine the relative health of Catholicism in New Mexico.

On a cold, clear day in January 1852, Lamy rode into Santa Fe the second time. No welcoming party awaited him. In fact, few even noticed his quiet return. Machebeuf had kept the home fires burning and the two sat down to a long discussion of their experiences in the previous months. Lamy's trip to Durango had been a success. Bishop Zubiría had endorsed the transfer, but for the two French vicars, the real work in New Mexico had just begun.

TEN

Mountains and Canyons

On Lamy's return to Santa Fe from Durango, the two French priests sat down to a serious discussion of the work ahead. The pair made a powerful combination, a force to be reckoned with, opposite yet complementary, with a friendship stretching over two decades behind them.

As Lamy and Machebeuf evaluated the condition of the church in New Mexico, the people and the clergy of New Mexico carefully evaluated the two of them. The tenuous relationship between the French and the Spanish might best be described as an uneasy alliance. European divisions between the two cultures had carried over into the New World.

The French view of New Mexico's Hispanic population was undoubtedly influenced by the legacy of the Black Legend. By the sixteenth century the Dominican Bartolomé de Las Casas challenged the rights of Spanish conquest, particularly the institution of the encomienda, a system of serfdom in which land given to conquistadors brought the services and tributes of the indigenous peoples who dwelt there. He accused the conquistadors of "endless crimes and offenses against the Indians who were the king's subjects," considering the system "more unjust and cruel than Pharaoh's oppression of the Jews." Following the publication of de Las Casas's *Destruction of the Indies*, those opposed to any expansion of Spanish power in the New World lost little time popularizing a dark version of Spanish culture. The Black Legend portrayed "a brutal, sanguinary, and sadistic Spain, torturing and killing wherever she went—in tacit contrast, no doubt, to the lily-white colonialists from France, England, and the Netherlands." While these northern European nations were quick to criticize Spain for its treatment of conquered peoples, it must be remembered they never submitted themselves to the same scrutiny. The Spanish debate on the rights of conquest became, in effect, "the first full-fledged modern debate on human rights," an issue none of the other world powers bothered to address. But the legacy of the Black Legend encouraged northern European immigrants, like Machebeuf and Lamy, to view themselves as purity personified and their own culture as inherently superior to Spanish culture. It was not difficult to view themselves, if only unconsciously, as European white knights, bringers of light in a land ruled by the dark forces of Spain.[1]

The situation was further complicated by the traditional fear of encroachment from the French in Louisiana, which was shared by many New Mexican Hispanics. The presence of raiding Comanches and Apaches in the eastern part of the territory was tolerated, in part, because they were thought to provide a buffer against any French ambitions to expand their domain to the west. This fear diminished somewhat when the ownership of the Louisiana Territory was turned over to Spain in 1762, but increased again when the region was returned to France prior to the Louisiana Purchase.

Still adjusting to the abrupt transition from Mexican to American government after the Mexican-American War, as well as the absorption of increasing waves of the American arrivals that followed in its wake, the people of New Mexico had reasons to be wary of their new bishop and his aide. Not only were the two men French, they had been sent not by the bishops of Mexico, but by the American bishops. To some it may have seemed that the French succeeded ecclesiastically in what they failed to accomplish militarily. There may have been concerns, too, that the two Frenchmen would show greater allegiance to the new American government than to the traditional cultural values of Hispanics in New Mexico. Throughout the territory, people settled down in front of fireplaces, and evening conversations turned to impressions of the two French priests.

Lamy, at thirty-seven, was young for a bishop, but the years of hard work and discipline had matured him. His face was weathered from missionary travel and the strain of frontier life. It was a handsome face, gaunt beneath a full head of curly dark hair. His dark eyes sparkled with intelligence, determination, and not a small amount of ambition. Occasionally, when brooding or distracted, his face took on a melancholy aspect. But most often it was softened by his determined kindness, his gentility, and his patience. His jaw was square and resolute, and although usually quiet and soft-spoken, Lamy was clearly not a man to be trifled with.

Machebeuf was thirty-nine but appeared much older. His face was even more weathered than Lamy's, his eyes a watery pale blue against his sun-darkened skin. His hair was no longer the white blond of his childhood, but a faded, sandy blond, bleached dry by sun and wind. He was by no means a handsome man. His neck was thin, his face lean and angular, his mouth somehow too big for his face, and he had a large mole on the right side of his chin. He wore small, gold-rimmed glasses, and the eyes behind them twinkled with quick humor and compassion, alert and ever watchful. He had a ready smile, continually breaking out, softening his irregular features.

Returning from Durango, Lamy told Machebeuf the details of his trip, of the terrain of the land between Santa Fe and Durango and his meetings with Bishop Zubiría, many of them under the vigilant eye of Vicar Ortiz. Machebeuf, in his turn, gave Lamy his evaluation of the New Mexican clergy.

Beginning with the Spanish colonization of Juan de Oñate in 1598, New Mexico had been known as the Franciscan territory, the Territory of St. Francis. The Franciscan friars had been the sole ministers of the Catholic faith, the official representatives of the Church of Rome. The faith of the loyal Franciscans was sorely tried. New Mexico repaid their fervor by producing more Franciscan martyrs than any other territory in the world. A plaque at St. Francis Cathedral in today's Santa Fe shows a total of thirty-eight. Closer inspection shows that twenty-one of those martyrs lost their lives in 1680, the year of the Pueblo Revolt. Just over a century later the Franciscan monopoly on New Mexican Catholicism came to an end.

In 1798 the bishop of Durango secularized the parishes of Santa Fe and Santa Cruz. These two important parishes would be headed by secular priests, independent priests who took no vows in community, did not belong to a religious order, and were subject to bishops only in ministerial matters. Following the secession of Mexico from Spain in 1821, New Mexico became a part of the Mexican Empire. The remaining Franciscans, almost all of whom were Spanish nationals, were removed from the territory. The bishop of Durango began ordaining native New Mexicans as secular priests, gradually increasing their numbers. By the 1830s most of the Franciscans had been withdrawn; the last one died in 1848. With the loss of the Franciscans, only a handful of secular clergy were available to direct the faith of the entire population, both Native American and Hispanic. By the 1850s Machebeuf and Lamy would be working with mostly native, Hispanic, secular priests.[2]

One of the most influential of the native clergy was Don Juan Felipe Ortiz, Zubiría's official representative in the area. But he was not the only influential priest among the New Mexican clergy. Another was pastor of Albuquerque, José Manuel Gallegos. From all accounts, Gallegos was a personable man, known for his intelligence, charm, and good humor. Middle-aged, he was a thin, balding man, with a fringe of dark hair and sparse side-whiskers. His mouth was wide, and his full lips set off by deep creases on either side of his mouth. His face had an almost quiet sadness, which sometimes revealed a cast of shrewdness or skepticism, a face strangely well-suited to a man with an established reputation for charm and wit. In his personal life, Gallegos was somewhat flamboyant. Well known among the more prominent politicians and traders, he served grape brandy and cakes to his friends and traded gold pieces for rare provincial currency. Perhaps most disconcerting, however, at least to his new French superiors, was Gallegos's choice of housemates. Gallegos lived with a widowed Hispanic woman who, reportedly, had adopted three children. Together she and Gallegos ran a general store, which incidentally, remained open on Sundays.[3]

Lt. J. W. Abert visited with Gallegos in 1846, stopping in Albuquerque to purchase sheep. When Gallegos invited the men inside to sample his grape brandy, Gallegos's hostess did not escape their notice. "A very handsome lady, who graced the establishment, entered the room and he presented us to her," Abert recorded.[4]

The "very handsome lady" in question was Dona Maria de Jesús Trujillo de Hinojos. The 1850 census records her as "Jesusita," thirty-five years old, and lists her alongside six other women and four men as members of Gallegos's household. Hispanic historian Angelico Chavez indicates that such an arrangement was not uncommon. "Such a large household of 'familiares' was nothing unusual among the secular clergy and religious missionaries in Spanish America," he writes. "Particularly in New Mexico, it sometimes took the place of an orphanage whereby the pastor took in — over and above poor relations — children of poor families or no family at all, who thus found some sort of asylum in the midst of the backward economics of the region." At least one other source supports this view. Rev. L. Smith, a Baptist missionary, on a visit with Padre Martínez of Taos noted, "Like all the Benedicts of the territory he has a large family." Others were not so understanding. Eyebrows arched, and some of the local residents found it particularly unsettling when the woman appeared in a carriage after Sunday mass to take Padre Gallegos for a ride.[5]

Nothing in Lamy or Machebeuf's background could have prepared them for an understanding view of Gallegos's lifestyle. Products of strict French Catholic families, provincial and severe, their education in the Sulpician Grande Séminaire de Clermont-Ferrand was not untainted by Jansenism. At the time of their formation, in a backlash against the excesses of the French Revolution and the decadence of figures like Richelieu and Talleyrand, the French church was in the midst of extreme clerical reforms.[6] These reforms emphasized, above all, deportemént, conduct becoming the revered position of priest. Doubtless Machebeuf would have filled Lamy in on the rumors surrounding the activities of Padre Gallegos. Five years later his views would be clearly expressed. "It was," Machebeuf wrote in 1856, "a great scandal for the people to see a woman such as that in the rectory, travelling alone with the priest in his coach, and active in his business. . . . The parish administered by a priest so scandalous and so given to business and politics finds itself plunged in the most profound ignominy and corruption."[7] A confrontation between Gallegos and Machebeuf was inevitable.

Another Hispanic priest with whom Lamy and Machebeuf would come into conflict was a distant cousin of Gallegos, Padre Antonio José Martínez of Taos.[8] When Lamy and Machebeuf arrived in New Mexico, Padre Martínez was fifty-eight years old and one of the most fascinating and gifted men in the territory. Martínez was a heavy-set man, with full downturned lips and a soft round sadness to his eyes. Somewhat balding, he carried himself with the quiet authority becoming to a man of his birth, position, and education.

Born in January of 1793, in the small village of Santa Rosa de Abiquiú, Martínez was a member of a respectable provincial New Mexican family. His lineage could be traced back throughout New Mexico's Spanish colonial history, to the colonists who accompanied Oñate in 1598 and those who took part in Vargas's Reconquest in 1693. By the time he was five, Martínez began to read and write. When he was twelve, his family moved to Taos. Taos had no school, but Martínez continued to study privately. Overall, Martínez was largely self-educated, but given the relative scarcity of educational materials, he did a remarkable job developing his intellect. In 1812, at the age of nineteen, he married Maria de la Luz Martín. His young wife died in childbirth fourteen months later. His daughter, named for her mother, survived and Martínez placed her with her maternal grandparents. After four years, not having remarried, Martínez traveled to Durango and began studies for the secular priesthood, entering the Tridentine Seminary of Durango on 10 March 1817. Among his fellow seminarians were several members of the distinguished Ortiz family in Santa Fe. Juan Felipe Ortiz, who would later become Martínez's superior as vicar forane, was one. Two of Ortiz's cousins, twins Rafael and Fernando Ortiz, also studied alongside him. In 1822 Martínez was ordained to the priesthood. By 1823 he was assisting the elderly Franciscan, Fray Sebastián Alvarez, at Taos, and by 1825 was the cura encargado, or pastor in charge, in Taos.[9] Martínez immersed himself in the religious activities of the parish, tending to baptisms and marriages, opening a school and a minor seminary, and becoming entangled in a number of political affairs, some of them highly questionable.[10] By the time of Lamy and Machebeuf's arrival, Martínez was widely respected for his political acumen and his broad learning. He was one of nineteen delegates selected for the preparation of a full territorial plan of government in 1849, and in June of 1850 was among those who watched as the First Territorial Constitution of New Mexico was adopted. Following the inauguration of Territorial Governor Calhoun, Martínez headed up a group of five representatives to the newly formed legislature. Calhoun wrote to Martínez "as a learned and intelligent citizen of broad experience in regard to what is needed in this country" and offered his own house as headquarters for Martínez during his stay in the capital for the First Territorial Legislature.[11]

In 1851 Baptist missionary H. W. Read visited Martínez in Taos. His report, published in the *Home Mission Record* and preserved in the Danielson papers, offers a glimpse of Martínez's ecumenical hospitality and the recognition accorded him at the time. "The priest, who by the way, is one of the most influential men of New Mexico," Read writes, "called on me to enquire more particularly about the school I propose to establish." After assuring Martínez that the education would be of the same calibre as other institutions in the United States, "He said he was satisfied, and again promised to render me and the school all the assistance in his power." Martínez's hospitality did not stop with the promise of assistance. "He said he would invite me to preach in his church, but their ecclesiastical regulations forbade it," Read recorded. "I thanked him for his kindness, informed him that the Court-House had been offered me, when I should preach at 5 o'clock, and invited him and his people to attend."[12]

The following morning Read attended mass, but seemed to have doubts as to the efficacy of the edification that resulted from the service. "Many hundreds of Mexicans present," he reported, "probably not one of whom understood a word that was said, as what little was read was not above a whisper and in Latin." Nor did he seem to feel that the populace had much of an opportunity to learn from thoughtful homilies or inspired sermons. "It is not customary for the priests of this country to preach to the people, and as only about one in three hundred can read, their opportunities for instruction are very limited."[13]

For some fortunate students, opportunities for instruction came through Martínez's school in Taos. In September 1851 another Baptist missionary visited Martínez at his school. Reverend L. Smith's comments again emphasize Martínez's influence and standing in the community. "In the p.m.

we called on Padre Martínez, one of the most influential priests in the territory. Found him teaching a small school." Given Martínez's influence, it is not surprising that Smith remarks "In the evening preached in the Court-house to the largest congregation I have yet had."[14]

Martínez was a man widely respected and supported throughout New Mexico, by both Hispanics and Anglos — a man deserving every due political consideration. There were other considerations that had not yet become apparent to either Lamy or Machebeuf, considerations that would ensure their becoming very, very familiar with Padre Martínez of Taos. But that complex relationship would develop over the course of years.

The first of the Hispanic clergy to come under immediate scrutiny by Lamy on his return from Durango was the pastor of San Miguel, Padre José Francisco Leyva. Leyva had been one of Martínez's companions at the First Territorial Legislature. At sixty-five he was an old assemblyman and politician. In November 1851 Padre Leyva had fallen off his horse and broken his leg in three places. The fact that Leyva was particularly drunk at the time, combined with a reputation that did not exclude dalliance with women and gambling, did not help him much in Machebeuf's estimation. With Lamy still in Durango, Machebeuf temporarily suspended Leyva. He sent Father Grzelachowski, the Polish priest who accompanied them from San Antonio and had been assigned to San Felipe Pueblo, to replace Leyva at San Miguel. It was up to Lamy, as duly authorized superior, to chastise Leyva appropriately. Apparently Lamy reconsidered the action. Records at San Miguel indicate that he reinstated Leyva early in March, after consulting with Padre Martínez in Taos.[15]

As Lamy and Machebeuf evaluated the challenges presented them by the New Mexico Territory — the scarcity of priests and the numbers of Catholics for whom they were responsible — it became increasingly apparent that their first and foremost priority would be obtaining additional manpower. By the beginning of February, Lamy made the first of countless efforts to secure priests, religious, and sisters for his new territory. He wrote to Father Roothaan, the general of the Jesuits in Rome, requesting two Spanish-speaking Jesuits be sent to him. Unfortunately neither was available; one was studying at Georgetown, the other fully occupied as president of St. Louis University. But another opportunity for recruitment quickly presented itself. The U.S. bishops were to convene again in Baltimore. Lamy would leave on the first of April to attend the Plenary Council. He would focus on recruiting additional priests and, if possible, sisters to open a school. Machebeuf would remain in Santa Fe, supervise the vicariate, continue his circuit riding to outlying parishes, and attempt to secure an appropriate building to house the proposed school.[16]

By the end of May, Machebeuf's views on the New Mexico Territory were firmly established. Not surprisingly, given his youth in the Volvic mountains, Machebeuf had fallen in love with the rugged landscape of northern New Mexico. Writing to his sister from Peña Blanca on 31 May 1852, he recorded, "From the window of my room I can see the richness of the soil in the abundant harvest of wheat, corn and wine promised to the laborer, and beyond the limpid Rio the picturesque mountains with their slopes covered with majestic pines, and their summits crowned with almost eternal snow, which the winds and heats of summer fail to dissolve." He was enchanted by the rugged majesty of the area. Continuing, he apologized to his sister, "I am now quite accustomed to scaling the mountain heights and crossing the winding streams, but I have not the grand and beautiful boats as once upon the Ohio, only a pair of neat Mexican ponies with no poetry in them, and in their company the Muse refuses to mount to Parnassus." But if Machebeuf's muse was unable to convey his admiration for the New Mexican landscape, he had no such difficulty in conveying his criticisms of local Catholicism. After explaining Lamy's absence and his visits to outlying areas he reported, "The lack of instruction and other helps has left religion in a deplorable condition in New Mexico. Its practice is almost entirely lost, and there remains little but the exterior shell. With such ignorance the consequent corruption can easily be imagined, and all the immorality that must flow from it." Machebeuf firmly placed the blame for New Mexico's deplorable state on the lack of education, "As the source of evil here is the profound ignorance of the people, the first remedy must be instruction, and for this we need Christian schools for the youth of both sexes, but especially for young girls. The means of forming them to virtue . . . is rare in New Mexico." Machebeuf told his sister of the modest school for boys begun in the house he and Lamy shared in Santa Fe, and he described his recent purchase of another building to house the school, a house that Lamy selected and instructed him to purchase. "It has a frontage of more than two hundred feet, and a large court in the middle with a portico all around in the form of a cloister. . . . There are twenty-six rooms, five or six of which are very large. . . . I bought it from a Frenchman who lives in St. Louis, and he was very generous in his price and in the manner of payments. It costs us $6,500. I do not know where we shall find that sum of money but the acquisition was indispensable."[17] *Deus providebit.*

In spite of his blithe assurance to his sister that he was "not too busy at the Capital," Machebeuf was extremely busy during Lamy's absence.[18] From Peña Blanca he traveled to Mora. When old Padre Leyva had been reinstated at San Miguel, Lamy had transferred Father Grzelachowski to Mora. Machebeuf found the Polish priest sharing quarters with an extremely attractive housekeeper. Informed by local residents that she was, in fact, a woman of ill-repute, Machebeuf suspended Grzelachowski.

In the interim, the Plenary Council ended, and Lamy began his return journey to Santa Fe with six Sisters of Loretto. Prior to his appointment as vicar apostolic of New Mexico, Lamy had served briefly as pastor of a church in Covington, Kentucky. During that time he had come to know the Sisters of Loretto at their motherhouse in Kentucky, and it was natural for him to direct his recruitment efforts toward them. Lamy's journey with the sisters had not gone well. On their boat between St. Louis and Independence, Missouri, cholera broke out and the superior of the women, Sister Matilda, died. She was buried at Independence.[19] Two other sisters had also been taken ill. One of them recovered rapidly. The other, too weak to make the journey across the plains, was left to recover in Independence and return to Kentucky. On the banks of the Missouri River, Lamy asked Sister Mary Magdalen to continue the journey, to succeed Mother Matilda as superior of the fledgling group. She agreed, subject to the approval of the motherhouse.[20]

Lamy's six had become four, but sisters he had acquired. Following the Santa Fe Trail, the famed trading route between St. Louis and Santa Fe, Lamy's party reached Cimarron on 14 September. Crossing the Red River, they grew wary at the sight of approaching horsemen. To their surprise, it was Machebeuf, complete with escort and fresh horses, coming to welcome his friend and bishop home, and to greet the sisters who accompanied him. Together, the group stayed overnight at an army outpost, then moved on to Las Vegas.

On 26 September 1852, under the careful direction of Vicar Ortiz, the people of Santa Fe greeted their bishop and welcomed the Sisters of Loretto. It was "a reception such as we had never seen before," wrote Mother Mary Magdalen.[21] More than a thousand people came out to meet them, leading them into the city under "triumphal arches" to the old cathedral of St. Francis, while the bells of the church rang out over the hills. Vicar Ortiz greeted them in full vestments, and as they proceeded to the altar, the people again broke out in the Te Deum while violins, guitars, and drums played. Proceeding to the altar, Lamy gave the episcopal blessing. All the celebration lacked was a display of fireworks, but there would be plenty of those in the months ahead.

Even before his trip to Durango, Lamy had received petitions from the congregation at San Felipe Neri Church in Albuquerque about the conduct of Padre Gallegos. Lamy issued him a warning but saw no change in his behavior. In late summer of 1852, as Lamy returned from Baltimore, Gallegos began preparations for a trip to Mexico, taking seven wagonloads of merchandise to trade. Telling his congregation that the vicar general, either Machebeuf or Ortiz, had given him permission to make the trip, he handed over his parish duties to Padre José de Jesús Lujan. Historian Fray Angelico Chavez writes, "Well before this, if we can believe some later testimonies in his defense, he had previously sent a letter to the absent and long-awaited bishop requesting permission for the trip, and for Lujan to take his place during his absence — and all this had been granted orally by Vicar Machebeuf."[22] As Gallegos began final preparations for his trip, he heard of Lamy's return, but still departed as planned. Apparently Gallegos had not received permission for the trip from Machebeuf. Lamy, upon return, issued a decree of suspension against Gallegos and sent Machebeuf to take charge of the Albuquerque parish. Machebeuf personally undertook administration of the church and ordered Lujan to remove himself from the parish.

Lamy's recruitment efforts were having the opposite effect. He had now lost three priests since his arrival: Leyva, who was later reinstated, Grzelachowski, and Gallegos. Machebeuf's new duties in Albuquerque did not make him any less indispensable in the outlying parishes, so he continued his circuit riding, traveling around northern New Mexico, visiting various communities, and returning to Albuquerque as his home base. Machebeuf had no way of knowing that his circuit-riding technique, so effective on the Ohio frontier, would be less successful in New Mexico. The settlements he visited in Ohio were new communities, towns and villages carved out of the frontier, eager for the civilizing influence of the church and willing to accept it on any terms. Communities that never saw a priest were happy to see one arrive three or four times a year. New Mexican communities were a different story. The church had been established for centuries. The pueblos and several other communities were used to having a resident pastor, whether secular priest or Franciscan friar, who became an important member of that community. Hispanic cultural values, with their emphasis on community and family, saw permanency in the priesthood as more important than minor personal failings. Machebeuf's sporadic if well-intentioned visits were no compensation for the loss of their resident pastors, whether that loss came through death or suspension.

That native Hispanic clergy, as well as parishioners, had little understanding of his circuit-riding approach is fairly clear. Parish registers indicate that Machebeuf was in residence at San Felipe Neri on 17 October, when he performed four baptisms. He had probably been in Albuquerque since the tenth, when he first undertook administration of the church. But shortly thereafter he must have left on one of his circuits, because entries from 19–28 October are in the hand of Padre Vicente Montano of Sandía. He had come over, he recorded, "because there was no padre in the parish."[23]

In November Machebeuf traveled back through Peña Blanca, then up to Santa Clara. He had been told that the pastor at Santa Clara, Ramón Salazar, was "a drunkard living with a married woman." Salazar, Machebeuf wrote, was "so guilty that he did not reply with even one word to charges of almost daily drunkenness and adultery."[24] Lamy had warned and charitably reinstated the man previously, but his behavior had shown no improvement. Machebeuf, in his usual impulsive fashion, suspended him.

As the year 1852 came to a close, having now had time for a considered evaluation of the church in New Mexico, Lamy drafted a Christmas pastoral letter. He issued it on 24 December 1852, indicating that the changes outlined in the letter would go into effect on 1 January 1853. The letter addressed a number of Lamy's concerns. The first was the amount of money the clergy were charging to administer certain sacraments. It was not uncommon for a couple to be charged twenty to twenty-five piastres in order to be married. A piastre, then equal to the Mexican peso, was worth more than ten of today's U.S. dollars.[25] This meant the price of the marriage ceremony prevented many couples from being able to marry. For baptisms the price was one and a half piastres — for internment of the dead, sixteen piastres. Those who refused to pay, or could not afford to do so, were deprived of the sacraments, imperiling their spiritual life. In his pastoral letter, Lamy slashed the costs by two-thirds: weddings would be eight piastres, baptisms one, and burial would be reduced to six. Lamy directed strong words to the clergy. Pastors were required to sing the mass at least once a month in every church which had more than thirty families and was more than three miles from the parish. The pastor's share of revenues would be lowered to one-fourth, another quarter would be reserved for maintenance and supplies for the individual churches, but those funds could only be expended with the bishop's approval. In consideration of the cost and scarcity of candles, the poor of the territory were dispensed from their use. Lamy urged respect for fidelity in marriage, discouraged believers from attending dances, and condemned gambling. The response to the letter was nothing short of explosive.

The first fuse to blow was that of Vicar Ortiz. Upon reading the letter, he ordered Lamy out of his house, the house he had previously decorated as an episcopal palace. Confused, Lamy suggested that as the house was on parish property it belonged not to Ortiz but to the church. No, Ortiz said, the house was his personal property and he had a deed from Bishop Zubiría to prove it. He produced the deed, "a priest who claimed to be authorized by Mgr of Durango [Bishop Zubiría] in 1831 or 1832 . . . gave everything to Ortiz," the property having been sold to Ortiz "for 300 sheep," not yet paid, but to be given to the church "after his death or resignation."[26] When Lamy consulted local residents, they told him the property had always belonged to the Church of St. Francis, that they were "astonished" by Ortiz's claims. Nor did Ortiz's claims stop with the rectory house. Ortiz also claimed as his private property the Church of San Miguel, the oldest church in Santa Fe, built by Native Americans under the direction of two missionaries in the early 1600s. He had another deed to support that claim.

Ortiz's anger about the contents of the pastoral letter was fueled by another of Lamy's decisions. Lamy had decided St. Francis Church would serve as his cathedral. He had divided the parish of St. Francis in half, keeping one half for himself to administer as bishop, offering Ortiz the other half. Ortiz did not accept the offer. He had been appointed by Bishop Zubiría as the parochus proprius, the life pastor of the parish. No one, Ortiz maintained, could deprive him of that status. Lamy tried to be conciliatory. He offered Ortiz the larger half of the parish for the rest of his life, a pension, and one of the houses on church land. Instead of accepting the offer or attempting to negotiate, Ortiz responded by demanding a payment of thirteen thousand dollars. Hoping to heal the rift, one of Ortiz's well-intentioned friends offered Lamy the three hundred sheep, mentioned in the deed. Lamy declined. "I have refused to accept them as I do not think the sale was legitimate."[27]

Possibly the final blow to Ortiz was the suspension of his former assistant José de Jesús Lujan. In their early months in Santa Fe, Machebeuf and Lamy had been informed that Lujan was "living in a most scandalous manner, keeping a very young and beautiful married woman in his house."[28] Periodically her husband would appear at the house, begging his wife to return to him. Finally, the husband approached Lamy. Embarrassed, Lamy ordered Lujan to send the woman back to her husband, but Lujan refused. When Lamy reassigned him, first to Albuquerque, then to replace a priest who had died, he took his mistress with him, lodging her in a house next to his own. Once there, Lujan refused to read Lamy's pastoral letter, meeting

Machebeuf's delivery of it with insults. Lamy suspended him. It was all too much for Ortiz. He prepared a list of written accusations to send to the pope and angrily prepared to leave for Durango.

Lamy's early recruiting drive could be considered less than successful. The toll since his arrival was ominous. Ortiz was departing for Durango. Gallegos, suspended, had not yet returned from his trip to Mexico. Lujan and Salazar were suspended. Of the priests who had accompanied him from San Antonio, Grzelachowski was suspended and the Spaniard, Borrajo, did not choose to stay. Two other priests, Jesús Baca and Antonio Otero, had resigned upon receiving the pastoral letter. Lamy gave them a month to reconsider, and when neither did so, he formally suspended them as well.

The divisions between the French and the Hispanic clergy had deepened drastically—the fissure had become a canyon. Lamy's rectitude, writes Horgan, "deeply rooted in the ancient faith and discipline of provincial Europe, could not condone what made mockery of the very sacraments of matrimony, ordination, and penance." But Hispanic historian Fray Angelico Chavez has a different view. Chavez suggests that the suspensions were not due to Lamy's rectitude, but to Machebeuf's influence on him. "There is no other way to explain it," he writes in his biography of Padre Martínez, "except to say that their 'particular friendship,' whether either one realized it or not, was something less than an admirable one—and with no imputation on our part as regard to their own personal morals." He concludes, "History is replete with such examples even down to our times, as when a high statesman, while most upright in every other regard, gets easily hoodwinked by those whom he cherishes as his dearest friends and then stands by them no matter how serious their misdeeds."[29]

In his biography of Padre Gallegos of Albuquerque, *Très Macho—He Said*, Chavez is even more explicit in his praise of Lamy and his derision of Machebeuf. The first of the charges Chavez levies against Machebeuf is that of chauvinism, of extreme nationalism in terms of his loyalty to his fellow Auvergnats. Lamy is as pure as the driven snow. "Here it must be said," Chavez writes, "that Bishop Lamy himself never betrayed any such chauvinistic faults, for in all of his life's conduct, and in every statement that he made, he never flaunted his French nationality." According to Chavez, however, "Machebeuf proved himself just the opposite." Machebeuf, he informs us, "kept on boasting about himself and other clerical countrymen of his as superior Frenchmen, more specifically as Auvergnats." Chavez seems unaware of the intense pride displayed by natives of the various provinces of France and the rivalry between them, divisions that remain viable even to this day.[30]

The charge of nationalism becomes even less incriminating when one remembers that in the mid-nineteenth century nationalism did not carry today's negative connotation. Discussing liberalism and nationalism in his essay "The Many Faces of Padre Antonio José Martínez" historian E. A. Mares reminds us, "Nationalism, that other great force that animated so many leaders of the nineteenth century, has had the most tragic of histories in the twentieth century." Remembering this, Chavez's aspersion smacks of a facile form of presentism, the evaluation of historical figures and their actions by standards set in the present. Chavez also fails to notice evidence of nationalism in his own subjects, Padres Martínez and Gallegos. The trait has not gone unnoticed by other historians. Mares comments, "Padre Martínez, like so many of his generation, appears naive to the wary eyes of this century when he extols the virtues of national patriotism. He, of course, cannot be faulted for not seeing that in the next century nationalism would be one of the significant forces leading the way to two major world wars."[31] Chavez extends no such courtesy to Machebeuf, laying all of the blame for the "world war" between French and Hispanic clergy squarely at Machebeuf's diminutive feet.

Chavez's contribution to the study of nineteenth-century New Mexican history is inestimable. His research delineating the web of familial connections and the lives of various members of the Hispanic clergy is unquestionably the finest available. But while arguing for every cultural consideration from his readers of Anglo or European descent, he does not always extend the same courtesy to cultures other than his own. Simply put, Chavez's understanding of French culture, and particularly French clerical culture, does not always inspire confidence.

Chavez's most serious charges against Machebeuf can be found in his discussion of Machebeuf's views on sexuality, which he considers, somewhat disingenuously, the source of all of the difficulties between the Hispanic clergy and French hierarchy. Chavez's fascination with Machebeuf's sexuality becomes the basis for an elaborate, if sometimes tenuous, structure of Machiavellian conspiracy and deceit that served as foundation for all the unjust persecution of the Hispanic clergy in New Mexico.

The core of Chavez's theory is a comment made by one of Machebeuf's acquaintances during his days at seminary. Chavez writes, "As he himself put it, Machebeuf had suffered certain most bothersome interior trials since boyhood — pleins de chasmes et illusions." In a curious translation Chavez tell us "The phrase means 'fraught with deepest confusion due to certain self-misgivings' better than the too literal 'chasms and delusions.'" He assures us that after examination of "all of his consequent actions and no less his copious correspondence, it poses no mystery at all." The key, according to Chavez, is a "certain spiritual malaise" called "scrupulosity."[32]

Chavez makes several errors. The comment that serves as his foundation, "pleins de chasmes et illusions," was not made by Machebeuf, but by someone else about him.[33] The French word "illusions" is a cognate of the English illusions. A "too literal" translation would not change it to "delusions." Finally scrupulosity is a term usually reserved for overly zealous reporting of one's own sins. Primarily concerned with their own sins, the overly scrupulous do not necessarily demonstrate the confidence of the spiritually righteous, they rarely express the "tense fanaticism against any impurity detected or even suspected in others" implied by Chavez.[34]

Scrupulosity is a term well known to those involved in spiritual direction. According to no less a source than St. Ignatius of Loyola, a scruple is when "I freely judge something to be a sin which is not a sin."[35] So common was this tendency in zealous penitents that Ignatius specifically includes two pages of "Notes Concerning Scruples" at the end of his *Spiritual Exercises.* Due, in part, to the international success of the Jesuits, many orders, including the Sulpicians, adapted Jesuit techniques in the formation of their members and in the administration of their seminaries. Knowledge of scrupulosity, and methods of dealing with the same, were widely known.

Yet, according to Chavez, writing for a largely secular audience, "for the faithful Catholic victims of such scrupulosity there was no . . . outlet, except to pester every priest-confessor they met to have him absolve them from their constant reeling off of imaginary sins." In Chavez's opinion, "Only this type of religious scrupulosity can explain Machebeuf's fanatical obsession with matters of the flesh, and the basic cause can then be traced to a latent homosexual inclination which at first attracted him to the exclusive male companionship in the barracks, but which his innate piety supplanted with that of seminary."[36]

As far as the charge of Machebeuf's latent homosexuality is concerned, nothing in the records of Machebeuf's life substantiates the charge. Chavez's only basis seems to be Machebeuf's interest first in the military and later in the priesthood, and if that served as sole criteria we would have a preponderance of candidates. While interest in both the priesthood and the military were fueled by Machebeuf's passion, it was hardly the passion of Eros. It was the siren call of adventure that drove Machebeuf. Machebeuf's dreams for the priesthood focused not on the availability of men in the seminary, but on the romance of the distant missions, the opportunity for solitary service on what Europeans of his age viewed as the frontier of the civilized world. Jesuit historian Thomas Steele comments, "Machebeuf himself, whose letters so appealed to Willa Cather, was a clerical, celibate, male Emma Bovary. If Emma was 'a little adventuress,' then Machebeuf was a little adventurer—in the sense that everything he did had to be an adventure. He had as little tolerance for boredom as Emma; he had instead a lively sense of the dramatic and a deep need of it."[37] Machebeuf's decision to join the priesthood was his response to the seductive call of missionary adventure.

Having succumbed to the call of adventure himself, Machebeuf felt driven to send the stories of his adventures back to his sister in France in over a hundred letters. Machebeuf's letters to his sister in the Convent of the Visitation in Riom have become an important source of historical information for Pulitzer Prize-winning writers such as Willa Cather and Paul Horgan, as well as numerous other authors. Those letters, according to Jesuit historian Thomas Steele, were "prime examples of a very definite and deservedly obscure genre of literature known as the edifying letter—lettres edifiantes in French, cartas edificantes in Spanish." Letters in this genre served three purposes: keeping in touch, raising funds for distant missions, and primarily, edifying the reader. Steele continues, "They were read during dinner and supper in the refectories of seminaries and convents like the one to which Machebeuf's sister belonged, and Machebeuf surely knew that his letters would be read to such an audience. "In such a setting," Steele explains, "they served as appeals for prayers, which were assumed to do as much for the conversion of pagan nations as the best actual field work." In discussing this type of letter, Steele describes Machebeuf's letters themselves, "They were very pious; they made a clear differentiation between good and evil, sketching the world with dark shadows and sparkling highlights and very little grey. There were good guys and there were bad guys, just like a John Wayne western."[38]

Chavez seems to completely miss the tenor of these letters. In somber tones he uses the letters to accuse Machebeuf of lying, then meticulously tracks down any discrepancy he can possibly detect. Each discrepancy he assures his reader, in an intensity that borders on the paranoid, is evidence of a grand conspiracy to deprive New Mexico's nineteenth-century Hispanic priests of their rightful place in history. Nor is Machebeuf alone in his mendacity—Lamy is also a liar, as are Willa Cather, Sister Blandina Segale, and others. When his own subject, Padre Gallegos, is caught bending the truth, Chavez advises us, "This has to be taken with a good lump of salt."[39] He offers no such courtesy to New Mexico's Europeans or Americans.

Perhaps most disturbing about Chavez's charges against Machebeuf is not the content, but the vehemence. Chavez sees a dark world of conspir-

acy, where almost every interaction is shadowed by malevolent intent. The
suspicion of malevolence is rarely justified by the documents. Machebeuf
was never a great intellectual, nor was he marked by exceedingly high intelligence. Quite frankly, there is little indication that Machebeuf was capable
of the kind of Machiavellian intrigue for which Chavez holds him responsible. As to any possible exaggerations contained in his letters, Steele comments, "I suspect that in addition to seeking out a place and a vocation
which would offer him a thrilling life, he consistently enhanced — 'embroidered' — his autobiographical writings to achieve the proper combination
of Christian fortitude and the sublime dangers, obstacles, and temptations
to exercise it."[40] If Machebeuf "embroidered" his accounts, it was more
likely that he did so in an effort to inspire others than as part of a malevolent
plot to displace native clergy.

Still, Chavez's views are indicative of how the climate of misunderstanding that began with the U.S. annexation of New Mexico keeps compound-
ing itself. Chavez's vehemence demonstrates how divisions between those
of Hispanic and European descent continue to this day, with the backdrop
of a church that still has not completely come to terms with the sexuality of
its clergy.

Curiously, Chavez's certainty that Machebeuf was at the root of all the
divisions between French hierarchy and Hispanic clergy substantiates Machebeuf's success in at least one area. There is little doubt that Machebeuf
and Lamy engaged in an ecclesiastical form of "good cop, bad cop" in terms
of their relationship to their public. Machebeuf served as hatchet man, the
one sent to "whip the cats," so that the saintly Bishop Lamy could remain
unsoiled by the dirty work of direct confrontation. Chavez's vilification of
Machebeuf, combined with his soaring praises of Lamy, indicate that the
public relations campaign was a complete success.

ELEVEN

Interpellato

✣

Machebeuf's troubles surfaced in the first days of 1853. On January fifth, Padre Martínez of Taos drafted a letter to Bishop Lamy making formal complaints about Machebeuf's behavior. The letter was signed by Martínez and a number of other priests, most likely Padres Abeyta of Arroyo Hondo, Lucero of Picuris, and Lujan of Santa Clara. The first page of the letter condemns "Don Preyecto Machiuf" for having acted with "quasi-episcopal authority." In addition, Machebeuf was charged with being hostile to the native clergy, "whom he seems to look upon with an eye of rancour." The narrative continues, denouncing Machebeuf's suspension of Don Ramón Salazar at Santa Clara, his interference with parish affairs in Santa Cruz during Padre Trujillo's absence, and his dismissal of another priest, Don Antonio de Jesús Salazar of Abiquiú. Machebeuf suspended Salazar "without there having preceded the steps set forth in the sacred canons and curial authors." It particularly condemns Machebeuf's seizure of parish funds: "The Señor Machebeuf appropriated the obventions of both parishes. . . . Such fraudulent usurpation is not far from having been the real reason for the suspension imposed on him." Salazar, Martínez agreed, had his faults and distractions, "but there is still the right for a case to be instituted and judgment passed according to justice."[1]

Martínez's letter then turned to recent events in Albuquerque: the suspension of his distant cousin José Manuel Gallegos. "It is said, and it appears with all moral certitude, that the Señor Machebeuf publicly suspended from office and ecclesiastical benefice the cura propio of Albuquerque," Martínez wrote. "The aforesaid Gallegos," he explains, "is absent and away from his curacy for a just cause, and he went to Durango in September of last year on pending matters of great importance before his Excellency Bishop Zubiría."[2] Apparently Martínez was under the impression that Machebeuf seized the parish without Lamy's knowledge, unaware Machebeuf acted on Lamy's directive. In doing so, Martínez reports, Machebeuf violated canon law and proper procedure; he neither respected the rights of the cura propio, nor had he issued warnings after taking the formal steps required to do so.

Throughout the remainder of the letter, the charges against Machebeuf take a pointedly personal form. "It is also said, your Excellency, that the Señor Machebeuf, by agreement with some to gain further lucre, celebrates Masses in private homes. . . . With regard to the conduct of the Señor Machebeuf in his clerical actions . . . he is a revealer of the seal of sacramental confession because, after having heard the confession of one or various persons, he has spoken about their faults, at least 'in genere.'. . . This horrifies one, and many persons on hearing about such conduct, say they will never make their confession to him; several other things are omitted, your Excellency, judging that what has been told suffices."[3]

Machebeuf was not in Santa Fe when Lamy received the letter, so the two could not immediately discuss the accusations. Prior to Machebeuf's return, Lamy wrote to Martínez, asking for proof of the most serious of the charges, that of violating the seal of confession.

Within a few days another attack on Machebeuf arrived from a different quarter. An unsigned complaint was sent by the Hispanic parishioners of Santo Domingo and Cochití. They complained of their loss of a resident priest following the death of Padre Rafael Ortiz, cousin of Santa Fe's vicar forane. Although Machebeuf, the "French vicar," sometimes visited the two communities, they had seen members of their communities die without extreme unction, the sacrament of the sick, because he was "tan ambulante," moving around so much, as he continued his circuit riding to Taos, Mora, San Miguel, Albuquerque, and Socorro. They complained about his preaching as well, saying that when he was not talking about the fifth commandment, he was revealing the secrets of the confessional.[4]

Lamy soon discovered the author of the complaint to be Francisco Tomás C. de Baca, a brother-in-law of the former vicar, Ortiz. Nor did the timing of the letter seem completely coincidental, arriving within two weeks of Martínez's letter. Learning that C. de Baca was in Santa Fe, Lamy wrote to him on 14 January requesting "judicial proofs" for what he considered a "most malicious calumny" against a priest's character. C. de Baca responded on 16 January, denying the people's petition was an attack on Machebeuf—they simply wanted a resident priest. On the eighteenth

Lamy wrote to him again. This time he requested specific information on the violation of the seal of confession, including who the injured party was and what had been revealed.

Meanwhile, in Taos, Martínez, having received Lamy's demand for proof of the charges, wrote a second letter on 24 January repeating the same charges. When Machebeuf stopped in Santa Fe and had a chance to review them, he sent a letter to Martínez on the third of February. "Most respectable Sir," Machebeuf wrote, "on my return from Las Vegas, and while still en route, I learned that you along with other clergymen had made a protestation to his Lordship against me, full of the gravest accusations." Machebeuf defended himself against the charges of violating the seal of confession, referring to the comments he felt may have been misinterpreted and assuring Martínez that he well understood the sanctity of the sacrament. He concluded, "I do not want to say a single word . . . regarding the suspension of some padres . . . his Lordship will inform you: I have to obey his orders. Without anything more to say, I am always your affectionate servant and squire."[5]

Martínez was either somewhat mollified by Machebeuf's response or strategically chose to retreat. On 24 February 1853 he wrote a reply to Lamy. "I remain satisfied with what Señor Machebeuf answers, and from it I observe the motive of his good faith while functioning here. . . . I see that the resolve he keeps to go on with his preaching and the motives which animate him, were in his soul the basis of religious zeal when alluding to the parties referred to."[6] His letter may have created a temporary reprieve, but it was not the last time a flurry of letters would fly between Padre Martínez of Taos and Bishop Lamy, nor was it the last time Martínez would come into conflict with Machebeuf.

C. de Baca, however, had not given up his accusations against Machebeuf. On 1 February he wrote Lamy a long and rhetorical letter, providing what he deemed the proofs of Machebeuf's violation of the seal of confession. He referred to Machebeuf presiding at a novena of masses in May 1852. After hearing confessions, Machebeuf made reference in his homily to a boy of ten who did not know his catechism nor how to make his confession. Everyone in the small community knew to whom he was referring. In a homily two days later, Machebeuf said he was pleased by the number of people attending confession, including a leading citizen who had not been to confession for eight years. "Your Lordship will judge if this is not a revelation," C. de Baca remarked, apparently, in this case, considering himself the injured party. Finally, Machebeuf had publicly refused holy communion to a man who had openly lived in sin with his sister-in-law, and refused to give sanction to the man's plans for marriage. These, C. de Baca considered, proofs "as clear as the light of noon." If Lamy would not act on this information, C. de Baca indicated he would have no choice but to consider it an "act of autocratic vengeance on his part."[7]

Lamy was not prepared to have his parishioners dictate the terms in his administration of the vicariate. In his letter of 22 February, Lamy chided C. de Baca for not providing the "judicial proofs" he had requested. He went on to say he regretted that a gentleman of his good education should be so confused as to criticize his administration and ended the letter by ominously suggesting that he must have written these things while suffering under some "private preoccupation."[8]

Lamy's sharp response is understandable. He could not afford to set a precedent in which his decisions were challenged by the laity and reversed on the strength of innuendo. But neither could he disregard the gravity of the charges against Machebeuf. Given Machebeuf's impulsive nature, he seemed most certainly guilty of indiscretion. And one doubts whether Machebeuf fully understood the network of political alliances created by intermarriages between New Mexico's wealthier Hispanic families or how his actions in one community would spread throughout the territory. Used to operating with autonomy on the newly settled Ohio frontier and accustomed to actions of the church hierarchy being accepted without question, he certainly underestimated the ability of the Hispanic community to launch an organized attack against him. Lamy had temporarily extinguished the fires in Cochití and Taos when Padre Gallegos returned to Albuquerque on 1 March 1853.

Ambrosio Armijo, probate judge and member of the influential Armijo family, acted as spokesman and authored a letter on behalf of 950 citizens of Albuquerque who signed a petition in defense of Padre Gallegos. Gallegos, they insisted, had traveled to Mexico on "important business" for Bishop Zubiría and left Lujan in charge of the parish. Since Lujan's removal, they had been spiritually abandoned, given only the "infrequent visitations of Señor Machebeuf." Machebeuf, "under the fictitious guise of an apostle," Armijo wrote, was neglecting the people of Albuquerque, even the dying. His preaching was "boring and annoying," and his sermons began with the Gospel, but ended with "the private lives of the Faithful."[9] The signers of the petition welcomed the return of Gallegos. They asked Lamy to withdraw Machebeuf and restore Gallegos as pastor of San Felipe Neri Church.

Lamy was firm in his response to Armijo. Writing on 17 March he stated that "the rehabilitation of Father Gallegos will be very difficult indeed. . . . He did not obey my orders during my absence, and furthermore, he left his parish without permission of his superiors." As far as the removal of Machebeuf was concerned, "let me tell you this: that this is my business alone, and I myself will decide what is to be done about the errors of which you accuse him. . . . Let me give you some advice, . . . you ought to adhere closely to Ecclesiastical Authority; otherwise you place yourselves in the gravest of difficulties."[10] His response could hardly have pleased Gallegos's supporters, nor were they prepared to docilely accept Lamy's "Ecclesiastical Authority."

The conflict soon came to a head. Visiting one of the pueblos, Machebeuf heard Gallegos had returned "and was going to dispute the possession of the church with me next Sunday." Writing to his sister he gave a full account of the confrontation. "This did not alarm me, but I thought it best to be prepared, so I sent a messenger in haste to the Bishop to get a confirmation in writing of the sentence pronounced on the Padre, and my authorization in clear terms to administer the affairs of the parish."[11]

By Saturday night Machebeuf had returned to Albuquerque, and on Sunday morning he arrived at the church an hour earlier than usual. "What was my astonishment upon arriving there to find the Padre in the pulpit and the church filled with people whom I knew to be his particular friends. These he had quietly gathered together, and now he was exciting them to revolt, or at least to resistance." He found the doors to the sacristy, which adjoined the rectory, locked, and so went around to the main door of the church. Assuming an air of confidence, he commanded the crowd to stand aside, then forced his way up past the pulpit, "just as the Padre pronounced the Bishop's name and mine in connection with the most atrocious accusations and insulting reflections." Reaching the highest step of the sanctuary, Machebeuf turned and listened quietly until Gallegos had finished. The faces of the crowd looked to him, silently awaiting his reply. Responding carefully, he "refuted all his accusations and I showed, moreover, that he was guilty of the scandals which had brought on his punishment." This stated, Machebeuf theatrically unfolded the letter he had requested from Lamy and read it in a loud voice, then called on Gallegos to justify himself, "if he had any reply to make." Gallegos made no response, "not a word; he went out as crestfallen as a trapped fox and left me in peaceful possession of the church. I sang the high mass as usual, and preached on the Gospel of the day without making the least allusion to the scene which had just taken place."[12]

Gallegos was not a man to accept defeat placidly. Neither were his friends ready to let the matter rest. A few days later, a group of twenty or thirty influential "rancheros" paid Machebeuf a visit. Most were from the outlying community of Los Ranchos de Albuquerque; Machebeuf recognized only three as being from Albuquerque itself. Arriving at Machebeuf's residence, they ordered him to get out of the parish, saying that if he refused, they would "have recourse to other measures." Machebeuf faced the men. "At that moment the good God must have given me patience and strength that were more than natural, for I answered them with firmness. . . . I told them they might take such measures as they saw fit, but . . . I was ready to die for my sheep rather than abandon them." Apparently his stand disconcerted them, because the group left without a word, to report back to Gallegos. "They did not know I was an Auvergnat," Machebeuf concluded, " 'Latsin pas.' Never give up!"[13]

According to Machebeuf, the second confrontation marked a turning point in his relations with his parishioners. "From that moment the Padre lost all hope of driving me away, and, abandoning the Church, he went into politics." Machebeuf did not seem to think much of Gallegos's political aspirations, "He worked every kind of scheme until he succeeded in getting himself elected to the Congress of the United States as Delegate from the Territory of New Mexico."[14] Regardless of his opinion of Gallegos's character and his conclusion that he had lost all hope, Machebeuf had not heard the last of Gallegos.

In April yet another attack was launched. Padre Martínez of Taos traveled to Santa Fe and held a meeting with at least three other Hispanic priests, Ortiz of Santa Fe, Lujan of Santa Clara, and Chávez of Belen. Together they drafted a letter to Lamy, protesting his failure to suspend Machebeuf. "The undersigned pastors," the letter read, "submitted to you a written complaint denouncing your Vicar Don Preyecto Machebeuf for unruly behavior which he practices in the churches of New Mexico, now vexing the clergy, now exercising jurisdiction and taking possession of obventions with the infraction of Canon Law." They challenged Lamy for dividing the parish of Santa Fe "without observing the canonical dispositions," for "appropriating" part of the parish for himself, and for "keeping under suspension the lawful pastor of Albuquerque." Not considering Lamy's responses to be adequate the four were prepared to go over his head. Their purpose, they indicated, was to notify him of their intentions; "we have gathered together to serve notice to your Reverence through this present letter. . . . We intend to appeal said matter with the cases it touches upon to higher authority."[15] The battle lines were clearly drawn.

Lamy did not seem overly concerned with the threat. Writing to Purcell on 10 April, eight days after the meeting of the padres, he seemed confident. "The fact is," he explained, "if I would comply with all the formalities they want, I would never stop abuses." Nor did he seem overly concerned about the charges against Machebeuf, expressing his own theory as to their origin. "Some of the clergymen who look upon Mr. Machebeuf with jealousy, on account of his zeal and good qualities, have taken up the pretended accusation and they would try their best to injure him." He could give little credence to the accusation, in part because of their failure to provide what he considered proof and in part because of the behavior of Machebeuf's parishioners. Lamy writes, "In the same place where the accusations originated, and also in the neighborhood, he was kept in the confessional day and night for weeks."[16]

Not all of the events of the year were unpleasant. Rome showed few signs of taking complaints about Lamy's administration seriously, for on 12 August 1853, Cardinal Franson, the Prefect for the Propaganda Fide announced that Santa Fe had been elevated from a vicariate to a full diocese.[17] By September Lamy had received the good news. He was now a full "Ordinary," first bishop of the Diocese of Santa Fe. Lamy would leave in January 1854 and travel to Rome to formally accept the appointment and make his visit ad limina with Pope Pius IX. The trip would also provide Lamy with opportunities for further recruitment. In the interim, Machebeuf would be the acting head not of the vicariate, but of the new diocese.

Machebeuf settled down to the affairs of his parish in Albuquerque, and yet another disagreement with Gallegos to be resolved. At the side of San Felipe Neri Church, a long adobe building, divided into numerous rooms, fronted the remnant of the town plaza. The building contained the sacristy, served as the rectory for the church, and was known to the locals as the convento. Gallegos had rebuilt the building and used it as his residence for a number of years. His election to the Territorial Congress necessitated his presence in Washington, D.C., but Gallegos refused to give up the house. The house, he maintained, belonged to him. It was his personal property, and had been deeded to him by Bishop Zubiría.

According to Jesuit historian Thomas J. Steele, Gallegos probably did own the house. "When he arrived he found the rectory next to the church so badly tumbled down that not even a single room was habitable," Steel writes, "so Gallegos got Zubiría's oral permission to rebuild the rectory and have outright ownership of the structure." By 1846 Gallegos had secured title from the chairman of the Albuquerque town council not only to the building but also to the church and the church land as well. This may have been an attempt on the part of civil authorities to prevent the property from being taken over by the U.S. military.[18]

Shortly after Lamy's departure, a month after Gallegos was elected New

Mexico's delegate to Congress, Machebeuf filed suit against Gallegos to recover the rectory. Gallegos asked first for a postponement, in order to gather documentation, and then for a change of venue. Both were granted. The postponement also allowed Machebeuf additional time to prepare. On 11 May Machebeuf wrote to Zubiría asking him if Gallegos did indeed have a deed. "I do not deem it possible that he possesses such a document, since I feel certain that the Lord Bishop Don Juan Lamy, on his return from Durango, told me that Your Illustrious Lordship had assured him that you had sold the ground for the Santa Fe rectory to Padre Don Juan Felipe Ortiz but that you had never sold the Albuquerque rectory." On 30 June Machebeuf sent a second letter in the event the first did not reach him. Zubiría's response made its slow way back to Santa Fe. The bishop formally declared he had never sold the house to Gallegos. "Behold the impostor unveiled!" Machebeuf crowed, and promptly moved into the rectory.[19]

The matter was far from settled. In April 1855 Machebeuf's lawyers asked that Gallegos's housekeeper, Jesusita Trujillo, be named as an additional defendant. Before the trial could begin, at only forty years of age, Jesusita died, "and Machebeuf himself buried her under the floor of the church." The house appeared in the inventory of her estate, "a house situated in Albuquerque, next to the church, of eleven rooms with two zaguans [roofed passages for wagons] and a corral, valued at $800."[20]

In October 1855 the trial finally took place. Most historians indicate that the civil courts found Gallegos's claim to be fraudulent and gave Machebeuf the house. "Quite the contrary," Steele explains. "Despite Bishop Zubiría's statement that he had not sold Padre Gallegos the house, the trial ended in a hung jury, and so Gallegos as heir and executor of Jesusa's estate remained in possession of the rectory." In spite of Gallegos's clear title to the house, Steele speculates that he must have realized the "church wasn't ever meant to be his possession any more than the church was meant to be his career."[21] On 14 February the following year he sold the house to Lamy for $1,501, almost double its appraised value. In May Machebeuf filed a brief with the Valencia County Court promising he would not prosecute but dismiss his suit and pay the costs of both parties. Machebeuf's celebration proved more than a little premature.

It may have been due to distractions. Attending to the affairs of the diocese, traveling back and forth as needed to Santa Fe, Machebeuf began a series of improvements in the parish. He began, also, to develop a strong, if thoroughly paternalistic, attachment to his parishioners in Albuquerque. "They are dear to me," he explained to his sister, "for the more a mother suffers from a sick and petulant child, the more she loves it. So it is with me." And at last the people of Albuquerque seemed to return his affection. The letter continues, "Every day I have new proofs that my parishioners share my sentiments. They never before testified such respect and confidence as they did at my last visit."[22]

Machebeuf had not known the relative security of stable parish life since his departure from Sandusky, almost three years before. Although he scarcely acknowledged it, it seems that at least a part of him longed for the human contact that comes only through time, through shared hardship and joy. Another incident may well have brought his memories of Sandusky to the surface. One of the parishioners, after hearing Machebeuf's descriptions of formal church services in Europe and the East, seeing his efforts to repair and restore the church, offered to purchase a pipe organ for the parish. Machebeuf gratefully accepted. One problem remained, he knew of no one trained to play the instrument. "Deus providebit," as Machebeuf would say. He received a letter from a man who had been his organist in Sandusky for two years. Would it be possible, the organist inquired, for him to come to New Mexico and rejoin his former pastor? Organ and organist arrived at almost the same time. Soon, "the music fairly enraptured the Mexicans, who, from time immemorial, had been accustomed to hearing the mass sung to the accompaniment of a violin."[23]

Even the rancheros, who had previously ordered him out of the parish, began to return to the fold. When he held his first novena, "Every day the church was filled, and not even one of those leaders from the Ranchos was missing. . . . What pleasure I . . . have in seeing my Rancheros coming back — these same men who came to my room to insult and threaten me!" Machebeuf was beginning to feel at home in New Mexico. He had long realized the magnificence of the New Mexican landscape, but the human landscape held his greatest challenges and rewards. As he wrote to his sister, "These are the things which console us in our isolation."[24]

On 18 November 1854, Lamy returned from Europe. Three thousand of Santa Fe's citizens turned out to greet him, to escort him for the last few miles of his journey. The Sisters of Loretto rode out in coaches with the students of their growing school, and the dragoons from Fort Marcy arrived to serve as escort. Once again the streets leading into Santa Fe had been transformed, "all was most beautifully ornamented. Arches of beautifully colored silks, gold crosses, artificial flowers, mirrors, etc. were thrown over the streets in all directions."[25]

Lamy's Roman trip was a success. He recruited four priests, a deacon, two subdeacons, and two laymen who would begin studies for the priesthood on arrival in New Mexico. One of the priests, Dom Domaso Taladrid, was a Spanish priest Lamy met in Rome. The rest were all Frenchmen from the diocese of Clermont. He had waited almost a month in Willow Springs for the arrival of three more Sisters of Loretto, but their journey had been delayed.

Lamy's meeting with the elegant and articulate Pope Pius IX had gone well, as had his introduction to Alessandro Cardinal Barnabo, the new Prefect of the Propaganda Fide, who would become his most important financial ally in the years ahead. On his return journey across the plains, he had run into a bearded stranger carrying a rifle, who turned out to be Bishop Miège, the vicar apostolic for the Kansas Territory.[26] Within a few days of his return, Lamy had given assignments to the new recruits. N. Julliard would go to Belen, Antoine Avel would remain in Santa Fe, and Machebeuf could return to what he called "mon cher Albuquerque."

By March 1855 the three wayward Loretto nuns had been located. Another sister from St. Louis would also be able to join them. Everything was arranged for their journey to New Mexico. Lamy decided Machebeuf should be the one to retrieve them, and he could take time to renew contacts with the Ursulines he had brought to Ohio years before. Machebeuf returned to Brown County and watched happily as the students of the Ursulines' now-flourishing school performed *Uncle Tom's Cabin* in honor of his visit.

Machebeuf met up with the four Lorettines in Independence, Missouri, and undertook the preparations necessary for their passage across the plains. In June they began their journey westward, traveling with a wagon train of merchants. All went smoothly for the first month. Years later Mother Ann Joseph recalled the events of 16 July. "Looking toward the east we saw the whole bluff covered with Indians on horseback, the faces and arms painted in warlike style. They swooped down on us like so many eagles."[27] Machebeuf ushered the four nuns into their ambulances and fastened heavy canvas storm covers over them. The plains tribesmen rode up to the circle of wagons, and the merchants presented them with gifts of blankets, sugar, molasses, and tobacco. Machebeuf distributed a number of his holy medals and unsuccessfully tried to negotiate the purchase of a young Hispanic boy, who seemed to be a captive of the group. For over four hours the sisters stayed in the hot airless wagons, praying for deliverance. By nightfall the last of the Indians had left, the wagons had been moved to a better location, and the grateful, sweaty sisters were released.

With the exception of that one incident, Mother Joseph had fond memories of her travel across the plains. "Father Machebeuf," she said, "often sent some of his men ahead of the caravan to select a good spot in which to camp for the night and instructed them to plant young trees so as to represent a grove whenever we came to a wooded part of the country. . . . He would go on in advance and be on the spot to welcome us to our little garden or grove." Nor was his attentiveness limited to overnight campsites. "He would often bring into camp beautiful flowers, or shells found upon the prairies, and in every way try to cheer us after a long weary day of travel."[28] On 24 July the group arrived safely in Santa Fe.

During Machebeuf's absence Lamy had been canonically installed as bishop and old arguments had again come to the surface. Vicar Juan Felipe Ortiz had also returned. Lamy reported to Purcell in Cincinnati, "the old ex-vicario Ortiz has returned from Durango, and we receive new vexations from him every day."[29] In June, at the request of his cousin, Ortiz had officiated at the blessing of the acequias, the irrigation ditches, on the eve of the feast day of St. John the Baptist. Lamy had suspended him for assuming faculties not granted to him. Ortiz and Lamy met, and Ortiz asked Lamy to return the Santa Fe parish. Lamy refused, but offered him the river lands between Peña Blanca and Algodones. Ortiz declined the offer; he would take no charge that was not in Santa Fe.

Relations between the two men continued to be strained. Ortiz claimed as personal property a number of items his family had donated to the churches in the area, some holy vessels and a bell. Ortiz's brother-in-law, the municipal prefect of Santa Fe, gave him a writ of possession, so Lamy saw no alternative but to report the losses to Rome. Lamy began to tire of the seemingly endless conflicts with the Hispanic clergy. "Some of our Mexican padres are more troublesome to us than the 'know-nothings' with you," he wrote to Purcell; "we have not all roses in New Mexico."[30]

New Mexican thorns continued to plague Lamy's diocesan garden. The clergy were preparing formal charges against Lamy and Machebeuf, lists of offenses to send to the Vatican. Anticipating the fresh onslaught, Lamy decided to send Machebeuf to Rome, where he might personally offer a defense for himself and his battered bishop. The two of them spent the early months of 1856 preparing the documents Machebeuf would carry with him, the documents that would allow him to present their case at the Holy See. Lamy wrote a long letter in his own defense; he prepared an outline covering the long dispute over the Texan villages of Ysleta del Sur, San Elizario, and Socorro, which Zubiría still considered part of his jurisdiction. He also made a formal request to sell the Castrense chapel on Santa Fe Plaza. Finally he gave Machebeuf a general document authorizing him to recruit "priests, seminarians, brothers, nuns, or monks" wherever he traveled. Machebeuf must have cherished it, for he kept the document the rest of his life.[31]

In March Machebeuf set out across northern New Mexico toward the plains. The New Mexican March brings cold winds and lingering winter storms, and that year brought bitter cold and particularly heavy spring snows. Four days outside of Fort Union his carriage was damaged. Not willing to overload his other cart, filled with rations and luggage, he and an unnamed companion abandoned the vehicle and walked for two days through the snow until they came upon a wagon train of Mexican and American merchants headed for St. Louis. The merchants took pity on the wayward priest and made room for him and his luggage in a huge wagon — so massive it took a team of ten mules to pull it. He rode in relative comfort, with six other "passengers" on the fodder for twenty animals, making his way slowly across the plains.

Undeterred by inconvenience, Machebeuf found remarkable beauty in the snowscape of the frozen plains. Thousands of buffalo, deer, and antelope swept across them in undulating waves. Dinners were taken in the open air, their plates on a pristine tablecloth of snow, or standing, "like the Israelites" with weapons close at hand. Nightfall brought sleep nestled between two buffalo robes, insulated by five or six inches of snow. One fellow traveler reported seeing wolves prowling around Machebeuf's bed on several occasions, but judging by his reports to his sister he was "not of this world" and neither saw them himself nor was in any way disturbed by them.[32]

When he boarded the steamboat *Sultana* in St. Louis, bound for Cincinnati, Providence continued to watch over him. Nine years later the *Sultana*'s battery of boilers would explode, killing 1,647 people in the worst steamship disaster of the inland rivers.[33] By the last days of May Machebeuf was home, in Clermont-Ferrand, visiting his sister, Sister Philomène, in the Convent of the Visitation at Riom, making a round of recruitment efforts at his old seminary. By 7 June he was in Lyon, probably to visit with his brother, Marius, and a week later he was in Paris at 120 rue de Bac, seeing his old friends at the Seminary of Foreign Missions.

He reached Rome at the end of June. This visit would be far different from his first. There would be no time to visit pilgrim sites or to wander as a tourist through the religious monuments of the great city, no time to explore catacombs or sing masses at the altars of great saints. Formal charges against Lamy and himself had already been received by the Vatican. His old acquaintance from Albuquerque, José Manuel Gallegos, had written to

Pope Pius IX in April. Writing from Washington, D.C., Gallegos had complained of Lamy's hostile conduct toward the Hispanic clergy of New Mexico, of how they had been deprived of their posts, "leaving our poor previous ministers without their posts of spiritual administrations, and forcing them into the hard position of having to work in menial and crude tasks, in order to make a living." One can't help but wonder if Gallegos considered his position as Territorial Congressman one of those "menial and crude tasks." The litany of complaints went on. Anticipating Machebeuf's trip, Gallegos warned the Holy Father that Lamy "ordered the Vicar P. Machebeuf to hurry to Rome, for a reason which we suppose was the principal object: to try to mislead with false information." In addition to the suspensions of priests, Gallegos complained of Lamy's division of the parish of Santa Fe, of ignoring petitions sent to him, of the imposition of heavy fines and penalties, and of other infractions he did not wish to list so as not to "presume upon the High attention of Your Holiness." Machebeuf was guilty of interference in political affairs and faults of "much gravity." The list of charges was signed by twenty representatives, ten members of the legislative assembly of New Mexico, and three country prefects. Significantly, all of the signees carried Spanish surnames, indicative of the depth of the division between the new French hierarchy and the traditionally Hispanic residents of New Mexico. Concluding his missive, Gallegos pleaded, "we do beg Your Holiness, and we pray in the most humble and respectful way, that You deign to decree for us, according to our petitions, the removal from his place as Bishop of Santa Fe, His Illustrious Lordship Lamy; and the nomination in his place of the Vicar Don Juan Felipe Ortiz." Clearly the leaders of the Hispanic population supported the now-displaced vicar forane.[34]

Upon Machebeuf's arrival in Rome, the charges were presented to him and he was asked to comment. At a desk in an office of the Propaganda Fide, he wrote his response. His words tumbled out in page after page of hurried scribblings. First, he reported, "it is necessary to observe that the inhabitants of New Mexico are generally deprived of all schooling and little accustomed to governing themselves according to the law of the United States to which they submit since 1846." So great was the level of ignorance, he explained, "The immense majority do not know how to read and those who are able to sign their names are considered educated." The legislative assembly he considered "composed of ignorant men, most of them corrupt, dishonest, who hold the people in fear of them." The people of New Mexico "are mostly related to each other by different degrees of affinity and the corruption of this society illustrates their prejudice toward a foreign bishop who is obliged to reform their morals." It was even probable, or "not wrong to say that several signed the presentation without knowing what it meant."[35]

Having made these general remarks to set the tone of his defense, Machebeuf continued by addressing the specific charges against Lamy and him. As to the suspension of native clergy, on the contrary these priests had resigned, "declaring they would never submit" to the bishop's rules. The accusations against Machebeuf himself were "absurd." Clearly the people supported him, even Padre Martínez of Taos defended Machebeuf. Here Machebeuf attached both the joint letter by the Hispanic clergy written on 5 January 1853 and the letter from Martínez of 24 February 1853. As to the charges of political interference, Lamy's "only policies have been to preach the word of God and work for the salvation of souls, and in this pursuit he has been unjustly attacked by ignorant, dishonest, and corrupt men." To strengthen his point Machebeuf wrote brief but devastating sketches of Padres J. F. Ortiz, Salazar, Lujan, Gallegos, and Martínez. His portrait of Martínez was particularly pointed. As far as Martínez was concerned, "his character is so false and deceptive, so hidden, so flattering, that while seeking to destroy Mgr Lamy, he appears as his best friend in front of other people. Duplicity is thus his dominant trait."[36]

Completing his defense, Machebeuf turned his attention to the question of the disputed villages of Socorro, Ysleta del Sur, and San Elizario. Machebeuf cited a new rationale for a decision, the Gadsden Purchase and a new borderline between Mexico and the U.S. He asked that it be determined, once and for all, who had jurisdiction over the villages. Something must be done, he indicated, because within the year a 160 persons had died without the sacraments in the region. Finally he presented Lamy's request to sell the Castrense.

The verdict was soon returned, in the form of two narrow columns of tiny Italian script, entitled "Reclami dedotti al S. Padre contro Mons. Lamy Vescovo de S. Fé il suo Vicario Machebeuf." The document proclaimed that Signore Machebeuf, "interpellato" while in Rome, had responded satisfactorily to all the charges against his bishop and himself. The "disorder of the American clergy in the provinces once belonging to Spain" were the result of clerical opposition to Lamy's Pastoral Letter of 1852. The main source of this opposition was identified as "a certain Gallegos priest and pastor of Albuquerque who found himself in a scandalous union with a 'donna di mala vita.'" The proof of the falsity of the accusations of Machebeuf's breach of the confessional was the 24 February 1853 letter from Padre Martínez, who was credible precisely because he was "purely one of the adversaries of the Bishop." To the dismay of New Mexico's Hispanic clergy, Machebeuf's mission was a success.[37]

Gallegos would never again pose a serious threat to Machebeuf. In September 1855 he had been reelected to Congress, but defeated his opponent, Miguel A. Otero, by a very narrow margin. Otero filed a Notice of Contest, claiming irregularities in the election. In February 1856 he formally challenged Gallegos in Washington. Gallegos lost his seat and was replaced by Otero. Gallegos returned to Albuquerque, liquidated his belongings, and moved to Santa Fe. He settled into a house near the plaza and continued to serve as a thorn in Lamy's diocesan garden. He continued to play a part in territorial politics, serving as the Representative for Santa Fe county in the Territorial House of Representatives and as treasurer of the Territory. In 1868, when he was fifty-three, Gallegos was married in the first marriage appearing in the records of the Episcopal church of the Holy Faith in Santa Fe. One month after Santa Fe was elevated to an archdiocese and Lamy became its first archbishop, Gallegos died. In the hours before his death he summoned a French priest, Pierre Eguillon, and reconciled himself to his mother church. His Requiem Mass was held in Lamy's cathedral.[38]

In early August 1856 Machebeuf hurried back to France to collect his new recruits and sail, once again, for America. He was in understandably high spirits as he prepared for the journey. His recruitment efforts also brought success. He would be directing a party of thirteen recruits, including six young French seminarians to fill the depleted ranks of the New Mexican clergy, the future Fathers Coudert, Ussel, Fialon, Fayet, Rallière, and Truchard. Once again, Machebeuf watched the European continent disappear behind him, sailing from Le Havre on the *Alma*. August eleventh marked Machebeuf's forty-fourth birthday, although there is no indication he mentioned it to the group. The young men soon recovered from their initial mal de mer and by 15 August they were able to join in a jubilee celebrating the national holiday of the emperor. Truchard, in a booming bass voice, gave a rendition of the "Ave Maris Stella" and the *Alma*'s Captain Bocandy hosted a splendid dinner, accompanied by "the explosion of champagne corks and many hilarious toasts."[39]

From New York, Machebeuf wrote to Lamy to arrange for wagons to meet his party in Kansas City. After a brief visit to Niagara Falls, the group headed to Sandusky so that Machebeuf might show them his former parish. Sandusky gave the group, especially Machebeuf, a warm welcome. As Gabriel Ussel recorded, the welcome gave them "a higher idea of our good Father, and a greater love for him."[40] Traveling downriver to St. Louis, they were met by Machebeuf's old friend the Jesuit missionary De Smet and watched as Machebeuf laid the cornerstone of a new church in the woods. They traveled by riverboat to Kansas City, where Lamy's wagons were waiting, and late in the day, on 4 October, began their passage across the plains.

The first night out the young men were disturbed by the vast, unfamiliar landscape, their distance from home, and the chorus of coyotes, singing throughout the night. After hearing their complaints the next morning, Machebeuf remarked, "You dread the monotony of the plains; these are a few of their many distractions. You ought to be glad to have a free hand to serenade you. If you do not like the music, Mr. Truchard with his magnificent voice can intone the 'Ave Maris Stella,' as he used to do on the ship."[41] The tone was set. For the remainder of the journey, "Ave Maris Stella" became their theme song.

On 6 October, the second day out, Machebeuf asked why the young men didn't speak Spanish with the drivers. They responded they didn't know how. "Oh, yes, you do!" he replied, "and I shall prove it to you. Now, here are the conversation books; I shall read the Credo very slowly while you follow me in Latin." Then he gave the group some simple guidelines for pronunciation and the formulation of words, which they learned in a few minutes. From that point on, they "had no great difficulty in conversing" in Spanish. One can only hope Machebeuf's own Spanish was somewhat improved since his first homily in Santa Fe.[42]

Some evenings the young seminarians grew quiet, brooding over the dangers surrounding them on the plains, homesick and apprehensive of the trials ahead. Machebeuf, now an experienced hand on the Santa Fe Trail, knew how to raise their spirits. One morning the group seemed particularly quiet. "Well, young men, what is the matter?" Machebeuf queried. "Have you lost your voices? You do not seem to be enjoying your breakfast; perhaps the coffee does not agree with you? Well, let me work a miracle."[43]

Machebeuf disappeared, going to his carefully loaded wagon. He reappeared bearing a bottle of French wine in either hand. According to Ussel, it was "good wine, and it brought our spirits back like a charm."[44]

The group made about twenty miles a day, encountering herds of bison, some friendly but hungry Plains Indians, reconnaissance parties of U.S. cavalry, and a few prowling wolves on the windswept prairies. By 3 November they were twelve miles outside the first New Mexican town. Sitting before the campfire, while his young companions slept, Machebeuf penned a quick note to his brother, Marius. "I have only a moment to write that we are all in good health, we have not had the slightest accident, we have been visited twice by Indians but they did not seem hostile and were satisfied with a little sugar, wheat, and some biscuits. We hope to reach Santa Fe before Sunday."[45] On 10 November 1856 Machebeuf and company were warmly welcomed on the road outside of Santa Fe. The successful advocate was ceremoniously escorted back into the city he had left eight months before.

TWELVE

North and South

✧

While Machebeuf was in Rome, defending Lamy and himself against the charges of the Hispanic clergy, Lamy struggled on in Santa Fe. In the spring of 1856 Lamy received a letter from Padre Martínez in Taos. Writing on 22 April, Martínez complained of age — he was sixty-three — and ill health: "As I said to you in my letter of this year concerning certain ills that plague me, I now tell your Illustrious Lordship that if there were some priest whom you could send to serve this parish, I in the hope of conserving my health would like to be relieved of the one I have, for I find myself burdened a-plenty, perhaps for not being able to discharge the parish duties perfectly." Martínez suggested that Lamy appoint a younger Hispanic priest, so that he might watch over him for a period of time, thus retaining control over the parish without being burdened by its full administration. He suggested Ramón Medina for the position, "if it were possible, and your Illustrious Lordship found it convenient that Padre Ramón Medina would finish the year by coming here, he would acquire practice and direction under my supervision and within a short time he could remain and ably continue, I myself then tendering my resignation." Closing the letter he emphasized the importance of having a priest who was a native of New Mexico, "because the populace here is so seriously dead-set against priests who are not natives of this land . . . they judge them to be Americanos."[1]

Martínez had not really resigned. He indicated he would do so once a native priest had been assigned to support him in his parish duties, but Lamy, seizing the opportunity to place one of his own men in Taos, accepted his resignation as immediate. On 4 May Martínez announced his upcoming retirement in the *Santa Fe Gazette*. After outlining the reasons for his decision he mentioned his letter to Lamy, concluding, "although I did not then resign, I told him I would when the replacement arrived. So far he has not replied. But I suppose that in time he will send someone capable."[2]

Martínez was unprepared for Lamy's response. On the fifth Lamy wrote to him, accepting his resignation. He would send not Medina, who was behind in his studies, but Don Damaso Taladrid, the Spanish priest he had recruited in Rome. "In this way you shall be left free and unburdened of every worry so as to be able to rest, so much the more in the advanced age in which you find yourself."[3] Taladrid arrived with official letters of appointment, and on 8 May Martínez turned the parish over to him. In the following weeks Taladrid sent a flurry of letters to Lamy, complaining of Martínez's interference in parish affairs.

Taos was really made up of three separate communities, which dotted the high-altitude Taos Plain below a fringe of towering peaks. The ancient Taos Pueblo stood at the base of the mountains, a timeless community that had watched the invasions of both the Spanish and the Americans over the centuries. Three miles south was the main Spanish village, Don Fernando de Taos, the seat of the parish and base of civil authority. Further south was the smaller settlement of Los Ranchos de Taos, its mountainous adobe church of St. Francis serving the outlying farming families. In 1850 U.S. Army Colonel George Archibald McCall recorded his view of the three communities: "[T]he inhabitants of the Valley of Taos are the most turbulent in New Mexico, and the Indians of the Pueblo of Taos still entertain a smothered feeling of animosity against the Americans, which it is well to keep under." The animosity of the Taos Indians was not restricted to the Americans; they had not welcomed the Spanish either. Taos Pueblo, after all, played no small part in the 1680 Pueblo Revolt.[4]

By October, a month before Machebeuf's return from Europe, the situation in Taos had deteriorated. On the first of the month Martínez wrote a long letter to Lamy complaining that Taladrid was trying to take charge of the Penitentes, or the Tertiaries of St. Francis of Assisi and Order of Penance, at Ranchos de Taos. He could not give up his position with the Penitentes, Martínez explained, because he had received this privilege not as a diocesan priest from Taos, but from the second to the last Custos, or regional superior, of the Franciscans in New Mexico.

The Penitentes of northern New Mexico were shrouded in mystery and remain largely misunderstood. They are widely assumed to be a derivative of the Third Order of Franciscans. St. Francis of Assisi, in the thirteenth century, was the first founder of a religious order to add a third order. The First Order of Franciscans were the priests and laybrothers, the Second

Order was the order for women, the cloistered Poor Clare nuns. The Third Order of Penance was for men and women living in the secular world who wished to be a part of his apostolate. Members of the Third Order came to be known as Tertiaries.

The rules for the institution of Tertiary were first made public in 1221. Tertiaries had to be members of the church and of good repute. They were required to renounce luxurious living and dress, to use arms only in self-defense, to hear mass daily, if possible, and to observe the fasts of the church and certain prescribed austerities in daily life.[5]

The Franciscans of the Third Order traditionally wore coarse gray robes beneath their clothing, knotted with the familiar cord of the Franciscan brothers, and were permitted to be buried as true Franciscans. Their gray robes were worn for processionals and chapter meetings. Women could join the Third Order only with the permission of their husbands.[6]

Many historians, as well as European and native-born Hispanic clergy, assumed that the Penitentes were a form of the Franciscan Third Order. Franciscan historian Fray Angelico Chavez disagrees. Chapters of the Third Order were established in New Mexico only after 1700, when the Franciscans were at their peak. "It was not until more than a century later, between 1800 and 1821, that the idea of flagellant Penitentes was first introduced somehow from Southern Mexico," Chavez writes. While it was possible that some members of the Tertiaries had joined the Penitentes, it was actually a distinct society, "composed of males only, men who, unlike the true Tertiaries did not wear the Franciscan habit and cord underneath their clothing at any time, much less in public procession." For processions held on the Fridays of Lent, or during Holy Week, the Penitentes "stripped themselves down to a pair of drawers . . . in order to scourge themselves to blood and carry heavy timber crosses during their 'exercises.'" Even if the Penitentes were a distinct society, they were likely modeled after and influenced by the Franciscans of the Third Order. Historian Richard Ahlborn concludes, "Some degree of direct influence of the Third Order on 'penitentism' seems fairly certain."[7]

Padre Martínez had been born in the Penitente stronghold of Santa Rosa de Abiquiú and lived there until he was twelve. On 6 April 1831 the Franciscan visitor Rascón personally granted Martínez permission to direct sixty brethren of the Third Order in their exercises, so long as no abuses were reported that would call for correction during the course of his visitation. Thus, in a sense, Martínez himself seems to be one of the sources of penitential identification with the Third Order. It seems clear that he considered the group fully legitimate, officially recognized and accepted by the church. He also saw himself as the only legitimate director of the group.

Taladrid wrote to Lamy on 23 October reporting he had composed a set of rules for the Hermanos Mayores de la Hermandad, the Penitentes, in Taos. Even if Taladrid had clear ecclesiastic approval for such a move, he could never have gained the full support of the members of the brotherhood. No outsider could. Only a man like Martínez, born and raised in northern New Mexico, could act as liaison between the members of the hierarchy and the Penitentes. After all, their previous bishop, Mexican Bishop Zubiría, told them on one visit to guard and protect their faith jealously, especially from what Fray Angelico Chavez refers to as the "ever-growing number of blond foreigners whom he naturally regarded as heretics."[8]

Martínez was enraged by Taladrid's presumption. He complained to Lamy that he had handed over his parish duties "with the best disposition." In spite of that, Taladrid "does not behave well toward me, defaming me behind my back, even in some of the outlying missions of the parish."[9] Lamy made two trips to Taos in an attempt to reconcile the two men, but the situation continued to worsen.

Fr. Gabriel Ussel, who served in Taos from 1858 to 1876, had the opportunity to develop a fairly accurate picture of the events that followed. He suggested the beginning of animosity between the two men was the marriage of one of Martínez's relatives. "The pretext came by a marriage," he explained. "The bride was the niece of the old priest. He insisted on the privilege of presiding at her marriage." Taladrid refused Martínez permission to perform the marriage, citing a "cause for complaint" against the girl's father. The town divided into two factions, one that sided with Martínez and one that sided with Taladrid. "The specified day for the celebration of the marriage arrived, and Padre Martínez married the couple. This was his first act of the long schism."[10]

Taos was not big enough for the two priests. Jesuit historian Thomas Steele notes, "it was part of that pattern of increasing tension on the Taos Plaza . . . another episode in the series of troubles between Taladrid and the Martínez family that included the foreign priest's setting obstacles to the old Padre's saying Mass in the church." Taladrid not only complained to Lamy but "published a pair of articles profoundly insulting to Padre Martínez in *La Gaceta de Santa Fé* [the *Santa Fe Gazette*] in November 1856, calling him 'egotism personified,' and followed up with a succession of attacks the following month."[11]

Tension between the two men came to a climax when Martínez arrived early one morning to say mass. Taladrid seized the older priest and threatened him, saying, "I know how to hit hard and fight!"[12] Furious, Martínez composed a long letter giving his side of the story and arranged for its publication in the *Santa Fe Gazette*. In the letter Martínez objected to the greedy accumulation of mass stipends by certain foreign priests, decried the plight of suspended Hispanic priests, defended the right of the legislature to write to the Pope, and complained of unfair regulations in Lamy's Christmas Pastoral of 1852 and in his 1853 and 1854 circulars for the clergy.

On 24 October Lamy responded to Martínez's charges. Three days later he sent a second letter announcing his suspension. On 12 November, two days after Machebeuf's return, Martínez wrote to Lamy saying he did not accept the suspension as Lamy was operating outside of the dictates of Canon Law. His argument was based on the view that the position of cura propio was a lifetime appointment. Accordingly, he could neither resign nor be suspended. Additionally, Lamy had failed to give three formal warnings before imposing penalty on a subordinate, also required by Canon Law. "As to the contents of said letters," Martínez wrote, "I say that I give and am ready to give complete acknowledgement to my lawful superior, in everything that he may dictate or dispose according to the Canon Law which rules us; but when acting beyond it he seeks to impose penalties arbitrarily, I protest the nullity of such procedures for thus I am backed by Canon Law, by virtue of which I do not consider myself suspended, nor am I so."[13]

In the following weeks Martínez seemed to gradually lose his sense of reality. Repeatedly, throughout the early months of 1857, he wrote to Lamy claiming immunity under "canonic rights," declaring his suspension a "nullity," demanding to be recognized as "the rightful pastor of Taos."[14] When Lamy did not respond to the letters, he wrote to Machebeuf, telling him Lamy was "disobeying the laws of the Church," that his actions had placed Martínez's life in danger, and armed forces were threatening his personal safety.

It is difficult not to sympathize with the aging priest as the dreams of a lifetime crumbled around him. Following the Mexican Revolution in 1821, Martínez saw himself as a chivalric hidalgo, a noble country gentlemen who could lead his people to new glory by virtue of his education, eloquence, and political sophistication. Martínez had role models as well. Most likely during his time in seminary in Durango, Martínez learned of Padre Miguel Hidalgo, the parish priest who organized a revolt against Spain. Historian E. A. Mares comments, "Although he was captured and executed by royalist forces in 1811, the movement toward independence gathered momentum and found a new leader in another priest, José María Morelos, who continued to resist royalist armies in the south of Mexico for many years." Martínez must have known of Morelos's and Hidalgo's efforts, for as Mares points out, "Morelos was also captured and executed in 1815, just two years before Antonio José Martínez entered the Tridentine Seminary in 1817." Mares concludes, "It was while he studied there that Padre Martínez became imbued with liberal political philosophy and great admiration for the late Padre Hidalgo. Padre Martínez became an ardent Mexican patriot and championed the Mexican liberal, republican and nationalist cause." While Martínez prepared himself for the role of champion of the people of New Mexico, he was woefully unprepared for the impact of Manifest Destiny and the thousands of Americans who moved westward in its wake.[15]

With the transfer of New Mexico to U.S. rule, sealed by the Treaty of Guadalupe Hidalgo in 1848, history crashed through Martínez's carefully constructed plans. He had done his best to adapt to the sweeping changes by involving himself in the new U.S. political structure. As one of the key players, he had helped create the new order in New Mexico. Strategically he attempted to place himself as amicus curiae, sage adviser to his new French bishop, as the diplomatic elder statesman of the Hispanic clergy, who could serve as a liaison between the two cultures. Instead he found himself suspended from the priesthood, his carefully argued protests ignored. He could no longer officially sing the mass in his own parish. No longer could he see himself as the distinguished hidalgo and learned champion of his people. His sole clerical supporter was Padre Mariano de Jesús Lucero, pastor of the neighboring parish at Arroyo Hondo, his former pupil and loyal friend. Taladrid's letter of 23 October the previous fall accurately portrayed Martínez when he described "our wise man of the north" as "much disturbed."[16]

Taladrid's own behavior was far from pristine. Martínez considered him to be a libertine, a drunkard, and a gambler. This may not have been entirely accurate, but army microfilms of his discharge from the post of chaplain corroborate the last two. He may have been incompetent as well. Fr. J. B. Salpointe suggests as much by his evaluation of the condition of the Mora church when Taladrid "ended his regime there."[17]

Neither Martínez nor Taladrid evidenced much in the way of Christian charity. In the summer of 1857, the population of Taos was divided and the divisions in the community continued to increase. On the one side was the imperious Spaniard Taladrid, backed by a collection of Frenchmen, Canadians, Americans, and Hispanic families with marital or other ties to the

Anglo-American community. They supported Taladrid and the French clergy. On the other were many of the Hispanic residents, most of whom had been baptized or married by Martínez. The proud and increasingly unstable Padre Martínez was backed by the more conservative Hispanic community, longing for the relative peace they had known before the arrival of the outsiders. Rumors flew. Martínez's backers continued to suggest that his physical safety was endangered. Taladrid's supporters felt sure an armed rebellion was imminent.

Martínez gathered his followers and mounted a guard over his oratory, the small chapel he used for masses since the arrival of Taladrid. Rumors flew that the chapel had been threatened with arson. Martínez's followers announced they would protect the oratory, by whatever means necessary.

One Wednesday, 27 May 1857, the situation seemed to reach crisis proportions. Christopher "Kit" Carson dictated and signed a letter to the commander of the nearby Cantonment Burgwin. "Captain Macrae, Sir:" Carson's missive read, "There is a report in circulation here and of such a nature that induces me to believe from the strictest investigation . . . that there will be a brake [sic] out here tonight. I therefore respectfully ask of you a detachment of twenty-five men, immediately for our protection." The troops were necessary, he explained, because "We are generally prepared, but fear that we will be outnumbered."[18]

Carson had first come to Taos at sixteen years of age. He fell in love with the town, returning to it whenever possible, and eventually it came to serve as his base of operations. It was in Taos, on 28 January 1842, that Padre Martínez baptized Carson into the Catholic Church, prior to his marriage to Josefa Jaramillo the following year. Following the U.S. conquest in 1846, a conspiracy led to the massacre of Governor Charles Bent and eleven others, in an attempt to overthrow U.S. rule. It came to be known as Bent's Rebellion. At the time of the massacre, Josefa Carson had been staying with her common-law brother-in-law, none other than Gov. Charles Bent. She barely survived the massacre. After Bent was attacked by a mob at the front door of the house, she and the other women used a fire poker to dig through an adobe wall to the next house and dragged the mortally wounded Bent through the hole. Bent died, but the women, still in their nightclothes, lacking food, hid for two days and two nights until a neighbor smuggled them to safety.[19] Josefa's uncle, Cornelio Vigil, and her brother, Pablo Jaramillo, were also killed in the massacre. The Carson family had no love lost for anyone, including Martínez, they believed involved in the conspiracy that led to the massacre nine years before.

Their conviction, in terms of Martínez's participation in Bent's Rebellion, was probably as misplaced as their fear of imminent attack. In response to Carson's letter, the commander, Nathaniel Macrae, sent Capt. Robert Morris "with the thirty-two men of his company of mounted rifles to proceed to Taos prepared to use force against the Indians or offer aid to law officers against disorderly citizens." Morris and his men reached Taos after midnight. At the supposed command post of the reported insurrection, the house of Padre Martínez, the officer entered the house and "himself and household were found asleep." As to the riotous streets of Taos, he reported "patrolling the town and finding it quiet, with no indications of either a riot or a coalition between the Mexicans and the Pueblo Indians." The basis of the expected rebellion? Morris reported "large numbers of Mexicans were assembling at priest Martines' [sic] house, about dark of the evening of the 27th. . . . As many as twenty were said to have been seen [to] enter and remain there; as they wore blankets it was not known whether they were armed."[20] It would seem that Padre Martínez was not the only one feeling a little paranoid.

The episode should have ended there. It didn't. "Some people were very displeased," observes Jesuit historian Thomas Steele in classic understatement. "Bishop Jean Baptiste Lamy seems to have been one of them, for he instantly removed Father Taladrid as pastor of the parish."[21] His placement there had done nothing to soothe the troubled parish; it had only created further difficulties for the embattled bishop. Taladrid was reassigned to Isleta. As his replacement, Lamy chose Padre José Eulógio Ortiz of San Juan, half-brother of the former vicar forane of Santa Fe. Taladrid signed the parish over to Ortiz on 5 June 1857.

Displeasure echoed in other corridors as well. By the end of the summer of 1857 both "Sheriff Ezra N. DePew and District Attorney Thomas G. Smith had submitted their resignations. None of the letters offered any but pro-forma explanations for the reassignment or resignation, but it would figure that the fiasco of the night of 27 May was a major factor." Displeasure was also expressed by the 212 citizens of Taos. They wrote a formal letter of complaint to the acting governor of the Territory of New Mexico, W. W. H. Davis. They demanded that "he tell the U.S. Army to stop pestering them." Davis placated them and placed the blame for the incident on the military commander of New Mexico, Col. John Garland, chastising him for his presumption in sending in the troops and the "violation of the civil rights of the citizens of Taos."[22]

Garland did not passively accept the reprimand. Where did Colonel Garland get the idea that Padre Martínez might be so malevolent and dangerous? From Governor Davis. Garland directed the governor's attention to his own book, *El Gringo*, published earlier that year. Governor Davis wrote of the attack on Governor Bent: "A large body of the rebels, composed mainly of Pueblo Indians, and incited to the act by Priest Martínez and others, attacked his residence, and murdered him and several others in cold blood."[23] A primary source of the rumors of Martínez's involvement in the rebellion seems to have been Davis himself.

While feathers continued to be ruffled in political and military circles, there was a calm before the storm in ecclesiastical ones. Ortiz's assignment seemed to quiet Martínez somewhat. After all, he had gotten what he originally requested, a native Hispanic priest, fluent in both Spanish and English. But Martínez's grasp on reality was shaky. In his mind, he was still cura propio of the Taos parish; it was a lifetime appointment, and his suspension by Lamy was invalid. He continued to perform marriages and burials and to sing the mass in his oratory, or private chapel. Two weeks after Ortiz's arrival, Martínez explained to Ortiz that he and the rest of the parishioners of Taos accepted him only for the administration of the sacraments; they considered him an assistant rather than full pastor.

Sometime thereafter Lamy began formal proceedings of excommunication against both Martínez and Lucero. Over the course of three Sundays the "canonic" admonitions were read in both Taos and Arroyo Hondo, demanding that Martínez and Lucero submit to the bishop's authority. Like the furious thunderstorms that sweep across New Mexico each summer, a dark cloud of tension descended on Taos. Is it coincidental that the governor's embarrassment preceded the action? Is it suggestive of cooperation between political and ecclesiastical authorities? We shall never know. There is a conspicuous lack of written records. The exact dates are not even recorded. Most likely it was in the spring of 1858. Jesuit historian Thomas Steele places Martínez's excommunication on the Sunday after Easter, 11 April 1858, and Lucero's the following week, on 18 April 1858. Records indicate Machebeuf performed a baptism in Santa Fe on March thirtieth. He probably would have stayed in Santa Fe through Easter to help with the Holy Week festivities before setting out for Taos.[24] Whatever the exact dates, it was Machebeuf who traveled to Taos to make the official pronouncement.

Machebeuf drew his support from the Anglo community, with their ties to the new military and civil authorities. They feared for his personal safety, worried that Martínez's followers might resort to violence against him. Some members broadcast their intent to protect him, even if they had to use armed force, and assigned bodyguards for the purpose.

Machebeuf's supporters were a formidable group. One was Céran St.

Vrain, widely known as a scout and trader, respected, if suspected of being a "francmason," or freemason.[25] Another was a French Canadian emigrant, Charles Beaubien. Beaubien's son Narcisco had also been murdered during Bent's Rebellion in 1847, and Beaubien had already gone on record concerning his dislike of Padre Martínez. Writing to Manuel Alvarez in June 1856, he expressed his delight in Taladrid's displacement of Martínez. "He nibbles his thumb," Beaubien wrote of Martínez,

> unfortunately too late, and can not see, without profound chagrin, the gradual diminution of his power, and the fading, little by little under his own eyes, of his colossal prestige, which he exercised in these valleys and elsewhere. . . . But especially his anguish increases when he can not refrain himself from recognizing in his successor a superior pastor [Taladrid], better instructed and more capable than him, who holds him with dignity and more politely in his place, who has not need of him nor of his advice in anything.[26]

Beaubien also considered Martínez to have been one of the prime organizers of Bent's Rebellion in 1847, although no evidence exists of his participation. Beaubien's long history of animosity toward Martínez was evident in Gabriel Ussel's version of the events. " 'La grosse tete — the big head,' came from the lips of that peaceable man, Mr. Charles Beaubien, and he meant the old priest, 'has always been treacherous.' "[27]

Another of Machebeuf's supporters was Kit Carson. Carson stood firmly behind Machebeuf and made his feelings toward Martínez's supporters clear. In his memoirs Ussel recorded Carson's reaction. " 'Are we to be murdered,' proclaimed Gentle Kit, 'as it came to pass in 1847? Are we to suffer that pillaging of old days? I hate disturbances amongst the people, peace is my motto, good will to all.' " Ussel makes Carson's alliance with Machebeuf clear. " 'Fight? yes, indeed, I am ready to do anything to protect my wife and children. Let them provoke us by their menaces to make it hot for the Vicar-General! We will — I will stand by him.' "[28]

There was no response the three Sundays when the admonitions were read by Ussel in Arroyo Hondo and Ortiz in Taos. On the fourth Sunday the church at Don Fernando de Taos was filled to overflowing, and crowds gathered outside unable to get in. Friends of Martínez were scattered through the crowd. As Machebeuf sang the High Mass the tension was palpable. In his homily he explained the nature and effects of excommunication. According to Gabriel Ussel, in what is probably the only eyewitness account, he emphasized the separation of the excommunicant from the general graces of the church.[29] He then advised the waiting parishioners that from that day forward Padre Martínez was to be shunned, to be avoided in commerce and society. Technically speaking, Machebeuf exceeded his authority.

There are two classes of excommunication. One, *tolerati*, indicates those who are to be "tolerated," allowed to remain a part of the community but barred from sacramental life. The other, *vitandi*, is reserved for those who have already separated themselves from the church, whose offenses were of such a heinous nature that they were to be avoided in all things, at all times. In the latter case, one can only become *vitandus* after "he has been excommunicated by a published decree of the Holy See itself."[30] Machebeuf did not have the authority to issue the second class of excommunication. But excommunication itself was the ultimate condemnation Lamy and Machebeuf could pronounce. It demonstrates Lamy and Machebeuf's complete frustration with Martínez at that point, as well as their recognition of his influence and the sense that his views could still endanger the good standing of other members of the parish.

In a solemn voice Machebeuf read the instrument to the hushed congregation. He announced he would remain in Taos for several days in order to hear confessions, his own way of giving those who wished to an opportunity to return to the bishop's fold. The crowd parted silently as he left the church.

Later in the day, he joined Carson and other supporters at Beaubien's house, where he had been given a room. "The after-supper hour was given to a sober review of the day's events," records Gabriel Ussel. "Still, the private sentinels, for prudence sake, occupied their posts." Ussel also reports Kit Carson's presence at Beaubien's. "Kit Carson," he writes, "by the way a Catholic and a sincere friend of Bishop Lamy, Father Machebeuf and the French priests, was one of the jovial party. He could not half enough exalt the courage of Father Machebeuf." Machebeuf, modestly deferred the praise. "And why should I be afraid?" Ussel quotes him as saying. "After all, I only did my duty. Next Sunday, the repetition of today at Arroyo Hondo. That poor Father Lucero! but he compels the good Bishop to inflict on him the same penalty."[31]

The following Saturday Machebeuf set out for Arroyo Hondo with Fr. Gabriel Ussel. Ussel replaced Julliard, who had served as interim pastor after Lucero. His friends in Taos offered to provide an armed escort, but Machebeuf declined, saying he felt there was no real danger. On Sunday he repeated the scene in Arroyo Hondo, excommunicating Lucero, Martínez's most loyal supporter. Again he met with no response. His distasteful duties completed, Machebeuf told Ussel he thanked God it was over. "It is always the way," he explained. "Bishop Lamy is sure to send me when there is a bad case to be settled; I am always the one to whip the cats (a fouetter les chats)."[32]

It is particularly curious that neither Lamy nor Machebeuf left any written account of the incident. Perhaps it was because they found the excommunication of a priest an unpleasant affair. Perhaps they did not want to add more fuel to the fires of division. In any case, none of their letters contains a detailed account. Lacking any record of the dates the excommunications were imposed, some have even questioned whether they actually took place. The only formal records are an entry by Lamy in the Taos burial book on 1 July 1860, and in the Arroyo Hondo baptismal book on 8 July of the same year. Citing Martínez's failure to heed his censures, Lamy wrote "We then saw ourselves obliged to excommunicate him 'servatis servandis' with all the required formalities. Since that time this unhappy priest has done all he can to make a schism both publicly and privately."[33] Lamy left no other official record of the excommunications.

On 23 July 1857 Ortiz sent Lamy a copy of a letter from Martínez. In that letter Martínez designated himself four times as the pastor of Taos and once as the assistant pastor. "Pobre Martínez desgraciado!" wrote Ortiz. "He desperately wanted to visit me: he first sent word if I would receive an excommunicate, and my answer to his messenger was that, if he was already condemned, I also had the faculties from the lawful head of the New Mexican Church to receive the condemned."[34] Martínez did come to see him and told Ortiz that his differences with Taladrid had been out of pure caprice on his part, promising to acknowledge Ortiz as pastor of Taos and to cease exercising any parish duties.

In spite of these assurances, or perhaps because of his diminishing grasp on reality, the defeated padre continued to perform infant baptisms and the sacrament of confirmation. At one point, he even seemed to believe he had been granted the privilege by no less than direct papal authorization.[35] Martínez retreated into a world untouched by the U.S. annexation of New Mexico and the French clergy that swept through the newly created territory in its wake.

Perhaps the real reasons behind the tragic breakdown of communication, the division between the French and Hispanic clergy in New Mexico, lies not in New Mexico but in France. Priests like Lamy and Machebeuf were products of one of the most conservative periods of French ecclesiastic history, culminating in the decree of papal infallibility in 1870. The French Revolution decimated the ranks of the French clergy. Thousands of priests and religious were executed, and some historians have put the number of those in exile as high as forty thousand.[36] After the Revolution, the church in France embraced a growing Ultramontane trend, increasingly looking to Rome for guidance in spiritual and political matters. A new emphasis on obedience was given to Catholics everywhere, but was enthusiastically received in France.

In contrast to this renewed emphasis on obedience, Padre Martínez and other members of the Hispanic clergy had embraced a liberalism and thirst for democratic reform. Martínez modeled himself after Mexican revolutionaries such as José Miguel Hidalgo and José María Morelos. Historian E. A. Mares comments, "There is great irony in the fact that while priests in Latin American such as Padre Hidalgo and Padre Morelos in Mexico, or Padre Martínez in New Mexico had been strongly influenced by political liberalism, the Papacy remained staunchly conservative and fearful of the many changes occurring in the world."[37]

Padre Martínez was singularly successful in his adaptation to the new U.S. democratic government. In fact, he could be considered an important contributor in the formation of the early territorial government. He could not have anticipated how his efforts would be received by members of the American hierarchy, particularly conservative French members. Martínez's emphasis was on participatory democracy. He seemed unaware to what extent he offended the sensibilities of those whose primary emphasis was on hierarchy. He had no way of knowing that his laudatory civil participation might be viewed by his new superiors as reminiscent of those priests who had chosen to serve the secularized church under the liberal government following the Revolution. While Martínez's actions could be considered appropriate in terms of adjusting to U.S. democracy, they were possibly the worst course he could have chosen in terms of securing approval from his new ecclesiastical superiors. In their eyes unquestioning obedience would have served him far better than the most eloquent defense of his own position.

As Martínez's mental acuity deteriorated, he expressed a certain level of confusion regarding basic American tenets. Martínez showed little evidence of understanding the separation of church and state or freedom of religion. In a sense, this is understandable. Such philosophies were a part of neither the Indo-Hispanic culture of the Southwest nor the cultural traditions that Spanish descendants carefully maintained and preserved. But the inability to recognize these divisions pushed him further and further from the good graces of Bishop Lamy. Martínez seemed frustrated by Lamy's priests revalidating the marriages and baptisms he performed, as if he failed to understand the necessity.

In 1859 he issued a proclamation against Bishop Lamy, "Obispo Y Su Oficio" [the bishop and his office]. He suggested a reunification of the clergy in Taos. "Wouldn't it be better," he wrote, "if the Bishop were to put things straight with his roman Ecclesiastics bringing them to their one duty, and thus united they might harvest better fruit for their Religion?" He also suggested new applications of democracy, but he seemed confused about democratic rule. The people of New Mexico, he suggested, should elect their priests. "In 1848 the Governor of the Territory circulated the right and liberty that the faithful had to elect Ecclesiastics who should serve them in the acts of Ministry," he reasoned, "and not be subject to any specific parish priest, who many times might be an enemy or have other circumstances adversarial to them." He continued by exhorting the faithful to employ these rights. "It is to be hoped," he suggested, "that the faithful knowing their rights might use them, and keeping their respect for the Bishop, and for Religion, will employ Ministers who are responsible for their faith."[38] While such a suggestion might be welcomed by some of today's more progressive theologians, it was hardly in keeping with the climate of the times.

Historian E. A. Mares dryly comments, "Given this ambiguity concerning constitutional rights and church regulations, it is not hard to understand why some Protestant ministers and some members of the Martínez family have claimed the Padre for Protestantism." Reverend J. M. Shaw, in a report written in 1860, clearly saw Martínez's views as a potential ally in his missionary activities. "In Taos," he writes, "the priest, Martínez has set up independently of the authorities of the Church of Rome, and declares the Word of God to be the only rule of faith; he has his congregations, and preaches against the errors of the Romish Church, and also writes against them." Shaw was obviously pleased by what he interpreted as Martínez's Protestant leanings. "He is fast approaching, if he has not already attained, the position occupied by Luther, to say the least," Shaw confidently reports. "He will be an entering wedge to split the Romish Church." Shaw gives a description of Martínez's continuing ministrations to the community. "He appears the most sincere and candid of any of the priests I have seen; performs the offices of religion gratuitously, receiving what the people voluntarily give; is strongly opposed to the exacting system of his old church, and wrote and printed quite a strong article on that subject and others, that contains the true principles and spirit of Protestantism." Shaw

seemed unaware of the encroaching confusion that came to dominate Martínez's later years.[39]

Padre Martínez seems to be a part of a tradition of idealistic, revolutionary Latin priests in Central America and Mexico. In his exclusion from the
church he has shared the fate of some modern adherents, while his democratic Catholicism might be considered to echo the theologies embraced by
some liberation theologians. But no matter how much Martínez might have
been ahead of his time, it didn't protect him from his own share of suffering.

Ten years after the summer of 1857, on 27 July 1867, Martínez died. He
was never reconciled to his Mother Church. His faithful fellow excommunicant, Padre Lucero, administered the last rites and buried him in his
little oratory, on the Plaza of Don Fernando.[40] Later, probably when the
church was returned to the bishop's fold, his remains were reportedly transferred to the cemetery in Kit Carson Park in Taos. If the reports are true,
today he lies a little too close for comfort to the remains of his old adversary,
Kit Carson.

Just before his death, Martínez is said to have predicted that the division
between his followers and those of Bishop Lamy would be resolved when
the Jesuits came. Martínez had come into contact with the Jesuits during his
time in Durango, when he attended seminary. In a sense, it is a pity that
Padre Martínez did not survive a few years longer, so that he might have
welcomed the arrival of the Jesuits in Taos. Fr. Donato Maria Gasparri
preached a parish mission in January 1869. Jesuit historian Thomas Steele
records, "The Mission destroyed the schism which had existed there ever
since the death of Cura José Antonio [sic] Martínez, who had provoked it.
Seventy-six marriages of schismatics were revalidated, and there were 3,593
communions. Fr. Gasparri departed on the 9th, with the principal men, and
even some of the former schismatics accompanying him for ten miles, and
he arrived in Albuquerque on 14 February."[41]

Steele suggests that in terms of the Jesuit attitudes toward Martínez, "the
Jesuits thought they knew some facts which modern historians would probably doubt to be facts." Among these he includes, "that Martínez was 'ruler'
of the Taos church . . . that Martínez refused to acknowledge Taladrid as
pastor, whereas it looks like an attitude that turned off and on; that the old
priest broke openly with the bishop, whereas vice-versa seems to have been
the case." Further chiding his Jesuit antecedents, Steele questions whether
"the division might properly be called a schism, whereas most likely it was
not." As to Martínez's deathbed prediction? The iconoclastic Steele continues, "Fr. Troy himself suggests that the deathbed prediction about the
Jesuits solving everything was probably not historical. Finally, the Jesuits

had trouble — as many persons did and do — getting Martínez' given names in the right order, calling him José Antonio more often than not."[42]

Martínez obviously had a fondness, deserved or not, for the Jesuits, and a faith in their ability to unravel ecclesiastical tangles. Curiously, it is the one thing he might have had in common with his antagonist Machebeuf. Machebeuf later became a solid supporter of the Jesuits in Colorado, greatly encouraging them to expand their work throughout the state.

After Machebeuf completed the distasteful business of the excommunications of Martínez and Lucero, he set out on a series of "little trips" around northern New Mexico before returning to Albuquerque. Years later Ussel wrote an account of accompanying Machebeuf on such excursions. The accoutrements for the mass were packed in one valise. Another valise was filled with a change of linen, a few prayerbooks, catechisms, beads, and holy medals, "a veritable Noah's Ark, filled with religious articles for free distribution among the people." Rolls of blankets served as bedding. These were loaded on a pack mule, sometimes given in charge to a young man who accompanied them. "We kept our saddle-bags and overcoats with us, and we each had an extra mule as a mount when our horses were tired."[43] They headed north to Rio Colorado, only fifteen miles away. After listening to confessions and singing mass, usually in the largest room of the largest house, they moved on to Costilla, thirty miles further north. From Costilla they traveled over the bluffs to the crossing on the Rio del Norte. After Conejos came the tiny village of Los Cerritos, then to Guadalupe in the Conejos Valley.

Along the way, Machebeuf talked to the younger priest about the rewards of his work. "Don't you like this kind of missionary life?" he queried. "I hate to stay at home, even for a month at a time. For me, to work is to live, and such trips as this are full of consolation." In spite of the difficulties of his work in New Mexico, Machebeuf's attitude toward the Hispanic population was also changing. He was beginning to develop a deep affection for his "Mexicans." Though not untouched by lingering condescension, he began to appreciate the deep faith of the people to whom he ministered. He explained to Ussel, "such days as these at Conejos I love to think over. I admire the simplicity and faith of these good people, and their testimonials of love for the priest are but expressions of their love for God Whom they honor in the priest." Machebeuf was eager to see Ussel, still new to New Mexico, share his affection. "The Mexicans may have queer ways in the eyes of some people — they are ignorant, they are poor and not very saving. . . . Everybody has his faults, but they have redeeming qualities, and more of them than their critics."[44]

From Conejos the two men traveled to Fort Massachusetts, later moved and renamed Fort Garland, to see to the needs of the soldiers. After a few days they traveled to Culebra, San Pedro, and San Luis. "This ended our mission life in this direction," Ussel concludes, "and we made our way leisurely back to Arroyo Hondo."[45]

Throughout the fall of 1857 and the early months of 1858, Machebeuf continued his work in Albuquerque, making sporadic trips around the countryside. Most of the people in smaller communities throughout the territory knew him on sight, the aging, weather-beaten vicar with his bulging valise of religious trinkets. Occasionally a newcomer would ask him where he lived. "In the saddle!" was his response. "They call me El Vicario Andando, and I live on the Camino Real."[46]

In the summer of 1858 Archbishop Kenrick presided at a provincial council in St. Louis. In order to attend, Lamy requested that Machebeuf preside as rector of St. Francis during his absence. After Machebeuf told his parishioners of his planned departure, they called "un meeting monstre," demanding he remain in Albuquerque. A petition was drawn up, addressed to Bishop Lamy, pleading that he be allowed to stay with his congregation. Over two thousand individuals signed it, more than twice the number that had protested his arrival. Machebeuf explained he must leave within two days, but they objected, asking him to stay long enough for the petition to be delivered to Lamy in Santa Fe. The women of the parish told him they would stand guard along the road to Santa Fe, acting as sentinels to prevent his departure. Machebeuf, amused by the suggestion, reminded them he knew the road to Santa Fe better than anyone, he would manage to "escape" if necessary. He remained an additional three days, but Lamy refused to reconsider. A mounted escort accompanied him out of town, while good-byes were cried from the houses they passed.

On his arrival in Santa Fe, a delegation greeted him — officials, religious, and priests — and the bells of Santa Fe's five churches rang out in welcome. Now he felt "as Napoleon III must have felt in the Boulevard Sébastopol." A reception was held at the cathedral to celebrate his arrival, and Lamy presented him with "a good bottle of wine to settle the dust." Should he ever make it to New Mexico, Machebeuf wrote to his brother, Marius, "you will see how we do things in style."[47]

In August a decree arrived from the Vatican granting the bishop of Santa Fe jurisdiction over La Mesilla, the areas of New Mexico and Arizona transferred under the Gadsden Purchase. This vast tract of land, more than 45,000 square miles, would make up the southernmost portions of the two modern states, stretching from El Paso to California, as no boundary yet divided them. Previously the western part of the area had been under the jurisdiction of the bishop of Sonora and Sinaloa, whose see was in the ancient city of Culiacán. Considering the confusion that had followed the transfer of New Mexico from the bishop of Durango, Lamy determined that Durango should be notified, and the bishop of Sonora, Don Pedro Loza, should personally approve the transfer. He relieved Machebeuf of his duties as vicar general, replacing him with the pastor of Socorro, Fr. Pierre Eguillon. This left Machebeuf free to travel to the south, to secure formal acknowledgement of the transfer of jurisdiction.

On 3 November 1858, accompanied by two unnamed Hispanic riders, Machebeuf left Santa Fe. Stopping for brief visits at Albuquerque and some of the other missions along the way, he reached El Paso by the end of the month. The handsome and charming Don Ramón Ortiz, who had shown Lamy and Machebeuf such warm hospitality in 1851, again received him graciously. But when Machebeuf brought up the official reasons for his visit, Ortiz balked. Machebeuf asked Ortiz, in his capacity as vicar general to the bishop of Durango, to officially recognize the transfer. Ortiz refused to do so. Ortiz "raised a cloud of objections and difficulties under the pretext that he had received no instructions to that effect from his bishop." Machebeuf presented him with the original decree, signed by Cardinal Barnabo, the Cardinal Prefect of the Propaganda Fide, the Vatican Congregation for the Propagation of the Faith. Diplomatically, Ortiz took a copy of the decree, promising "to send it immediately to Durango and to act according to the orders which he would receive from the Bishop of that city."[48]

Ortiz also granted Machebeuf permission to say mass along the way, "but I did not care to stop any length of time for mission work until I had all the necessary faculties and full jurisdiction." He did stop long enough to minister to the soldiers at a U.S. fort, and from the soldiers he learned that a troop detachment had just left Santa Barbara, destined for Tucson. Within two days Machebeuf overtook them. The commanding officer gave orders he should be furnished with whatever he needed. "This was just what I wanted, and I spent the night in peace."[49] From the troop detachment he learned there was little danger from Comanche or Apache raids at that particular time. Since the slow-moving contingent was traveling on foot, he decided he could make better time without them, and pushed on with his two riders to Fort Buchanan. The soldiers at Fort Buchanan had not seen a priest for some time, so Machebeuf spent several days there, hearing confessions and saying mass. On a Sunday morning he started for Tucson.

Entering the Sonoran desert, Machebeuf found himself in a landscape unlike any he had ever seen. Dry, ragged brown mountains stood starkly under the desert sun, fading to blue in the distance. Vegetation exploded in a myriad of strange fantastic shapes. Saguaro cactus stood like sentinels, ancient guards observing his passage. Prickly pear and chain cholla flourished beneath the scant shade of mesquite and palo verde trees. "Nine miles from Tucson I came to the Indian village of St. Francis Xavier among the Pima Indians, a tribe almost all Catholics. I had the pleasure of finding there a large brick church, very rich and beautiful for that country."[50]

San Xavier del Bac, an aging mission church constructed in the late eighteenth century, stood alone on a golden desert plain where desert mountains wove a distant circle of pale blues and lavenders. The church's towers and dome stood in stark relief against the single black hill beside it. Around the church were a few scattered adobes, among the traditional brush huts of the Papago, or Tohono O'odham. Machebeuf was mesmerized by the decaying elegance of the church, by its towering ornate facade, its magnificent statuary, and the murals that covered its interior walls.

The governor of the tribe, José Zapata, welcomed him, and the two men became friends. When the bells of the church rang out, the people of San Xavier, men and women, old and young, crossed the open field in front of the church. Much to his surprise, Machebeuf found that the people of San Xavier had not forgotten the prayers the Franciscan fathers had taught them. Some of them could even sing parts of the mass — taught to them by Mexicans who lived in the pueblo. Most touching of all, José, leader of the community that waited three decades for the arrival of a priest, presented the sacred vessels of the church to Machebeuf. Four silver chalices, a gold-plated silver monstrance, two gold cruets with a silver plate, two small silver candlesticks, two silver censers, and the sanctuary carpet had been buried in the desert to protect them from theft, then brought to José's house. The people of San Xavier, he explained, had guarded these treasures for over three decades.[51] Now they were his to use as he sang the mass. Machebeuf was deeply moved by the gesture. For the rest of his life, he had a special fondness for the people of San Xavier del Bac.

The church had had no resident pastor since the expulsion of the Franciscans over thirty years before. Impressed by their sincerity, their devotion, and their hospitality, Machebeuf vowed to return to the people of San Xavier del Bac. But first he must complete his mission. He set out to cover the final few miles to Tucson.

Tucson, he later wrote his sister, was "a village of about 800 souls, built around an ancient Mexican fortress." Originally an Indian settlement, Tucson became a Spanish military post. In 1792 Fr. Juan Domingo Arricivita identified it as the Presidio del los Españoles, with two churches built, one for the soldiers, Our Lady of Guadalupe, and another for the people, St. Augustine.[52] With the change of government brought about by the Gadsden Purchase, the Mexican town began to be infiltrated by Anglos, for the most part hard men driven by a thirst for the silver in the nearby mines. The Apaches frequently raided the area, and even army posts limited their patrols to the immediate vicinity. Isolated from any system of justice, it had become a haven for fugitives, murderers, robbers, and other criminals. No one could remember the last time the bishop of Sonora had visited the town, and the ministrations of a priest were a welcome, if rare, event. Machebeuf stayed long enough to hear confessions, bless marriages, baptize the children, and sing the mass. He announced to the people that the area now belonged to the bishop of Santa Fe and again set out, on 20 December, to find Bishop Loza.[53]

In Tucson he learned there was no point in traveling to Culiacán — the bishop of Sonora was not in residence. Juarez was leading Mexico through a period of revolutionary struggle, and the bishop had temporarily established his cathedral in the Spanish colonial silver-mining city of Alamos. Machebeuf changed his course. He would ride south to Guaymas, then inland from the Pacific Ocean. Leaving Tucson he passed the abandoned Mexican fort and derelict mission church of Tubac, then the ruins of what had once been another Jesuit mission, Tumacácori. South of the border he rode through Imuris and the ruins of San Ignacio mission. He faced a landscape of neglected people and derelict churches, small villages forgotten by bishops and priests if not by God. In each village he stopped only long enough to hear confessions, bless the marriages, baptize the children, and sing the mass, then traveled on. At Magdalena, on Christmas Eve, he finally found a church with a resident pastor. In the shadow of the blue-tiled dome of the church, the two sang midnight mass together in a private chapel. There were no evergreens or holly, only tamarisks and palms swaying in the warm breeze outside the chapel.

In Magdalena he also met another group of travelers. He and his two riders joined them, stopping to visit with Governor Gándara of Sonora at his magnificent hacienda, then moving on to Hermosillo, described in a May 1859 newspaper account as a center of commerce, with a population of twelve thousand, which included fifteen American residents, two Germans, and fifty Frenchmen. He watched the townspeople perform the play *The Shepherds — Los Pastores*, for Epiphany, rested a few days among the bougainvillea and lime trees, then began the hundred-mile journey to Guaymas.[54]

Machebeuf rode through the dry forbidding lands of the Yaqui, where each village had a church established by the Jesuits, and rituals combined Catholicism and traditional Yaqui beliefs. Around him the desert sky began to grow hazy, giving a dreamlike quality to distant mountains and savage canyons. The mountain range that separated him from the ocean finally gave way, and he emerged through a canyon to look down on endless sparkling blue. Riding down the quiet shore of Bacochibampo Bay, he followed the gentle curve of the coast into Guaymas.

The seaport of Guaymas had about thirty-five hundred residents. Their houses surrounded the great church, its twin towers and blue dome bright against the red rock behind it. Before long Machebeuf befriended an American convert, Brigadier General Stone, a surveyor working for the Mexican government, exploring and mapping the west coast of Mexico. Machebeuf hoped to take a steamer to Mazatlán, then ride across the Sierra Madre del Occidente to Durango, and present his documents directly to Bishop Zubiría. When the steamer failed to appear, Stone came to his rescue. He let Machebeuf use one of his company's sailing vessels, commissioned him a captain, and provided him with a crew. Captain Machebeuf sailed the coast to the point where the River of May met the Gulf of California at Navajoa. Again changing his plans, he decided to ride inland. Perhaps he would find Bishop Loza in Alamos, at his interim cathedral.

Crossing forty miles of flat, brushy plains, he came to the craggy ridge of the Sierras, and wove his way into their forbidding canyons, passing Los Tres Frailes, the three-humped mountain named after three Franciscan friars. Finally he saw the walled streets of Alamos. In a large plaza stood the cathedral, its single tower and cracked bell ringing out the Angelus or calling the faithful to mass. But Loza was not in Alamos, so Machebeuf settled down to wait. It was pleasant in Alamos, a town rich from silver mining, its streets lined with elegant villas. White walls met wrought-iron windows, tall palms and tamarisks emerged from protected gardens. Yaquis quietly came into the town to trade, then disappeared into the surrounding mountains. He did not wait long. The day after his arrival Machebeuf learned that Loza was in a village only three miles to the north. He rode to the house of Don Mateo Ortiz, the bishop's host, and finally presented himself to the illustrious Sr. Don Pedro Loza y Pardave, bishop of Sonora.[55]

A portrait of Loza, taken from an 1897 photograph, shows a kindly, judicious countenance. His long, narrow face supports a strong patrician nose. His features are softened by a wide mouth, with the slight suggestion of a smile, and gently drooping eyes beneath straight black brows. His graying hair comes to a widow's peak above a high, smooth forehead. Born in Mexico City in 1815, Loza was educated at the Seminario Conciliar de

México and continued his studies in Culiacán. As bishop he succeeded in establishing a number of schools and a college in Sonora. Loza was exceedingly gracious and quickly agreed to Machebeuf's requests. He suggested Machebeuf rest while the necessary papers were drawn up and invited him to join him the following day, to hear him preach and to attend the confirmations of new church members.

On 16 January 1859 Loza presented Machebeuf with a letter acknowledging the transfer. The "Señor Presbyter Don Jose Machebeuf," Loza considered "amply authorized" by virtue of his description and letters from the Propaganda Fide. With a stroke of his pen, Loza duly authorized that "La Mesilla within the condado of Doñana in the United States of the North has been joined entirely to the before mentioned diocese of Santa Fe." This transfer included "Tubac, San Xavier del Bac, Tucson, and a few other smaller towns." The reasoning behind provision of the document was explained: "We have thought it expeditious to give the present document with which one can, with neither difficulty nor obstacle, take possession of the temples that were in that region and whatever was contained in them."[56] Additionally, Loza provided Machebeuf with the faculties permitting him to exercise his priestly functions in Sonora.

Having secured written acknowledgment of the transfer from the bishop, Machebeuf decided to press on. He told Loza of his plans to return to his sailboat at Navajoa, sail to Mazatlán, travel overland to Durango, and obtain the same from Bishop Zubiría. Loza advised against it. Sinaloa was in a state of civil war, and priests were particularly endangered. His own departure from Culiacán had been that of a "half-fugitive."[57] Machebeuf, he suggested, should return to Arizona, rather than jeopardize himself by attempting to reach Durango. Nor did Loza think he should try to sail from Navajoa to Guaymas. The current in the Gulf flowed to the south. Better he renounce his commission as captain, leaving the crew to pilot the ship home, and ride north by the coastal road.

Machebeuf accepted Loza's advice, traveled overland to Hermosillo, then he retraced his route back to Tucson. On his arrival in Tucson he sent word to Lamy, by the Butterfield stage, of his success with Loza, and surveyed the considerable work at hand for a missionary, both in the wild town of Tucson and the quieter neighboring villages of Tubac and San Xavier.

The old church of Our Lady of Guadalupe, built when Tucson was a presidio, or military post, was in such poor condition that it could be neither used as it was nor repaired. Machebeuf approached one of the prominent citizens of the town, Don Francisco Solano Leon, and persuaded him to donate a house to serve as an interim church. With the help of his parishioners, he added a large wooden porch to the two-room structure and began singing mass regularly. Because of the frequency of murders in the town, Machebeuf decided to devote one of his more impassioned sermons to the subject. He was unaware that one member of his audience had killed a man the night before. The man was furious, convinced the sermon was directed at him, and felt Machebeuf was being unjust. He did not consider himself a murderer — he had killed in self-defense. Later that day, when Machebeuf went riding, the man followed him in a buggy. Confronting him in a nearby wood, he drew his pistol. Machebeuf spurred his horse so hard he knocked the heels off his boots, and taking off at a dead run, quickly outdistanced his attacker, slowed by the weight of the buggy. When the Catholics of Tucson heard of the incident, they no longer allowed him to travel alone, even within Tucson itself. Without his knowledge, they assigned guards. Each night, when Machebeuf finished hearing confessions, one or two of the men always stood outside the makeshift church, waiting to escort him to his residence.[58]

When not working in Tucson, Machebeuf traveled out to San Xavier del Bac, to sing the mass, and make a more careful study of the beautiful mission church. After several weeks seeing to the most pressing needs of the area, Machebeuf departed for Santa Fe in March 1859. The people of Tucson tried to warn him about traveling across Apache lands — just a few days before some soldiers had been killed. Undaunted, Machebeuf led his small party through Apache Canyon, later the site of Fort Bowie. In heavy rain, he left his wagon with his companions and mounted a saddle horse to ride to the changing station at the top of Mount Ciricasca. Approaching the stage house alone, he suddenly confronted a group of Apache braves. The leader of the group rode out to meet him.

"Tu capitán?" he queried.

"No capitán." Machebeuf responded.

"Tu padre?" the man asked.

"Si, yo padre."

"Bueno! Como le va?" said the smiling warrior, then sent for his companions, each of them taking turns to shake hands with the aging, blond priest. The leader asked if he had seen any troops along the way.

"Certainly," Machebeuf told him, there was a detachment on their way up the mountain. After conferring with one another for a few minutes, the group decided to depart, shouting "Adiós, Padre," as they spurred their horses and disappeared into the rain. Inside the stage house Machebeuf found three frightened, grateful Americans, convinced that Machebeuf had saved their lives. They took him in, fed him, and gave him a room for the night, then saw him off the following morning.[59]

By the time he reached the village of Doñana, Machebeuf began to feel feverish. He had contracted malaria in Mexico. He rested a few days, then moved on, finally arriving in Santa Fe on 24 March. For two months malaria forced him to rest, while he caught up on news from Lamy and recovered his strength. In May 1859 he again left for Arizona, hoping to visit all the western provinces of New Mexico and push on to California, where new silver mines had been discovered. Besides, he had a promise to keep, one made to the people of San Xavier del Bac.

Machebeuf rode down through the Gila Valley from its source in the Mogollon Mountains to central Arizona. He visited isolated settlements along the way and made his way to Tucson. For the next two months he traveled back and forth between Tucson and San Xavier. In Tucson he urged the people to begin raising money for the construction of a new church, and in San Xavier he began repairs on a very old one.

Many consider the Mission of San Xavier del Bac the finest example of Spanish colonial mission architecture in the United States. According to at least one historian, it is to Machebeuf "we owe its preservation today." The twin towers of the church rise up in delicate majesty on a level plain south of Tucson, prominent against the dark hill behind it. The mission was founded by the great Jesuit missionary Fr. Eusebio Francisco Kino in 1692. Visiting the Sopaipuri village of Bac, a word for the site where water surfaces from an underground passage, he started a mission and named it after his patron saint, Francis Xavier. In 1700 Kino laid the foundation for a church, but the church was never constructed. Between 1756 and 1759 another Jesuit oversaw the construction of a rectangular adobe church. The present church was not begun until 1778.[60]

In 1767, when Charles III of Spain exiled the Society of Jesus from Spanish lands, the Franciscans took over the care of the Jesuit missions in Sonora. The Franciscans also began construction of the church at San Xavier, designed by an unknown architect and built by Indian, Mexican, and Spanish laborers and artisans. The cruciform baroque church, with its two towers and central dome, was built out of fired adobe bricks. A dramatic stone portal, or facade, filled with life-size statues of saints was designed to cover the front of the church. Known as Churriguresque, after a family of architects in Salamanca, the style is rarely seen in the United States. Of the seven missions founded by Kino in northern Sonora, San Xavier del Bac is the only one that has survived.

With his usual energy Machebeuf directed the people of San Xavier in much-needed repairs on the church. First, he covered the roof with a cement mixture to stop it from leaking. Previous leakage had already damaged the side walls, so he constructed wooden braces to prevent the walls from spreading. The Tohono O'odham welcomed his efforts and worked alongside him. It was they who had protected the church from the ravages of the Apaches, the raids that reduced all the other missions to ruins. Machebeuf's repairs held. It was 1906 before further repairs were made, when Bishop Henry Granjon began his restoration of the church and first painted the mission its distinctive bright white.[61]

Having once again rendered the church suitable for mass, Machebeuf began to cast about for additional projects. He decided to visit the villages near the Gila, eighty miles west of Tucson, and the small settlement on the Colorado River known as Yuma. As he was preparing for departure, a letter arrived from Lamy summoning him back. Considering it a command, he promptly returned.

When Machebeuf reached Santa Fe, Lamy seemed to have no pressing business for him. Although he was glad to see his old friend, Machebeuf spent much of his time pouting and pacing, bored by the relatively slow pace of Santa Fe, by the lack of challenge and adventure. He was restless, and inactivity had always been toxic to him. He asked Lamy to send him back west. When Lamy refused, Machebeuf asked why he kept him in Santa Fe.

"Oh, there was nothing in particular, and you were so long away that I was lonesome for your return. Just stay here with me now for a while and rest. It will be pleasant to talk over old times. We have not had too much consolation of this intimate sort and I feel that we need some now. In a short time you can go again."[62] Actually, the delay in Santa Fe seemed fated, for, as the two French priests were about to learn, gold had just been discovered at Pike's Peak.

Part Four

Rocky Mountain Missionary: Colorado

1860–1868

THIRTEEN

After the Gold Rush

✙

"I see but one thing to be done." Bishop Lamy's dark figure was silhouetted in the window. "You have been complaining because I sent for you and have kept you here at Santa Fe — now, don't you see there was something providential in all this? I don't like to part with you, but you are the only one I have to send, and you are the very man for Pike's Peak." Machebeuf was restless, ready for adventure. "Very well," he replied, "I will go! Give me another priest, some money for our expenses, and we will be ready for the road in twenty-four hours."[1] With his usual impatience and impulsiveness Machebeuf accepted the challenge that would dominate the last three decades of his life. He began his missionary work at Pike's Peak, covering the vast area that would become the states of Colorado and Utah.

In late September 1860 two men mounted wagons and left Santa Fe for the fledgling city of Denver. Their journey took them almost four hundred miles to the north. They traveled first past the golden cottonwood and red river willow on the upper Rio Grande, past the savage golden bluffs of Embudo Canyon to Taos, built on the sweeping sage-covered plateau amid soaring peaks. From Taos they traveled overland through the northernmost range of the Sangre de Cristo Mountains, through miles of jagged granite, the dark blanket of ponderosa pine broken only by the scattered sparkling gold of aspen already sensing the approach of winter. The Rocky Mountains with their endless hidden valleys, their sweeping plains, and vast alpine meadows enveloped them. Crossing the Huerfano River at Fort Garland they reached the great southern plains of Colorado and traveled north again, to the town of Pueblo, to Pike's Peak, and finally to Denver.[2]

At forty-eight Machebeuf looked much older than he was, his weather-beaten face carved by years of wind and sun, his blond hair like dry straw. He was well qualified to undertake the impossible mission to the miners. He now had over twenty years of experience as a missionary — ten years on the Ohio Frontier and another ten in New Mexico — was fluent in Spanish, spoke passable English, and was inured to the hardship of travel in the West. His young assistant, John Raverdy, was still green by comparison: fresh out of France, not yet able to speak English, with only a working knowledge of Spanish, and a novice in terms of frontier life. The two men, along with their gear, represented the total resources and manpower of the Catholic Church in northern Colorado.

From experience, Machebeuf knew to travel relatively light. "Their actual preparations consisted of a wagon to carry the necessaries of church service in his new field where he might have several chapels, a few personal effects, blankets and buffalo robes for bedding, and provisions for the journey. This, with a lighter conveyance called an ambulance, for their personal comfort and for later travel among the mines . . . and four mules . . . [that] furnished the powers of locomotion."[3]

Machebeuf carried with him a letter to serve as credentials in his new territory. "To all those whom it may concern," Lamy had written, "we make known by the presents that Very Rev. Joseph P. Machebeuf has received from us all the faculties necessary to administer the Sacraments of the holy Catholic Church in the various districts towns and settlements of Pike's Peak and also that he has the same extraordinary faculties which he has had as Vicar Genl in our Diocese these nine years." It was signed, "John B. Lamy, Bp of Sta Fe." An additional letter for Raverdy identified him as Machebeuf's assistant missionary.[4]

Lamy had been as reluctant to part with his friend as he had been to accept responsibility for the huge territory to the north. When he received word from Archbishop Kenrick of St. Louis that the Pike's Peak country, previously under the jurisdiction of Bishop Miège in Leavenworth, Kansas, was to be temporarily attached to the Diocese of Santa Fe, he wrote to Rome saying he had no "desire to extend the jurisdiction."[5] In spite of his objections, Rome confirmed the transfer. It was up to Lamy to provide the manpower needed to service the spiritual needs of the territory.

Machebeuf and Raverdy reached Pueblo in early October, stopping briefly to bless the marriages and baptize the children of an isolated Hispanic family. Such families waited years before encountering a priest and were relieved to bring their accounts with God and the church up to date.[6]

Within a few days the two priests reached Pike's Peak. The peak stands alone, towering in faded blue above the pale green plain that surrounds it, challenging all comers. One of the first Europeans to take the challenge was Lt. Zebulon Pike in 1806. He failed to reach the summit, and when he crossed the Arkansas River into Spanish territory, he found himself arrested by Spanish soldiers. Nonetheless, Pike managed to leave his name on the peak. Fifty-two years later Julia Holmes, described as "young, handsome, intelligent . . . a regular women's righter, [who] wears the bloomer, and was quite indignant when informed she was not allowed to stand guard," strolled casually to its peak, and accomplished what Pike did not.[7] Her great accomplishment was universally ignored. Everyone was too busy looking for gold. Pike's Peak had become the focal point of the Colorado Gold Rush.

Probably the first to discover gold in Colorado was a group of Cherokee Indians and whites traveling to California in 1850. On 20 June a man named Lewis Ralston panned some gold in a sandy creek a few miles west of what would later become the site of Denver. According to a diary kept by one of the party, they found, "Good water, grass, and timber. We called this Ralston's Creek because a man of that name found gold here." When the party returned from California they took samples of the gold back to Georgia with them. The first organized group of prospectors left from Auraria, Georgia, on 9 February 1858, under the leadership of William Green Russell. By November of the same year, Green's party had discovered enough gold to justify building a settlement. Green and his party platted a townsite at the mouth of Cherry Creek, naming it Auraria, on 4 November.[8] The town that eventually became Denver City was born.

News of their success spread rapidly. A few weeks later the *St. Louis Republican*'s headline read, "THE NEW ELDORADO!!! THE PIKES MINES. FIRST ARRIVAL OF GOLD DUST AT KANSAS CITY!!!"[9] Thousands of Americans, shaken by the financial panic of 1857 and with the California Gold Rush still fresh in their memories, flocked to Pike's Peak. Mining communities, groups of hastily constructed shacks with names like Manitou Springs, Mosquito Pass, Cripple Creek, and Russell Gulch, fanned out from the Denver area.

Machebeuf reached Pike's Peak in October 1860. A settlement named Eldorado City had been constructed at its base the previous year. He paused long enough to "set up their tent for the night, and here they offered" what biographer Howlett assures us is "the [Mass of] Clean Oblation for the first time in the history of the American settlement of Colorado." Thomas Steele, Jesuit historian and coeditor of the 1987 reprint of Howlett's biography, says, "Not so." According to Steele the first mass was offered by the Jesuit Bishop John B. Miège of the Vicariate Apostolic of Kansas and the Indian Territory. On 27 May 1860 "Miège and a fellow

Jesuit, Brother John Kilcullin (1823–91) were in Denver. . . . The Bishop offered the first mass in the Denver area in the home of Mr. Guiraud, a French Catholic merchant located at 15th and Market streets."[10]

Machebeuf and Raverdy reached Denver City on 29 October 1860. Before him Machebeuf saw a village in the middle of a level plain, dwarfed by the snowcapped mountains to the west. Years later he remembered his first night in Denver. "Having camped out nearly every night of our long and tedious journey from Santa Fe, we expected to camp out also in Denver, but a good friend had a store in a small frame building on the corner of Fifteenth and Holladay." The following morning, the early light revealed the community that would be Machebeuf's home for almost thirty years. "After a good night's rest, and a good breakfast we walked around to see, not the city, but the little village of Denver, made up of low frame stores, log cabins, tents and Indian wigwams on the banks of the Platte, and only two or three brick houses."[11]

A small but eager congregation had already been directed by Bishop Miège to purchase two lots on the outskirts of town, from the "express company, worth about $15 each." Following his suggestion, they issued a contract to Samuel Howe for $1,000, for the construction of a church.[12]

With the experience gained during his years in Ohio, Machebeuf was well prepared for the construction of the church. The first church was a plain brick structure that measured thirty by forty-six feet. Beginning sometime in November, he had the roof in place by Christmas, and on Christmas Eve, Raverdy officially opened it, singing the Midnight Mass. The church was not yet plastered and had canvas instead of glass for windows, but he had completed it within two months of his arrival. For seventy-five dollars he built a wooden frame house that would serve as his and Raverdy's residence for the next ten years. "Although a stranger and newcomer to Denver, I was rich in lumber. A good Canadian carpenter whom I employed in Santa Fe had been waiting for me in Denver for over a month, but as business called him back to Santa Fe, he left two orders for lumber to be delivered to me on my arrival. . . . I furnished all the lumber required and my house was built."[13]

Machebeuf had his work cut out for him. The city was far from civilized. Lavina Porter, who traveled by ox cart from Hannibal, Missouri, arrived in Denver about three months earlier. Disappointed, she recorded that Denver "was an exceedingly primitive town, consisting of numerous tents and numbers of crude and poorly constructed cabins, with nearly as many rum shops and low saloons as cabins." Nor was she pleased that "horses, cows, and hogs roamed at will over the greater part of the village." To increase her disdain, a number of Arapaho families lived near the river. Their "poor, overworked squaws were busily engaged," she imperiously recorded, "cooking their vile compounds, and making the skins of wild animals into the uncouth garments that they wore. Loafing around in the sand and dirt were the indolent and unemployed braves, while their filthy and vermin covered offspring played naked in the sand."[14]

The white men of Denver were just as unlikely to be pleasing to Mrs. Porter's fastidious nature. Most of them divided their time between "Gambling, whoring in dance halls, horse-racing, gun-fighting, [and] claim-jumping," and the greater population "consisted of lonely men, living a hard life, and taking loose pleasures in compensation." Horace Greeley described the city as filled with men "soured in temper, always armed, bristling at a word, ready with the rifle, revolver or bowie knife," and concluded he was convinced there was more general lawlessness "in this log city . . . than any community of no greater number on earth." The more respectable members of the community formed a vigilance committee, hired a sheriff, and began a series of regular public hangings, but "the fact that Denver had six successive marshals between December 1859 and December 1861 testifies to the difficulties inherent in the job."[15]

Machebeuf showed no sign of being intimidated by the work ahead of him. In December 1860 he left Raverdy behind to mind the parish and began a series of trips to the outlying mining camps, just as he had once visited railroad camps in Ohio. He established circuits: one to Central City that included stops at Fall River and Spanish Bar, one to South Park that would take in camps called Buckskin Joe and Fairplay on the South Platte, another up the Arkansas to Cache Creek and Dayton, a route through the mountains by Loveland Pass and down to Breckenridge, and a southern route to Pueblo, Colorado City, Canon City, and scattered Hispanic settlements. Usually he traveled in the ambulance, the heavy two-wheeled buggy he'd brought with him from New Mexico. It was light enough for mountain roads, but big enough to carry a load. "It was a peculiar shape," another priest later recorded, "with square top, side curtains, a half curtain in front to be let down in cases of storms, and a rack behind for heavy luggage." Distinctive and easily recognized, it soon became a familiar sight in the camps, a sign that the priest had arrived. It had enough room to stow "his vestments for mass, his bedding, grain for his horses, his own provisions and his frying pan and coffee pot. . . . It was a movable home . . . a movable church."[16]

Often as not Machebeuf would celebrate the mass on a little altar on the rack at the back of the buggy. Few of the camps would support the construction of a church because most of them were highly transient. Placer camps were abandoned when there was no more gold to be found in the sandy streambeds, and lode camps turned into ghost towns as soon as the particular vein or the mine played out.

Even some of the more stable communities seemed reluctant to contribute the money required for the construction of a church. But Machebeuf didn't hesitate to encourage his fledgling congregations, as the residents of Central City discovered. For weeks he held mass in any shelter he could find. He later recalled, "The only place I could find to say Mass in was a kind of theatre, and I had to put the altar on the stage. . . . At my second visit, Mass was said in a vacant billiard room, and it required the work of two good men to clean and scrape the floor; the third visit, in a ballroom used as a theatre; the fourth visit, in a large store."[17]

Tired of having to find a new place each visit, Machebeuf decided to take action. He posted a man at the only door of one of the camp's meeting halls, and after saying the mass, he gave the benediction. With the last "amen," a prearranged signal, the man slammed the door shut, bolted and padlocked it, and took the key to Machebeuf at the altar.

"Now, my good men," he thundered, using a tone he had never before used with his parishioners, "none of you will go out until you contribute for a church." John B. Fitzpatrick, described as "a mine superintendent and a practical Catholic," one of the founders of Golden City, was the first to volunteer a donation. He stood up saying loudly, "I give $20.00 for my contribution, and advance $50.00 toward the building of the church," then walked up and deposited the money on the altar.[18] One by one the startled miners brought out pouches of nuggets and gold dust. Four hours and five passes of the hat later Machebeuf opened the doors. The construction of the church began the following morning.

Machebeuf was able to write of success to his brother, Marius, in September 1861. By that time he considered himself "firmly established at the foot of the Rocky Mountains" and said he would soon "leave for my eighth trip across the Middle and South Parks." He suggested that Marius "consult a map and follow me if you can." Giving a slightly edited version of his activities, he was happy to tell Marius that "besides the principal parish, established at Denver, we have begun another in the center of the mountains at a flourishing place called Central City." Then he outlined his projected travel plans. "After several days there I'll go on to South Park. . . . I'll be able to see through the gorges far off to the territory of Utah where the Mormons live. I'll be returning only at the end of September [1861] to pass a few days at Denver and Central City, and then, in October, I'll move on again to the same South Park, and New Mexico, Santa Fe, and Albuquerque. . . . I'll return to Denver by Christmas at the latest."[19]

Machebeuf left on the proposed trip, but had to delay his planned trip to New Mexico. Returning to Denver he was taken ill. The doctors diagnosed it as typhoid. Once again Lamy was informed of his death.

In January 1862 Machebeuf wrote again to his brother in France. "Last September, while among the highest mountains at California Gulch, where the range is always covered with snow, I fell sick. . . . Bishop Lamy heard from some people that I was sick, and from others that I was dead. Not knowing which to believe he sent Father Ussel to find out, but when he came I was up and walking about in my garden with the help of a cane. I kept Father Ussel for two weeks," Machebeuf calmly reported, and "went with him to Santa Fe. I spent the greater part of the month of December at Albuquerque, where the care and good old wine of Father Paulet contributed not a little to the re-establishment of my forces."[20] The irrepressible Machebeuf had deceived death once again.

FOURTEEN

The Cripple

✧

For all his blithe assurances to his brother, Marius, Machebeuf had more than Father Paulet's wine in mind when he traveled to New Mexico late in the fall of 1861. His circuit riding had given him an opportunity to evaluate the territory, to ascertain the needs of the diverse population with whom he would be working, and to evaluate the material goods that would be needed for that work. He now had some idea of just what was required to undertake the physical as well as spiritual construction of the church in Colorado.

Gabriel Ussel, who had been serving as pastor in Taos, received Lamy's letter regarding Machebeuf's illness. With a young companion, he set out on horseback for the three-hundred-mile journey to Denver. Finding Machebeuf alive, Ussel suggested he return with him to Santa Fe, and Machebeuf readily agreed. Machebeuf still needed some rest before he would be strong enough to travel, so Ussel used the time to survey the surrounding countryside with Raverdy. "We visited Central City and vicinity," Ussel wrote sympathetically in his account of the journey, "and I could see the nature of the work and the inevitable privations under which the powerful constitution of Father Machebeuf had given way, and I wondered how he had been able to stand up under them so long."[1]

In some ways the challenges of the Colorado Territory were far greater than those presented by New Mexico. By the 1850s New Mexico had been under Spanish control for three centuries; villages and towns were long established, churches long built, and the Iberian influence of Spanish colonists could be seen in New Mexico's rich cultural legacy, the developed agricultural economy, and the established trade routes. The Pueblos of New Mexico provided another focus for missionary activities. They were stable, settled communities, inured, or at least resigned, to the incursions of the church. Catholicism had been grafted onto the culture of many of the pueblos, and although not a part of their original belief system, it was maintained alongside their seasonal observances. Colorado was a different story entirely.

The area that today makes up the state of Colorado was, for the most part, virgin wilderness. Most of the tribes that inhabited the region were nomadic. Nor had the Spanish influence carried into much of the territory. With the exception of nomadic tribes and a few Hispanic communities along the New Mexico border, in the San Luis Valley and beside the Huerfano River, the area was uninhabited. Unlike New Mexico, there were no stable Catholic communities to draw on for tithes or supplies. The church in Colorado would have to be built from the ground up.

The inhabitants of Denver and the smaller towns were not the same as those in New Mexico either. The population of New Mexico was primarily Hispanic and Native American, a well-settled populace with rich cultural traditions that formed and regulated their lives. Until the gold rush the only Europeans in northern Colorado were mountain men, the odd trader or trapper who could survive without civilized amenities. George F. Ruxton, an English traveler and member of the Royal Geographical Society, recorded his impressions of the mountain men after his 1846 trip. "The trappers of the Rocky Mountains belong to a genus more approximating the primitive savage than perhaps any other class of civilized man," the disdainful Ruxton reported. "Constantly exposed to perils of all kinds, they become callous to any feeling of danger, and destroy human as well as animal life with as little scruple and as freely as they expose their own. Of laws, human and divine, they neither know nor care to know."[2] Machebeuf would have his work cut out for him transforming these men into pious parishioners.

Nor could he count on influencing the men through the women of the area. The population that came to Colorado in the wake of the gold rush were primarily men, either U.S. gold-diggers from the eastern cities or recent immigrants from diverse European backgrounds. They were, for the most part, single men lacking the gentling influence of wives or children, intent only on finding gold and securing whatever limited pleasures they could in the process.

A month after Machebeuf wrote his confident letter to Marius, on 26 February 1861, Congress passed a bill authorizing the new Territory of Colorado. The same year the first territorial census recorded a total population of 25,329. The number of females, of all ages, was only 4,484.[3]

Women were few and far between, and the number of Catholic women exceedingly small. Throughout his missionary work previously, Machebeuf had always relied on women to provide the bulk of his social amenities — from food and bedding to altar cloths and vestments. Recognizing the population of Denver as unlikely to provide such niceties, he saw his trip to New Mexico as a perfect opportunity to garner much-needed supplies.

During his ten years in New Mexico, Machebeuf had developed a deep affection for Hispanic Catholics. His Spanish was much better than his English, his taste for chile stronger than his tolerance for ill-prepared meat and potatoes, and his childhood in the French countryside of Auvergne had bred into him a deep respect for simple, hardworking people. Although he could be quite authoritarian, with all the imperialistic superiority of nineteenth-century European culture, he did not share the blatantly racist attitudes that most of the Anglo residents of Denver held toward the Hispanic population. Nor did Machebeuf have any qualms about using those same racist attitudes to shame the people of Denver into finishing his rough church.

One Sunday mass he announced his departure to his growing congregation. "You may wonder at the pleasure I anticipate in New Mexico, for you never have a good word for the Mexicans, and you seem to despise them as an inferior race of people," he announced from the pulpit. "The only thing about them which you seem to care for is their 'pesos' — their dollars! Well, when I go among them I am going to ask them for some of their pesos to put windows in the church for the Catholics of Denver." Ussel, who recorded the event, remarks, "That evening several carpenters came and pledged their word to Father Machebeuf that they would have the windows in for Christmas."[4]

Machebeuf was in no way exaggerating when he told his congregation he was going to New Mexico to beg on their behalf. He traveled with Ussel back across the Huerfano River, to San Luis de la Culebra, Taos, and Santa Fe. After spending time with Lamy, he set out on a round of serious begging.

By the end of January 1862, Ussel got a message from Machebeuf asking him to meet him at Salpointe's home in Mora. Salpointe, serving as pastor of Mora, was another Auvergnat, a large-framed, dark-haired man described by historian Paul Horgan as having "an observant, original habit of mind, a keen practical sense, and a Frenchman's taste for a well-set table." Salpointe could well understand Machebeuf's eagerness to secure a few material comforts. Ussel recorded his arrival at Salpointe's home. "When I arrived there Father Salpointe took me to the corral to see the equipment of the Señor Vicario. There it was — a big ox wagon, besides his own ambulance, and both filled with provisions, furniture and various articles."[5] In a few short weeks Machebeuf had secured an ox cart piled high with plunder. He had six feather mattresses, handmade by the ladies of New Mexico. To go with them he had feather pillows, linens, and a dozen hand-trimmed pillow slips. For his dinner table he had ristras, or strings, of dried red chile, burlap bags of onions and beans, and fruit and vegetable seeds for the garden he envisioned. He had collected two oxen to pull the wagon and two men to drive the wagon and generally assist him on his trip to the north.

Seeing Ussel approaching the corral, Machebeuf yelled, "Hands off! That is my property." Then, teasing him about his poor manners on his previous visit, Machebeuf quipped, "When you come to Denver the next time you will not pull the straws out of the pillows and present them to me as American feathers as you did the last time!"[6]

Having secured a few of the basic necessities for a more civilized existence at his new home in Denver, Machebeuf focused his energies on developing the physical foundations of the church. The Denver church was almost complete. The land on which it stood, at the corner of Stout and Fifteenth Streets, had been purchased before his arrival. He began making improvements on his residence, planting a garden to provide fresh produce and flowers and building a fence around the property. He also began acquiring other pieces of land, anticipating future need for churches and schools and eager to secure the land before development brought higher prices. He purchased one small tract on the Platte River two miles outside of Denver for farming and another five hundred acres on Clear Creek eight miles to the west. He bought still another section three miles outside of Denver for use as a cemetery and additional land for farming in South Boulder. Long familiar with the irrigation techniques of Hispanic farmers in New Mexico, he quickly applied those techniques to the dry, fertile land of Colorado, starting with vegetables and grain. By August of the following year he would not only be growing fresh produce for his dinner table but would be successful enough to harvest three hundred bushels of grain to use as feed for his teams.[7]

Throughout the summer and fall of 1862 he divided his time between overseeing Raverdy's work in Denver, circuit riding to the missions, arranging land purchases, farming, and developing plans for schools and churches throughout the territory. W. J. Howlett remembered Machebeuf's plans for one piece of land. "In his mind's eye he had a picture of a grand institution, conducted by some religious order of men, in which homeless and destitute boys would be cared for, properly trained and taught some trade, or useful and honorable mode of making a livelihood." Machebeuf eagerly shared his plans with the young priest. "More than once in those early days he took [me] over the grounds and pointed out the very spot where he proposed to erect the buildings, and drew the plans of them on the ground."[8]

Machebeuf continued to spend one Sunday a month at his church in Central City and make regular trips to other growing communities. In June 1863, after his usual visit to Central City, he started out for Denver. Central City was still a ramshackle collection of wooden buildings, some rough log structures and a few clapboard houses, hugging the steep sides of a mountainous valley. Amid the thinning pines and granite-strewn hills, a few dirt roads had been carved into the hillsides, providing the only access to Denver and other nearby towns. Following the Denver road through Black Hawk, to the point where it rose out of Clear Creek Canyon, Machebeuf found himself on a narrow passage, literally carved into the side of the mountain. The four-mile ascent led him to the crest of a ridge where he met a group of heavily loaded wagons, a supply-train traveling in the opposite direction. As his was the smaller and lighter vehicle, he maneuvered his vehicle to the outside edge of the road. Apparently he miscalculated, for his outside wheel edged off the narrow road. The wagon lurched and Machebeuf was thrown out of it, while the vehicle tumbled down the rocky hillside.[9]

In Santa Fe, a few weeks later, Lamy received a letter from Denver, written in an unfamiliar hand and telling him that Machebeuf had been the victim of a terrible accident. The writer indicated that Machebeuf's carriage had fallen from a narrow road onto the rocks below, but gave few details and little information as to Machebeuf's condition. Lamy's response again expresses the depth of their friendship. Concluding that Machebeuf was critically injured and might not live, afraid he would never see his friend alive again, he set off immediately for Denver, not even taking time to pack food for the journey. By noon the following day he arrived in Mora, to collect Salpointe. Lamy asked Salpointe to accompany him to Denver, but when Salpointe suggested waiting long enough to pack food for the trip, Lamy insisted they take only remains of the meal Salpointe was eating and leave immediately. Salpointe, who didn't share Lamy's sense of austerity, had hungry memories of the journey. He later wrote, "The Bishop, who could do with one meal a day even at home, provided he had a cup of black coffee and a piece of bread morning and evening, always objected to making ample provision of victuals for traveling."[10] The two lived mostly on game until they crossed the Huerfano River and reached the ranch of a friend. Their friend was able to tell them that Machebeuf was recovering from the accident, but he had heard that Machebeuf would be crippled for life. Lamy pushed on the next day for Denver and finally, ten days after his departure from Santa Fe, arrived at Machebeuf's home.

Much to their surprise Machebeuf, on crutches, answered the door himself. Lamy found his friend not only alive, but on his feet, and Machebeuf, who had no way of knowing the two were coming, was speechless. Celebrating a warm reunion, Machebeuf supplied the details of his latest brush with death.

Machebeuf had miraculously survived the fall, but his right leg was "broken off completely at the thigh joint."[11] Although he had been taken to a nearby house on the ridge and a doctor was summoned to set the leg, Machebeuf would never be the same. Whether because of the severity of the break, damage to tendons, or the ineptitude of the doctor, the leg was not properly set, and for the rest of his life, his right leg was shorter and weaker than his left. The varying reports of his treatment are confusing. It is even possible his leg was never set at all, for when Lamy later wrote Purcell about the accident he reported, "No bones were fractured. the doctors say he will get well."[12]

Perhaps most difficult for Machebeuf were the limitations the injury brought to his mobility. Always intensely active and independent, he could no longer sit a horse, could no longer ride for days beneath the sky. The accident marked a turning point in his life, an end to solitary journeys on horseback, to his endless roaming of mountain and desert. From that point on, his travels would be limited to areas he could access by carriage, to those he could reach by road. But if he was troubled by these new limitations, he did not allow it to show, and it certainly didn't slow his pace. Instead he seemed to recognize the increased effectiveness it might bring to his habitual begging, to his ability to garner donations for his continually developing plans. Shortly thereafter, in typical Machebeuf fashion, he began to include a somewhat dramatic request in his letters, "Pray always for the poor cripple!"[13]

FIFTEEN

Water, Sand, and Blood

✦

In March 1864 Machebeuf purchased a two-story frame house on a lot adjoining his church. Making a down payment of two thousand dollars, he gave the owner a personal note for two thousand more, payable in sixty days. The Mother Superior of the Sisters of Loretto in Kentucky had promised to send him a colony of sisters in the summer, and the property would be ideal for a school. The only problem, in terms of the site of both the church and the school, was its distance from town. "We all said, 'What folly to build a church so far from the town,' " he later recalled. "Although in those days I was not lame, it tired me to walk to the spot, but as the church was then commenced and the material on the ground we had to resign ourselves to our fate, to live for a long time on the prairie and go on with the work."[1] It seems fate had his best interests at heart, for the church's distant location soon proved to be a blessing.

Indians and mountain men warned Denver's inhabitants against building the town too close to the banks of Cherry Creek. They told of flash floods that sometimes followed heavy rains, but bankers and businessmen ignored their warnings. On 19 May 1864 black clouds engulfed the nearby mountains. Just before midnight one citizen recorded "a strange sound in the south like the noise of the wind, which increased to a mighty roar as a great wall of water, bearing on its crest trees and other drift, rushed toward the settlement." A wall of water nearly twenty feet high swept down the usually dry creek bed, wiping out houses, tents, bridges, and everything else in its path.[2] Both East and West Denver were flooded and at least eight people lost their lives. The flood wiped out nearby crops and livestock, causing food prices to rise, and contaminated water supplies. Machebeuf, whose church and new house were out of range of the flooding creek, seemed unfazed by the event. He lent what assistance he could to those who suffered losses, but for the most part he was too busy planning his school.

In June 1864 four Sisters of Loretto arrived, Sisters Ann Joseph, Joanna, Agatha, and Louise. They dubbed Machebeuf's new building St. Mary's Academy and promptly opened their doors to the girls of Denver.[3] Not satisfied with a school for girls, Machebeuf wrote to the Benedictines in Atchison, Kansas, hoping to convince them to open a house of their order, along with a college, in Denver. The Benedictines later decided Denver's future was too uncertain; they would wait before investing manpower in the Colorado Territory. But another of his recruiting efforts paid off. He succeeded in convincing Fr. Thomas Smith to relocate from the East and join him in his missionary efforts, assigning him to Central City as its first resident pastor.

The following month Gabriel Ussel visited Machebeuf in Denver. Ussel had been granted a leave of absence to visit his family in France, and Machebeuf took the opportunity to send word to his sister in Riom. "For the first time in its history four priests are together in Denver to-day," Machebeuf proudly wrote.[4]

As the summer progressed, tensions between Anglos and Native Americans continued to increase. The plains tribes refused to sign a treaty with the United States for the purchase of tribal lands, and attacks on whites increased. Almost fifty prospective citizens of Denver were killed, either crossing the plains or in homes on outlying ranches. Wagon and stage stations along the Platte River were destroyed. At one point rumors swept through Denver that the city was about to be attacked. Panic swept through the city. Men and women went into hiding, some in cellars, some even resorting to the dry goods boxes on the streets. Machebeuf had nothing to fear; he was well-protected.

Sometime earlier he had hired a housekeeper. The woman, Sara Morahan, was a strong, well-built Irish woman with a fearlessness that matched Machebeuf's own. She promptly secured an old musket and began standing guard. Throughout the night she marched back and forth in front of the house, ready to protect it from the attackers that never came. Nor did she restrict her bravery to Indian attacks. When a group of soldiers broke into her hen house to supplement their diets, Morahan went on the rampage. She succeeded in capturing one of the men as he was climbing the fence, stolen chickens in hand. "Oh, let me go, let me go!" the man cried, terrified of the Valkyrie that descended upon him, then apologetically added, "I haven't got but two!" He managed to escape with his life—but whether with or without the chickens is not recorded.[5]

The situation was far more serious in the southern part of the state. In October 1864 Machebeuf set out for a trip to visit Santa Fe and return by the way of the Las Animas River in the San Luis Valley. Early French trappers seemed to have sensed something unsettling about the region. They named the river the Purgatoire, the River of the Souls. Hispanic settlers called it Las Animas. The Las Animas River flows within forty miles of the site of the Sand Creek Massacre. On 29 November 1864, one of the bloodiest tragedies in Colorado's history unfolded, and the territory entered a kind of political purgatory.

As battles between the Plains Indians and whites continued, reports of Indian raids on Anglo settlers streamed into Denver. The telegraph line between Denver and Julesburg, in northeastern Colorado, was repeatedly cut, and travel to Denver from St. Louis came to a standstill.

In September 1864 Black Kettle, one of the most influential of the Cheyenne chiefs, sent word to Ned Wynkoop, the commander of Fort Lyon, that he wanted to begin peace talks. His tribe, along with the Arapaho, Comanche, Kiowa, and Sioux, wanted to meet with representatives of the army and the government. The messenger offered himself as a hostage to demonstrate the sincerity of the offer, and Wynkoop accepted.[6]

Wynkoop and 125 of his men met Black Kettle at Smoky Hill River. Both Black Kettle and Left Hand, of the Arapaho, surrendered white female captives in return for safe conduct to a meeting with the territorial governor. On 26 September the chieftains rode into Denver for peace talks. Governor Evans was not receptive, harping on atrocities reportedly committed by the Arapaho and Cheyenne. He was joined in these sentiments by Col. John Chivington. Chivington, once a presiding elder of the Rocky Mountain District of the Kansas-Nebraska Methodist Conference, demonstrated little evidence of Christian charity or forgiveness toward the Native American population.[7] He was convinced that the only road to peace lay not through negotiation but through military conquest. The discussions proved far from satisfactory for either party.

Regardless, the chiefs of the Cheyenne and Arapaho seemed determined to demonstrate their good intentions. They moved their encampment to the Big Bend of Sand Creek, fifty miles from Fort Lyon. In doing so they turned to Wynkoop as their protector, voluntarily placing themselves under his jurisdiction. Wynkoop allowed the hungry tribesmen to trade openly in the fort and dispensed allowances to help them through the lean months of the approaching winter. News of his cooperation was interpreted by his superiors as a sign of weakness, and Wynkoop was replaced by Maj. Scott J. Anthony. Anthony publicly announced he would follow Wynkoop's policy of pacification, but privately wrote he intended to do so only "until troops can be sent out to take the field against all tribes."[8]

On 4 November after his defeat as a candidate for delegate to the territorial congress, Colonel Chivington gave marching orders to the Colorado First and Third Regiments. A motley group of semi-trained men set out, on plow horses and gaited geldings, carrying rifles and antique Austrian muzzle loaders. The force arrived at Fort Lyon on 28 November. Chivington announced to the troops there that they would depart immediately to march on Black Kettle's encampment at Sand Creek.

Capt. Silas Soule, a veteran from the Civil War battle at Glorieta Pass in New Mexico, was the lone dissenter. He reminded Chivington that the Cheyenne and Arapaho had put themselves voluntarily under the protection of the U.S. Army by coming to Sand Creek. In response to his plea of conscience, Chivington threatened to court-martial Soule. In the early evening seven hundred men left Fort Lyon.

Shortly before dawn on 29 November, Chivington's troops reached the bluffs bordering Sand Creek. To one side, shifting sand dunes reached a height of six hundred feet above the valley floor, to the other piñon merged into ponderosas on the mountainous perimeter of the San Luis Valley. With bugles blaring they swept into the village — 115 bleached hide lodges of the Cheyenne with eight Arapaho lodges beside them. Anthony's troops from Fort Lyon began firing into the encampment at will — Chivington had ordered them to take no prisoners. Chaos erupted in the Native American settlement. Historian Phyllis Dorset writes, "Suddenly Black Kettle himself swung into view holding a long pole with an American flag on it. Beneath the American banner fluttered a smaller white flag. Standing in front of the first row of lodges, the Cheyenne chief . . . shouted to his people not to be frightened, that it was a mistake." Before him his people were "cut down by hundreds of yelping, frenzied white troops who overran the sand holes, finishing off with bayonets those they missed with bullets."[9]

The slaughter continued until midafternoon. Drunk on the orgy of blood, army troops scalped and mutilated the bodies, proudly displaying bloody breasts and testicles, picking off the remaining toddlers with rifle fire. Only those soldiers under the command of Captain Soule failed to participate. He refused to allow his men to fire a single shot during the massacre. They watched the spectacle in silent horror.

No one is sure how many were killed in the Sand Creek Massacre. Estimates run from four hundred to six hundred. The majority were women, children, and men too old to participate actively in battle. All of them believed themselves to be under the protection of the U.S. Army. It is known that only six were taken prisoner, two women and four children, and that a few escaped on foot, Black Kettle among them. At sundown Chivington torched what remained of the village and prepared for his glorious return to Denver. The *Rocky Mountain News* proclaimed the conquest "among the brilliant feats of arms in Indian warfare."[10]

While the majority of Denver's predominantly white population approved of Chivington's action, a growing dissent echoed from more knowledgeable quarters. Ned Wynkoop, from his new post at Fort Riley, wrote letters denouncing Chivington's actions. His letters, along with those of unidentified "high officials" in the territory, brought three separate investigations, one by the Congress of the United States, one by the Army Department, and one by the commandant of the Military District of Colorado.

Silas Soule testified against Chivington and his troops at hearings resulting from the investigations. Following his outspoken testimony against the Colorado First and Third, identifying individual participants by name and action, he was assassinated on Lawrence Street, in broad daylight, by one of the regiment's soldiers. Soule's witness and subsequent death gave eerie credence to the French trappers' name River of Souls. The name of Sand Creek was changed to Medano Creek. Sometime after the tragedy the water disappeared from Sand Creek, as if unwilling to wash away the blood that once stained its golden sand.

Colonel Chivington, Major Anthony, and Governor Evans were all censured, with the blame laid primarily on Chivington. In his own defense Chivington wrote, "these Indians had threatened to attack the post, etc., and ought to be whipped."[11] After the Sand Creek Massacre the schism between white settlers and Native Americans deepened. The Cheyenne, Arapaho, Sioux, Kiowa, and Comanche increased their raids, waging a harder war against the flood of immigrants. The flood temporarily slowed to a trickle. Reports of the massacre and the escalation of Indian attacks made Colorado far less attractive to immigrants.

Machebeuf was within forty miles of Sand Creek when the massacre occurred. He would have been almost close enough to see the gathering vultures, certainly close enough to have heard reports of the massacre from the local, largely Hispanic, residents. But whatever misgivings he may have had about the events at Sand Creek are unrecorded. His own encounters with the tribes of the plains had always been friendly and not untouched by humor. On his return to Denver he could hardly have avoided the coverage the Denver papers focused on the subsequent hearings. But Machebeuf knew Chivington, and succeeded in making Chivington give something more than lip service to Christian ideals. Machebeuf succinctly recorded, "I once got $100 from a Methodist preacher for the convent, but he was a public man, a Colonel Chivington of the army. Thus Providence is assisting us in all sorts of ways."[12]

The years 1864 to 1866 brought changes to the character of many of the towns Machebeuf tended. Many of the stream beds were played out, and placer mining was on the decline. Many camps were deserted almost as quickly as they had been founded; others managed to survive, if not prosper. Caribou was one. Idaho Springs, Empire, and Georgetown continued as viable communities, but the camps and towns founded along the Arkansas River were beginning to disappear. The Blue River and Ten Mile regions no longer had the same intense mining activity, but enough people remained to occasionally require the services of a priest. As the mining activity declined, so, too, did the numbers of the most "unstable" element of the population, the opportunists drawn solely by the lure of gold.[13] Other parts of Colorado were just beginning to grow.

Colorado had proved itself to have good agricultural potential. Communities in the valleys, those whose economic base was tied to farming, grew at a slow but steady pace. Towns like Golden City, Mount Vernon, Morrison, Bradford, and Marshall began to take up more of Machebeuf's time. The fertile land around Boulder and the Big Thompson and Cache-la-Poudre Rivers had scattered Catholic settlers. In addition settlements on the Platte, on Cherry and Plum Creeks, and in the Bijou Basin now needed attention, as did the more southern communities like Colorado City, Pueblo, and Cañon City. New Mexican families continued to settle on the Purgatoire, or Las Animas River, as well as the Cucharas, the Huerfano, and the Greenhorn and move into the rich, vast San Luis Valley. Finally, the southern town of Trinidad was steadily growing and needed attention, although Lamy agreed to send Father Munnecom to tend to it.[14] And the demands on Machebeuf were not limited by the boundaries of the modern state of Colorado.

In October 1862 Col. P. E. Connor, heading up a group of U. S. volunteers from Nevada and California, established Fort Douglas in Salt Lake City. His duties were twofold — keep an eye on Indian activity in the region and keep an eye on the Mormons.[15] Since Utah was part of the Colorado Territory, responsibility for the spiritual needs of any Catholics that might be in that area fell on Machebeuf. In September 1864 Machebeuf sent Raverdy on a missionary visit to Utah to investigate the region and determine the number of Catholics that needed the services of a priest. Raverdy was warmly welcomed by Colonel Connor and spent some time ministering to the Catholic soldiers based at Fort Douglas. Otherwise, he found few Catholics in the area. Leaving Utah, he decided to extend his journey, traveling to Bannack City, Montana, where new gold strikes had been reported.

Before leaving Salt Lake, Raverdy decided to surprise Machebeuf. A great deal of fruit was being grown in the nearby valleys, while Colorado had few established orchards. As a special treat, he sent Machebeuf a big box of peaches. Machebeuf was surprised, but not by the fruit. He was shocked to find himself the recipient of a freight bill for sixty dollars. Knowing how rare peaches were in the area, Machebeuf made a quick series of calculations. He offered sixty of the peaches for sale, at the unheard of price of a dollar apiece. Having recouped his losses, he kept a few for himself, then distributed the rest to the students and Sisters of St. Mary's Academy.[16]

Peaches were not the only thing Machebeuf sent to the Sisters of Loretto at St. Mary's. In late August 1865 four Sisters of Charity arrived in Denver, en route to Santa Fe to establish what would become St. Vincent's Hospital. Sister Blandina Segale left an account of the stopover. "We made a stop in Denver, going directly to the Planter's Hotel. The Rt. Rev. J. P. Machebeuf was soon informed of our arrival, and he sent his carriage to have us conveyed to the Convent of the Sisters of Loretto, where, through the kindness of the Sisters, we soon forgot our past fatigues, and made preparations to continue our route to our destination." The Denver press caught wind of the sisters' visit but either misunderstood the purpose of their trip or were still caught up in the spirit of the gold rush. A footnote in Blandina's account reports, "The morning after their arrival in Denver one newspaper announced, 'Four Sisters of Charity are going to New Mexico to speculate.' "[17]

In the spring of 1866 Machebeuf wrote to his sister acknowledging the news of his aunt's death. "I cannot express to you the pain and sorrow I feel at the news of that dear aunt whom we have all had reason to love as a good mother," he wrote, then added philosophically, "if Providence gave her to us to lavish upon us the cares and affections of the mother whom we had the misfortune to lose so young, let us bless that same Providence which now takes her away, and show our gratitude to this good aunt and mother by offering our prayers and good works for her benefit."[18] The death cut one more tie with France. Both his parents were now dead, so was the aunt who had become his "second mother"; his brother, Marius, was married and had a family of his own; and Anne, Sister Philomène, was secure in the convent. Even had he wished to do so, he would have fewer and fewer reasons to return to France, and he would have more and more opportunities to offer good works in Colorado.

The previous fall had brought another trial to residents of the Colorado Territory — an epidemic of bloody dysentery swept through Denver. Even the strongest and healthiest members of the population contracted the disease, Machebeuf among them. Machebeuf, who had already survived cholera, typhoid, and malaria, seemed to be hit hard by the illness, and many people doubted whether he would recover. Over a two-week period reports of his death once again circulated, as they had done so many times before. He wrote of his illness to his sister: "Last September I had a severe attack of dysentery which was prevalent in Denver at that time, and claimed many victims, some of whom were my nearest neighbors." For once, he did not minimize the seriousness of his own illness, "I was so near the grave with it myself that more than once rumors of my death were spread throughout the city, and friends came to assure themselves of the foundations for the reports." His new friends in Denver might well have taken a few lessons from Lamy, who so many times had traveled to attend Machebeuf's funeral, only to find the irrepressible Machebeuf amused by his efforts. "I laughed at them and told them not to put themselves out about such reports, that at the proper time I myself would let them know of the day and hour of my funeral." Remembering his illness in Ohio and the nickname it produced, he quipped, "If Bishop Rappe knew of these rumors he would still have more reason to call me the Deceiver of Death (Trompe-la-Mort) than he had in 1849, when the newspapers of Sandusky put my name in the list of victims of cholera, or when I was reported dead in 1861."[19] Once again Machebeuf earned his title.

SIXTEEN

Reluctant Apostle

✦

In the final freezing days of February 1866, Machebeuf left on a trip through the Hispanic settlements in the southern part of the territory. His return brought him face to face with problems in Denver and Central City. Fr. Thomas Smith, whom he had assigned to the parish in Central City, would have to be removed. The Fenian movement had spread to Central City, and the good Father Smith, if not a part of the movement, was at least a strong sympathizer.

The Fenians, or the Irish Republican Brotherhood, were a secret, oath-bound society founded in 1858 by Dubliner James Stephens. Conspiring to organize an armed revolutionary overthrow of British rule in Ireland, the Fenians quickly came under episcopal scrutiny. Archbishop Cullen of Dublin and Bishop Moriarty of Kerry issued censures declaring the Fenians to be an "occult society." The Fenian paper, the *Irish People*, the bishops said, preached socialism and disrespect for all ecclesiastical authority. Cullen's pastoral of 10 October 1865, painted the movement as "a compound of folly and wickedness wearing the mask of patriotism." He declared it to be "the work of a few fanatics and knaves," giving a comprehensive summary of his ecclesiastical case against the Fenians.[1]

As early as 1858, founder James Stephens traveled to America looking for financial support from Irish American immigrants. Support was widespread in areas with large Irish Catholic populations, and the Fenians succeeded in raising hundreds of thousands of dollars for their cause. On 3 February 1866 Fenian orator J. J. Hynes boasted, "There are 4,000,000 Irish people in America. Four million at a dollar a head would fit out forty privateers with which every red flag could be struck down."[2]

The American bishops were slow to take any official position regarding the movement. In October 1864 Archbishop Spalding of Baltimore sent a circular letter to members of the U.S. Catholic hierarchy asking their opinions of the movement. His intent was to follow through by asking instructions of the Holy See so that the response of the U.S. bishops to the movement would be consistent.[3] The statement of the bishops' position would require some delicacy, as outright condemnation might estrange large portions of the Irish American community, one of the church's largest and most devout populations. Irish immigrants might feel pressured to choose between love of Ireland and Catholicism.

Unsettled by the revolutionary quality of the Fenians, Machebeuf wrote to Archbishop Kenrick in St. Louis, asking his advice on how to handle Smith's involvement. Kenrick's response left little room for doubt. "I have never changed the opinion I publicly expressed regarding the Fenian organization," Kenrick wrote to Machebeuf on 19 February 1866. "Its object is unlawful, to excite rebellion, and its spirit is decidedly hostile to Religion. The greater part of its adherents are dupes, for whom their blind spirit of hatred to England, which they identify with love of Ireland, justifies in their mind every act no matter how unlawful. The leaders are, for at least a greater part, abusing the confidence of their followers." Kenrick went on to tell Machebeuf, "For my own part I would not let any member of the organization to the Sacraments unless he were to promise to give up all connection with the Society." If Kenrick's feelings were so strong about members of the church being involved in the Fenian movement, Machebeuf could hardly allow one of his priests to participate openly.[4]

In May 1866 Lamy arrived for a pastoral visit. He found Machebeuf as busy as ever, making his rounds by buggy rather than on horseback, rarely finishing his paperwork before eleven at night. Machebeuf took Lamy everywhere. The two traveled to Central City to lay the cornerstone for a new church, and while there, removed Smith from the parish. Machebeuf was forced to send Raverdy to replace him, which he did on 1 June 1866. The transfer left Machebeuf solely responsible not only for Denver but for the rest of the missions as well.

Once back in Denver, Lamy and Machebeuf sang a pontifical high mass together on Trinity Sunday, with Machebeuf serving as deacon, Raverdy as subdeacon, and Lamy giving the homily. They found time to discuss Machebeuf's work in Colorado and the sharp contrasts between Colorado and New Mexico. Colorado was awash with Anglo-American residents. Its population had completely different cultural values from the residents of New Mexico. Yet with its money from mining and agriculture, Denver was already a richer city than Santa Fe. Lamy predicted that Colorado would soon be established as a separate vicariate apostolic and that there could be no doubt who should be its first bishop. Nothing would be settled until official acts had been promulgated, but Machebeuf seemed somewhat pleased by the prospect.[5]

Before returning to Santa Fe, Lamy promised to send another priest to replace Smith, but the replacement didn't arrive until the end of the year and didn't last long. The French priest, John Fauré, was excessively timid and spoke almost no English. The only help he could provide to Machebeuf was singing the mass, which he did, but even that was short-lived. Within a few months Fauré came down with typhoid. As soon as he was well enough to travel, he returned to New Mexico, leaving Machebeuf, once again, alone in Denver.[6] Machebeuf had little alternative but to "rest in action."

In October 1866 Lamy left Santa Fe to attend the First Plenary Council in Baltimore. Forty-five bishops and archbishops collectively reviewed the status of the church throughout the United States. Lamy presented proposals to the council for the creation of apostolic vicariates in Colorado and Arizona. The American bishops were impressed by Lamy, with his direct manner and rugged experience. In a show of confidence, they voted to name him courier to transport the reports of the council and present them to Pope Pius IX. On 16 December Lamy arrived in Rome.

As bishop of Santa Fe, Lamy had carried a tremendous burden for the past decade and a half. At fifty-two his dark hair had grayed and his handsome gaunt face was weathered by twenty-five years of missionary travel. After fifteen years of effort in the American Southwest, this was his initial report to the Vatican. Three territories, New Mexico, Colorado, and Arizona, made up the diocese of Santa Fe, which ministered to the needs of between 130,000 and 140,000 Catholics. The Catholic population of New Mexico stood at around 125,000. The vast majority, about 110,000, were Hispanic Catholics, but there were also some 15,000 Catholic Native Americans. The Catholic population of Colorado had grown to about 8,000, counting both New Mexicans in the south and the Anglo Americans in the north, but the Anglo population promised the most growth. Arizona held some 7,000 Catholic Hispanics and Native Americans.

Lamy now had fifty-one active priests, up from nine on his arrival: fourteen Hispanic priests, thirty-one French priests, and six from various other European countries. Eleven had either retired or been deprived of priestly functions. On his return to New Mexico, he hoped to take eight or ten more back with him, although he could use a hundred more. He now had thirty-one missions, but priests in residence in only seven churches and five chapels.[7] Lamy also had six convents of nuns, and a hospital and orphanage founded by four Sisters of St. Vincent de Paul, all established since his arrival.

Perhaps the hardest aspect to communicate to Europeans in the Vatican was the sheer vastness of the land he served. On his pastoral visit to Arizona alone he traveled more than three thousand miles on horseback. He had also made three pastoral visits to Colorado, each almost a thousand miles round trip. His 1851 trip to Durango, Mexico, was another three thousand miles. His diocese was three hundred leagues from north to south, just under a thousand miles, and almost as much from east to west. Although the railroad now reached St. Louis, one still had to cross nine hundred miles of plains and prairie to reach Santa Fe, all unsettled land subject to frequent raids by nomadic tribes. Regular visitations in the diocese could not follow the strict accordances of Canon Law — the distances were too great, the road conditions variable where roads existed at all, and the danger of Indian attacks a continuing reality.[8]

Lamy had cordial meetings with Pope Pius IX. After concluding his report to the Vatican, he filed a similar one with the Propaganda Fide, his greatest financial ally in Rome. He met with Cardinal Barnabo and asked for his help in recruiting Jesuits for Santa Fe. He had been trying to do so for thirteen years without success. The request to Barnabo brought a quick response. A few days later the general of the Jesuits, Father Beckx, called on him and assigned him three priests and two brothers from the province of Naples. They would sail with him on his return in May.[9]

For the next three months Lamy focused on recruitment efforts in Paris and Lyon, meeting with considerable success. In addition to the five Jesuits, he enlisted a priest and a deacon in Rome, six seminarians from Clermont, and two more Brothers of the Christian Doctrine. In the United States he hoped to collect more nuns from the Sisters of Loretto and the Sisters of Charity. By the time he reached St. Louis, in June 1867, he had a party of twenty-six in all.[10]

Lamy's trials, however, were far from over. On his return journey across the plains he met with hostile Indian raids. The *New York Herald*, on Friday, 19 July 1867, announced his demise to the world at large. The dispatch read, "A train was captured last Sunday, near Fort Larned, by the Indians. Bishop Lamy, ten priests, and six sisters of charity accompanied the train as passengers, en route to Santa Fe. The men were killed, scalped and shockingly mutilated. The females were carried away captive. This information comes through reliable sources."[11] The sources may not have been reliable, but the report might easily have been true.

On 23 July three hundred warriors attacked Lamy's train on the banks of the Arkansas River. About ninety armed men defended the train in a battle that raged for hours. Arrows filled the air with the sound of "a disturbed beehive" and bullets flew like hail. The youngest of the nuns, eighteen-year-old Sister Mary Alphonse was completely terrified. Another of Lamy's charges, a young business agent named Jules Masset, was dying of cholera, racked with abdominal cramps and crying for his mother. Masset was one of ten lost to cholera on the journey — buried on the grassy plains. Throughout the night the drunken voices of the Indians could be heard — they had captured one of the wagons and broken into a keg of brandy. "These seven hours of combat" made for "a terrible day" one of the priests said in a classic understatement. But the following morning there was no sign of the enemy. The nuns called Lamy to the bedside of Sister Alphonse where he "assisted her for death." She died at ten o'clock on the morning of 24 July. Alphonse, Lamy wrote, "was a girl beautifully educated, and a true model of piety and of all the virtues. . . . She died of terror."[12] The terrified young woman was buried by the trail in a crude coffin made of planks from one of the wagons.

Arriving in Santa Fe on the evening of Assumption Day, 15 August 1867, Lamy promptly wrote to the Propaganda Fide. He would send the details of the "long, laborious, and dangerous voyage across the prairies," but for now he merely discredited the erroneous reports of his death, assuring the society of his safe arrival in Santa Fe. The full report would have to wait a few days, for at the moment, he felt "a little tired."[13]

Lamy had been gone for almost a year. During his absence Machebeuf had struggled on with his missionary duties. He had Raverdy in Central City and Fr. Munnecom in Trinidad, but almost all the rest of the Colorado Territory was his sole responsibility. A few entries from his diary in August 1867 give a glimpse of his day-to-day-life. "Friday. — Mass at Mrs. Weaver's. Rec'd $7.00. Camped to-night on the Arkansas — alone! Saturday. — Crossed the Arkansas with buggy loaded on big wagon with two yoke of oxen. Camped at Weston's. . . . Sunday. — Start early. Mass at Guiraud's. Nice Trout. Monday. — Mass. Rec'd $10.00. Go to Farnum's. Tuesday, Aug. 20. — Junction House. Paid $5.00. Return to Denver. Found Father Raverdy in Denver." The entries cover twenty-two days, 350 miles of travel in his buggy, with mass, sermon, and confessions almost every day, and five special lectures. For his trouble Machebeuf collected a total of $200.00, an average of $9.00 a day. The diary also lists a recipe for the destruction of "vermin," or lice, just one of the smaller inconveniences he routinely encountered.[14]

In May 1867 he opened another church, this one in Golden City. Writing to his brother, Marius, he recorded, "I came home yesterday from Golden City — I should rather say Iron City, for there is no gold there, but they have found some very rich iron mines. Our little church there is almost finished, although there are but two Catholic families in the town, and these represent four different nationalities." Machebeuf never restricted his habitual begging to Catholics. He had no qualms about collecting donations from Americans of other religious background. "This winter I collected $1,600 for our convent from the Americans, who give with good grace," he explained. "I often state the sum that I expect them to give, and they smile and pay it to me. Then I show this to others and they give their share, too."[15]

By September 1867 he had news of Lamy's safe return. On the thirteenth he wrote to his sister to reassure her of Lamy's safety. "I hasten to answer your last letter, dated Aug. 11, in which you ask me to relieve your anxiety caused by reports of misfortune to Bishop Lamy and his party. I am happy to announce to you that Bishop Lamy arrived safely in Santa Fe." After giving her a short account of Lamy's harrowing journey across the plains he turned to happier subjects, the arrival of the three Spanish-speaking Jesuits who had traveled with Lamy. "The Belgian, whose name is De Blieck, is now giving a retreat to the Sisters in Santa Fe, and he will direct the retreat of the clergy in October." Delighted by the prospect of finally getting a little help, he wrote, "After that I expect this worthy Father, who was at one time president of the college in Cincinnati, and whom I knew there, to come to Denver."[16]

In his usual dramatic style he saved the more exciting news for the end of the letter. "Do you ask what he will do in Denver? Notwithstanding the hesitation I feel in touching upon a question which is no longer a secret from you, I must say the matter of a vicariate for Colorado seems to be settled. I have news from Bishop Lamy and others, and I only wait the return of the Archbishop of St. Louis from Rome for positive assurance that I am named to preside over it."

Machebeuf's feelings toward the appointment were far from settled. He had grave reservations about the possibility of being named a bishop. For the first time his letters carry something other than consistent optimism, an undertone of strain and fatigue. Continuing the letter to his sister he told her, "I cannot commit to paper my feelings in the matter, nor the reasons which make me tremble at the thought of such a position being offered to me." Far from being pleased by the prospect, he told her, "I have already taken some steps to avoid it, and I intend to protest still more before things go too far, but if I am obliged to bend to the burden and accept the inevitable, Father De Blieck will take my place here in Denver and remain during the time when I shall necessarily be absent." The letter closes with an air of resignation, an edge of almost despairing fatigue. "I hope that Providence will dispose events so as to relieve me of this burden, for my responsibility is already too heavy, rendered so by personal and local considerations and circumstances which I may take occasion to explain to you when we are face to face." But any further explanation in writing, Machebeuf judged indiscrete. He closed with his usual plea, "Pray always for the poor cripple!"[17]

As the long months of winter slowly passed, Machebeuf mulled over the prospect of becoming a bishop. He had good reasons for his misgivings. He was fifty-five years old. His mobility was greatly restricted since the accident six years earlier, and periodically his injury caused him considerable pain. He could no longer ride astride, but was restricted to travel by buggy, and of late, he had taken to using a cane. Even the limited mobility required to sing the mass was a problem for him. Nor were his problems limited to his physical condition.

The Irish in the Denver parish were showing signs of active hostility. The resistance, he admitted, was partly because of "my quick and passionate temper."[18] But the hostility was also, in part, a result of the dismissal of Thomas Smith for his involvement with the Fenians. Following his instructions from Archbishop Kenrick in St. Louis, Machebeuf had publicly opposed the brotherhood. It was a difficult position to take, as large numbers of Irish men had flocked to the mines of Colorado. Because of Machebeuf's opposition to the Fenians, most of his Irish parishioners refused to contribute to his church. Finally, Machebeuf's finances were in worse condition than usual. Long accustomed to robbing Peter to pay Paul, Machebeuf had borrowed large sums of money to secure land for future growth of the church and more to meet the constant payments needed to service the loans.

In the middle of March, De Blieck arrived from Santa Fe. Machebeuf was happy to have the help, especially from a man he had known for many years, since his time in Cincinnati in the 1840s. De Blieck promptly fell ill, forcing Machebeuf to complete his mission in Denver, but still Machebeuf was glad for the company. He discussed his reservations about accepting the bishopric with De Blieck. By the end of March he had made up his mind. He wrote Purcell in Cincinnati that "his Jesuit friend" had persuaded him it was his duty to accept. Besides, he realized that his self-respect demanded him facing and resolving his troubled financial affairs. "I would feel truly ashamed to leave the temporal affairs of the Church in such a bad shape. My earnest desire is then to pay the debts, with the assistance of God, and leave to another better qualified a clear field for future administration."[19]

Cardinal Barnabo, the Prefect of the Propaganda Fide, had written to Machebeuf on 24 January 1868, informing him of his appointment. The Brief erecting the vicariate was dated 3 March 1868, and the Bulls officially appointing Machebeuf were issued on 16 March 1868. In April Machebeuf wrote to his sister, "I am upon the eve of that terrible journey to Cincinnati which I can put off no longer." His new position was no longer theoretical: "Two months ago today I received from Cardinal Barnabo the official notice of my appointment as Vicar Apostolic of Colorado and Utah. The Bulls have not yet come, but I read today in the *Catholic Telegraph of Cincinnati* a copy of a letter from Rome which gives the title of each bishop elect, and that which falls to my heritage is Bishop of Epiphany in partibus infidelium." Machebeuf would leave the following morning, "I must go immediately while the Jesuit Father is here to take charge of the parish." He would first make a series of stops for fund-raising and recruiting, ending up in Cincinnati for his consecration, when he would become the first bishop of "a diocese larger than the whole of France."[20]

On 21 April Machebeuf left Denver. During his absence, De Blieck would tend his parish, assisted by a young French priest Lamy had sent up from Santa Fe, Father Matthonet. The first stage of the journey was across the plains — to Cheyenne, Omaha, Leavenworth, and St. Louis. From St. Louis it was a quick jump to Cincinnati. There he met with Purcell and made his first appeal for donations, on a journey described as "literally a begging tour for men and means."[21]

In July he found himself in New York. The city must have brought up memories of his arrival in America twenty-six years before. It also brought a sense of loneliness, which he sought to ease by writing to his brother, Marius. "Finding myself separated from Clermont by a voyage of only ten or twelve days, I cannot continue my journey without bidding you good day in passing."[22] He gave Marius a brief itinerary of his travels since leaving Denver three months before. "I leave here tomorrow for Montreal. . . . After fifteen days spent in Cincinnati and Brown county I went to Baltimore, where I spent more than a month, then seven days in Philadelphia and twelve in New York." Machebeuf's exhaustion can be clearly read between the lines.

During Machebeuf's visit in Baltimore, Archbishop Spalding clearly understood the problems the new bishop faced. On 25 May 1868 he gave Machebeuf an honest if not entirely flattering letter of authorization to solicit funds. "The bearer," the letter states, "the Rt. Rev. Dr. Machebeuf, Vicar Apostolic-Elect of Colorado and Utah, being very destitute and in great need of help, has permission to receive donations from the benevolent Catholics of the Archdiocese of Baltimore, and being an old, efficient, devoted and worthy missionary, he is warmly recommended to the charity of the faithful."[23]

With Marius, Machebeuf could be far more candid about his financial concerns than he had been with his sister. "As you are a man of business," he wrote from New York, "I must tell you that in 1863–4 I exhausted all the resources of New Mexico to secure at Denver favorable locations for churches, schools, convents, hospitals, cemetery, etc., hoping that the increased Catholic immigration would furnish me the means of existence, but since the war the high taxes are ruining us." He saw no hope for a reversal in his situation until the railroad came to Denver, and progress on the railroad had been slowed by the drain of manpower and materials created by the Civil War. "I was obliged to borrow money from the banks and from private individuals at very high rates of interest, and thus I have increased my indebtedness to a considerable sum." Some of these loans "from private individuals" carried interest rates of over 30 percent. For weeks Machebeuf had solicited investors in the cities he visited, with titles and descriptions of the properties in hand to use as collateral, but few understood the current or potential value of land in distant Colorado. He hoped to find someone willing to consolidate his loans and carry them at a more reasonable rate of interest. "It was only here in New York that I succeeded in finding a man who would help me. He is an American and a good Catholic. He knew the value of the church holdings in Denver and in the vicinity, and he assisted me greatly in my present difficulties." At last Machebeuf had found an ally who could help relieve some of the pressure he felt, a benefactor who would continue to play an increasingly important part in his financial future.[24]

Machebeuf's angel was Catholic philanthropist and banker Eugene Kelly. Their meeting was the beginning of a close relationship, one that would last until 1882. Before his death in the 1890s, Kelly was given special recognition by the Pope for the years of generosity and support he had shown for numerous Catholic projects. His patience, consistent concern, and fairness with Machebeuf over the years proved him to be deserving of the honor. In their 1867 meeting, the banker gave Machebeuf a loan of ten thousand dollars at 10 percent annual interest. He loaned Machebeuf the money, not from the resources of the Exchange Bank he headed, but from his own personal funds, taking the property in Denver as collateral. His motive, he later wrote, was "to prove to the world that a missionary Bishop who spends his life for the good of others can inspire some in this unfaithful world."[25]

Nor had Machebeuf's numerous other fund-raising appeals been unsuccessful. Concluding the New York letter to his brother he wrote, "I have made many interesting visits [in New York], and managed to collect over $600 for my missions and a number of presents of things necessary for a bishop."[26]

From New York Machebeuf moved on to Albany, Troy, Burlington, Montreal, Toronto, Buffalo, and Cleveland. In addition to the fund-raising appeals, he visited seminaries in Cincinnati, Baltimore, Emmetsburg, Philadelphia, Troy, Montreal, and Cleveland, hoping to recruit more priests or advanced seminarians for his missions, but with little success. By the end of July he found himself in Cleveland visiting with his old friend Amadeus Rappe, the bishop of Cleveland and the man who first dubbed him "Trompe-la-Mort." Writing to his sister he reported, "I have been obliged to postpone my consecration until August 16, to give me time to find a good priest, as I told Marius, and I have not yet succeeded in my search." Those willing to undertake work in distant Colorado were either too young or could not be spared by their own bishops. "I found several French and Irish students, but they cannot be ordained before two or three years. Several zealous priests offered to devote themselves to the missions in Colorado, but they could not get the consent of their bishops, all of whom complain of the lack of good priests." Again, he outlined the travel that lay ahead of him in the days ahead. First he would return to Sandusky to visit his old parish and his many friends there. After Sandusky he would stop in Cincinnati again, then he'd be off "to visit the Motherhouse of the Sisters of Loretto in Kentucky, to see if I can get two or three more Sisters. Then I shall go to the Trappists, who have a fine house close by at a place called Gethsemane. There I shall make my retreat and return to Cincinnati for the Assumption and the consecration."[27]

The same day he wrote his sister, 29 July, he first donned the robes of a bishop and as bishop-elect received the profession of several nuns at the Ursuline Convent in Cleveland. Afterward he sang the high mass and gave the benediction. The emotions of the experience overwhelmed him. His choking voice almost failed him.

Strong emotions also accompanied his return to Sandusky, the town that had been his home for almost ten years and that he had left eighteen years before when he accompanied Lamy to New Mexico. The parishioners held a huge reception for their former priest. For four days they showered him with praise, affection, and gifts. Nor had they forgotten his unorthodox approach to finances, his midwinter trip to Montreal to pay the creditors on their own church. He left Sandusky with an extra $180 in his pocket.[28]

Machebeuf spent a day in Columbus with Bishop Rosecrans, two more in Cincinnati making final arrangements for his consecration, and made a brief visit to the Sisters of Loretto. According to the sisters, the visit was too brief. They waited for him for three months, they complained, and he only stayed for three hours![29] The same Sisters of Loretto had donated land in a nearby valley to the Cistercians, sometimes called the Trappists, who established a monastery in Gethsemane. Bishop Flaget, formerly of Bardstown, the same leathery missionary who accompanied Machebeuf on his first trans-Atlantic crossing, had welcomed the Trappists in Louisville twenty years before.[30] Machebeuf left the Sisters of Loretto to begin his episcopal retreat at the Trappist Abbey of Gethsemane.

In the sticky, humid warmth of the Kentucky summer, he rode through thick forests of cedar and hickory, oak, maple, and walnut, the dense green broken occasionally by the mottled branches of a sycamore. Reaching the summit of a low hill, he saw below him a broad valley stretching out to a line of distant blue hills, the air tinged with the sharp scent of pine.

Crossing a creek shaded by cedar, his carriage rolled into open fields. On a knoll stood the log-cabin monastery, built at the site of the sisters' orphanage, Our Lady of Gethsemane, in the midst of what the monks called St. Joseph's field, a wide expanse dominating the center of the blue valley.[31] Entering the monastery for his episcopal retreat, Machebeuf found serenity amid the silent, white-robed monks. Under the direction of Father Jerome, he searched for the strength he would need in the trying days ahead. He renewed his devotion to the Blessed Virgin, to whom he had dedicated his missionary vocation so many years before, pleased that his consecration would come the day after the Feast of the Assumption. It seems his Second Mother continued to watch over him, for on 16 August 1868, the rather reluctant apostle would officially become the bishop of Epiphany.

Part Five

Bishop of Epiphany: Colorado

1868–1889

SEVENTEEN

Renewal

✧

Five days after his fifty-sixth birthday, Machebeuf was consecrated in Cincinnati. Sunday, 16 August 1868, Machebeuf received the title bishop of Epiphany in partibus infidelium. Epiphany, in a broad sense, means the manifestation of the Divine or a manifestation through miraculous effects. Considering it was nothing short of miraculous that Machebeuf became a bishop at all and only divine intervention had kept him alive long enough to be consecrated, it was a fitting title for the aging missionary.

The Greeks first used the word epiphany for the manifestation of a divinity, and later, to mark important events in the life of a king. Use of the word in a Christian sense can be traced back to St. Paul, and in the third century, Clement of Alexandria commemorated the baptism of Christ as the Epiphany. By the fourth century the Feast of Epiphany embraced the birth of Christ, His baptism, the adoration of the Magi, and the miracle of the wedding at Cana. The date, 6 January, marks the end of the twelve days of Christmas. As the three vows of religion have been compared to the three gifts of the Magi, members of religious orders traditionally renew their vows on Epiphany Sunday.[1] For Machebeuf the consecration marked a renewal in his own life, an even greater commitment to his life in the church. He had overcome doubts about his ability to meet the responsibilities of a bishopric. Fully aware of the difficulties before him, he knelt before God and church, accepting the challenge of the episcopacy.

The people of Cincinnati crowded into the Cathedral of St. Peter in Chains for the elaborate event and the opportunity to see three bishops as well as their own archbishop. Priests from all over the archdiocese traveled to attend — not missionary priests, such as Machebeuf had been in Ohio, but younger men serving in parishes carved out of the wilderness by the work of Machebeuf and his friends. Archbishop Purcell, as the consecrating prelate, presided as the man he recruited in France three decades earlier became the first bishop of the Vicariate Apostolic of Colorado and Utah. The final words of his title, 'in partibus infidelium,' referred to the transitional status of these territories, lands where the church was not yet fully established, where no diocesan see had yet been recognized. Assisting Purcell were Bishops Rappe and De Goesbriand, who had been recruited by Purcell on the same trip, accompanied Machebeuf on their first trans-Atlantic crossing in 1839, and worked beside him for ten years in Ohio.[2] The only one missing was Machebeuf's best friend, Lamy. Lamy wanted to attend, he explained in a letter to Purcell, but he could not afford a journey "so far and so costly." Nor could he justify imposing the expense of the trip on his impoverished diocese.[3]

After the moving ceremony of the consecration, Machebeuf said his first mass as bishop at the Convent of the Sisters of Notre Dame, his emotions so visibly powerful he barely finished the service. He spent two days resting, absorbing the impact of the event, then set out for Denver on 19 August. Apparently the Sisters of Loretto, although they had chided him for his neglect, harbored no hard feelings toward Machebeuf. Five more of the sisters met him in St. Louis to travel with him to Denver. There they would join the seven already at work at St. Mary's Academy.[4]

En route, during a stopover in Leavenworth, Machebeuf paused long enough to send his relatives in France his episcopal benediction. "May the good God grant you health and prosperity," he wrote. Remembering his own recent struggle to accept his new position, he added, "and above all, the fidelity to fulfill all your religious duties. May Divine Providence protect all of you and preserve you for many years in peace, in union, and in the grace of God." Having been told that one of Marius's sons, Jules, had shown an inclination toward the priesthood, Machebeuf eagerly encouraged the young man. "Bishop Lamy," he continued, "left at the seminary in Baltimore a nephew for his ecclesiastical education — how happy I would be if one day I could have near me one of my own dear nephews as a help and consolation to his bishop-uncle who begins to feel the weight of his infirmities, but whose health and courage, thanks to God, are not failing." Closing, he wished his family "a thousand blessings."[5]

Machebeuf and the five sisters traveled from Leavenworth to Omaha, where they boarded a train to Cheyenne. On 28 August, they transferred to a stage coach. No doubt Machebeuf compared the relative ease of the journey with his previous trips across the plains to Santa Fe. The advent of the railroad was bringing remarkable changes to the West.

The party arrived in Denver the following afternoon, and the Catholics of that city celebrated the return of their first bishop. Father Raverdy, the Sisters of Loretto, and a number of prominent citizens greeted Machebeuf several miles outside of town, escorting him to a grand reception, complete with an address by Gen. B. M. Hughes. The day after his arrival he returned the favor, officially beginning his duties as vicar apostolic to Colorado and Utah by celebrating a pontifical mass and officiating at pontifical vespers.[6]

The office of missionary bishop left little time for leisure. Nothing had really changed in Colorado, except the official designation of his status. Machebeuf still had only three priests serving under him in both territories; Raverdy in Central City, and two others, Munnecom and Rolly, in the southern part of Colorado. The trip had eased his immediate financial concerns, but he still had almost no money, more than enough debts, and a responsibility to thousands of Catholics over an area of hundreds of miles. He could no longer expect financial help from Lamy in Santa Fe, nor could he count on him to send additional priests. Now Machebeuf would be the one responsible for recruiting clergy in Colorado and Utah. He would be the one to assume the financial burden of building churches, schools, and hospitals.

A week after he arrived in Denver, he visited his principal parish, Central City. Within a few days he returned to Denver, loaded up his carriage, and left on his first official pastoral visit, an extended trip to visit dozens of Catholic communities in Colorado. He made his usual tour of the towns in South Park, then crossed the mountains to California Gulch. Moving down the Arkansas River, he ran into an encampment of eight hundred Ute Indians outside of Salida. With winter fast approaching, they were short on food. Machebeuf divided up his food supplies, giving them all but what he needed to make the next town, and headed from Salida over Poncha Pass in the north end of the San Luis Valley. After a stop at Fort Garland, he spent ten days stopping at each of the scattered communities in the valley. At each town or village, he sang the mass, heard confessions, and gave confirmations. In the larger towns he formed committees to build churches or chose locations for chapels.[7]

From the San Luis Valley he continued south, stopping to visit Gabriel Ussel in Taos. Ussel surprised him by gathering ten priests together to congratulate him on his new assignment, providing an excuse to spend a few days visiting with old friends. From Taos he went to Santa Fe, to see his best friend. One can imagine the conversations between the two men, remembering their furtive flight from Clermont as young idealistic priests, eager for adventure in the wilds of America. Now they were both bishops, both mature leaders with decades of missionary experience behind them. Having known enough adventure, neither was particularly eager for more.

Lamy had already sent official notification of the change in jurisdiction to Denver, but the letter arrived after Machebeuf's departure. On 21 September 1868 he had written to Machebeuf, telling him he was "happy to turn over to [Machebeuf's] jurisdiction the Catholics of Colorado Territory who were before in our diocese."[8] Two days after his arrival in Santa Fe, Machebeuf took the now familiar route back to Denver, through Las Animas, Trinidad, Huerfano, Pueblo, and Colorado Springs. By the middle of November, eight weeks after his departure, he had returned to Denver.

Colorado was not his only responsibility. He was also now vicar apostolic to Utah. On 23 November he set out for a pastoral visit to determine the needs of Catholics in the Utah Territory. A stagecoach took him north to Cheyenne, where he stayed with William Rowland, formerly a neighbor in Denver. The Union Pacific Railroad took him to the end of the line, Laramie, but a construction train reached as far as Green River. Transferring again to a stage, he arrived in Fort Bridger just before midnight. There was no hotel in the small Wyoming town, so the bishop of Epiphany wrapped himself in his buffalo robe and slept on sacks in a grain store. After a final leg over the mountains in another rattling coach, he arrived in Salt Lake City, six days after his departure from Denver.[9]

General Connor, the commanding officer at Fort Douglas, offered him every hospitality, and Machebeuf stayed with him for a week. He sang the mass, prepared a confirmation class for some of the soldiers in the fort, and confirmed them a week later. Machebeuf also took the opportunity to meet with Brigham Young and other leaders of the Mormon Church in an attempt to assure cooperation between members of the two religions. The Mormons could hardly have considered the Catholic presence a threat. Machebeuf found only four Catholic families in Salt Lake, but enough to begin work on a church. A site for the church was already secured, and one of the Catholic families, the Carrolls, occupied a house on the property. After completing the needed baptisms and marriages, Machebeuf returned to Denver.[10]

Machebeuf left Salt Lake in a blinding snowstorm on 10 December 1868. He met several delays on his return journey — his coach turned over in the Bear River one night, soaking all the passengers, he missed the construction train at Green River, and he stopped to tend to men working on the railroad at Bryant. Along the way, his buffalo robe was stolen, and when he finally made it back to Denver, he had caught cold riding in the drafty stagecoach the final hundred miles from Cheyenne.

Once back in Denver, he penned a report of the trip for the Society for the Propagation of the Faith in Paris. Explaining the stopovers on his return trip, he wrote, "there are a great number, perhaps eight to ten thousand workers employed in the construction of the railroad. . . . In the forts of Camp-Douglas and Bridger . . . there are many Catholic officers and soldiers that also demand the services of a priest. I hope to respond, during the course of the year, to all of their needs." Machebeuf seemed optimistic about his ability to service the Catholic population in distant Utah. "On my return from Europe, where I will be going very soon," he concluded the report, "I hope to make a second visit to Utah, to secure land for churches and schools, in the new towns that will certainly be constructed along the line of the Pacific Railroad."[11]

Machebeuf remained in Denver for the Christmas season, then left again in February, spending most of the month visiting Trinidad and the southern missions. By the end of his first six months as bishop, Machebeuf had traveled more than twenty-six hundred miles. He used the railroad and stagecoaches where possible, but the majority of his traveling, almost two-thirds of it, had been made in his own buggy during the coldest months of the year. Once again in Denver, in March 1869, Machebeuf received sad news from home. His nephew, Jules, the one family member who might someday assist him in his old age, was dead. "After the terrible blow which has fallen upon us in the death of our dear Jules," Machebeuf wrote his bereaved brother, "I feel the need of assuring you of my sincerest affection and my deepest feeling of sympathy in the great sorrow that has come upon you. . . . It is my sorrow also, for he was my Jules, and you know he gave himself to me with such a good heart. In the midst of my grave obligations and heavy occupations tears found time to flow in abundance." Jules's death was not the only bad news Machebeuf faced in the spring of 1869.[12]

While Machebeuf was singing mass on Sunday, 18 April, a fire swept through St. Mary's Academy. None of the sisters or their students was injured, and a portion of the building was saved, but the loss represented a setback in terms of time and money. Machebeuf immediately began raising funds to rebuild and enlarge the structure, and issued contracts for the work. He had planned to leave in April on a trip to Europe, for recruitment and his first episcopal visit to Rome. The trip had to be delayed.

Originally he had arranged to travel with Jean Baptiste Salpointe, then stationed in Mora, New Mexico. Four months after Machebeuf was appointed vicar apostolic to Colorado and Utah, Salpointe was appointed vicar apostolic to Arizona. Salpointe would be consecrated in Clermont, and Machebeuf had hoped to accompany him for the event. Salpointe could not delay his trip and left as planned, with Machebeuf's assurance he would follow as soon as possible. Machebeuf teased Salpointe about the hasty departure, saying he "may have special reasons for wishing to arrive in France before me. He will have his choice of missionaries and I shall come only to glean."[13] In reality he didn't mind; he was far more interested in recruiting Irish and German priests than the French priests Salpointe would find at Clermont.

Within two weeks Machebeuf had the repairs at St. Mary's underway. On 3 May he left Denver. Taking a coach to Sheridan, Kansas, he stopped in Leavenworth and Topeka, then proceeded to St. Louis. He visited with the Sisters of Loretto in Cairo and stayed in Louisville before visiting St. Thomas's Seminary at Bardstown in hope of recruiting seminarians. He stopped once again to visit the Sisters of Loretto at their motherhouse in Kentucky, visited with Purcell in Cincinnati, then made further recruitment stops at Baltimore, Philadelphia, and Troy. Arriving in New York, he missed the French steamer on which he had originally booked passage. Waiting a fortnight for the next, the delay meant Machebeuf missed Salpointe's consecration in Clermont. He arrived in Brest, France, on 21 June; Salpointe had been consecrated the day before. No longer having any reason to hurry, Machebeuf stopped at a seminary in Rennes for ordinations and a recruitment pitch. Once in Paris, he submitted a report to the Society for the Propagation of the Faith, along with the first of many requests for funds.[14]

Finally arriving in Riom, he spent a day with his sister and two more at Clermont. In Riom he officiated and gave confirmation in the college where he had studied forty years before, departing with Salpointe on 11 July. The two traveled leisurely toward Rome, stopping at Lyon, Fourviére, Chambéry, Grand Chartreuse, and Anecy. The Mont Cenis tunnel took them to Turin, and they paused briefly at Ancona and Loreto. On 23 July they arrived in Rome.[15]

This was Machebeuf's third trip to Rome. The first had been as a penniless missionary, a young, wide-eyed tourist infatuated with the city's history and spirituality. The second had been as an advocate, defending Lamy and himself against the charges brought by New Mexican Hispanics. This time he came as bishop, for his visit ad limina Apostolorum. Each visit marked a distinct period of his life, a change in his status and relationship with the church.

The two new bishops stayed in Rome for twelve days. The aging aristo-cratic Pope Pius IX was most gracious, meeting with the missionary bish-ops on three separate occasions. He examined maps of their territories, heard reports on the status of the church and the work to be done, and discussed the problems of their respective vicariates. Acknowledging the importance of their work and the many demands on their time, he excused the two from otherwise mandatory attendance at the Vatican Council of 1870. "You cannot wait for the Council," said Pius, "you have too much to do to organize your vast dioceses." With a twinkle in his eye, smiling affectionately at the new bishops, he added, "In any case, being only young bishops, you have not yet much experience and could not give us much assistance!"[16]

Excused from the council, their meetings in Rome concluded, Mache-beuf and Salpointe headed back to Clermont, traveling by way of Pisa, Florence, Milan, the Simplon, and Geneva. Salpointe decided to return directly to America, but Machebeuf lingered on in Clermont, where he was warmly welcomed by friends, family, and relatives. "I am overcrowded with a thousand things," he wrote back to Raverdy in Colorado. "I never was so busy receiving and returning visits, attending dinners which I cannot re-fuse, officiating, preaching, presiding." He had another reason for the de-lay, as he explained to Raverdy. "I am sorry that I am detained so long, but I cannot help it. I must wait until the opening of the seminaries, the colleges, and the academies in order to get some means from the boarders." In the interim he wrote to Irish seminaries hoping to recruit seminarians, then made travel arrangements to go to Dublin and surrounding areas.[17]

On 5 September Machebeuf officiated at the laying of the cornerstone of a new church in Volvic, the town where his father was born, where his grandfather's home was located, and where he had spent so many summers in his youth. In the course of the sermon Machebeuf lectured the town folk, saying that parishes half their size had churches of cut stone, admonishing them for living in the midst of quarries and not planning a stone church themselves. Ten years later, when he again visited Volvic, he found they had taken his advice and constructed a church of cut stone. Machebeuf's mo-tives when officiating were not always so altruistic. Relentless beggar that he was, he also took time to press his hosts for funds. "I have not lost my time," he told Raverdy, "for if I have to officiate, preach and accept dinners, I make them pay pretty well for it." His begging was not limited to pressur-ing his hosts. In Clermont Machebeuf received word that the Society for the Propagation of the Faith had approved an advance of twenty-five thou-sand francs, almost twelve thousand dollars.[18]

From Clermont Machebeuf headed to Ireland, hoping to find seminarians that might help to smooth his troubled relationship with the Irish
American population in Denver. The Fenian insurrection had been successfully put down the same year, and he had little fear of finding another
revolutionary in the Irish seminaries. He stopped first in Dublin, then
visited the colleges of All Hallows', Carlow, Kilkenny, and Maynooth. How
lush the Irish landscape must have appeared to Machebeuf, after his long
years in the American Southwest. He traveled through the countryside
James Joyce would later describe as "the peerless panorama of Ireland's
portfolio, unmatched . . . for very beauty, of bosky grove and undulating
plain and luscious pastureland of vernal green, steeped in transcendent
translucent glow of our mild mysterious Irish twilight."[19] How civilized and
contained the gray stone of the Irish seminaries must have appeared after
years of sleeping in adobe houses and rough wooden structures or under
the stars of the endless Rocky Mountain sky.

At the Irish seminaries Machebeuf found a number of students eager to
go to Colorado, but as he could not afford to underwrite their fare across
the Atlantic, he left without them.[20] He did manage to return to America
with four recruits: Fathers Joseph Percevault and Francis Guyot whom he
ordained in Rennes; one deacon, Philibert Domergue; and Rev. Thomas
McGrath, who would sail from Ireland and meet him in St. Louis. Landing
in New York on 17 November, he was back in Denver on 5 December,
urging the members of his diocese to help raise money for a new house to
better accommodate their four new priests.

In July 1870 the long-awaited railroad to Denver was completed. With
the railroad came a surge in population, and Machebeuf's Denver church
was soon too small to accommodate his growing congregation. Machebeuf
decided to expand it, adding side chapels, extending the front, building a
tower, and raising the roof to align with the new dimensions.

His financial resources failed to match either the growth of his congregation or his plans for the church. In the early months of 1870, letters to his
brother were not without the usual plea for money. "I am organizing two
new parishes, and I have applied for the Sisters of Charity for a hospital," he
wrote Marius on 3 January, "but this is a heavy expense and my house will
cost a good sum. For the house I count upon you to borrow some money
for me."[21]

In April Lamy finished attending the Vatican Council and notified Machebeuf he would be passing through France on his way back to Santa
Fe. "Bishop Lamy wrote me that he would return in May," Machebeuf
promptly relayed to his brother, "and this will be a good opportunity for

you to send me, if possible, 10,000 or 12,000 francs. I had to borrow money at high interest to finish my house."[22]

Machebeuf saved complaints of his difficulties in staffing the vicariate for his sister. "A young German student, almost ready to be ordained, let himself be frightened at the thought of the dangers and difficulties of the ministry here and refused to come," he reported. He also had problems with those who did come. "Even my young priest, Domergue, played an ugly trick on me. While waiting his turn for a place in the Mexican portion of the Diocese, he became discouraged and ran away with the intention of joining the Trappists. The Bishop of Omaha stopped him and sent him back to me, ashamed and repentant."[23]

Financially strapped, with ongoing difficulties finding clergy for Colorado, Machebeuf began to question his ability to provide for the few Catholic families living in Utah. He wrote to the Pope, the Prefect of the Propaganda and several American bishops. In 1871 Archbishop Alemany of San Francisco agreed to provide the manpower to staff it, and Utah was transferred to his jurisdiction. Finalizing details of the transfer, the two men began corresponding, and a lasting friendship grew out of their letters.

His friendship with Raverdy was also deepening. Raverdy had shown himself to be tried and true, a loyal man upon whom he could always rely. Toward the end of 1871 Machebeuf wrote of his increasing respect for the priest who had first accompanied him to Colorado and labored beside him for over ten years. "The good Father Raverdy is my secretary . . . administrator in my absence, and my man of business to keep my books and regulate my accounts." Considering Machebeuf's style of financial management, that role alone might recommend Raverdy for canonization; it certainly qualified as heroic virtue. The strain evidently showed. Worried about Raverdy's health, Machebeuf decided to send him to Europe as soon as he could spare him. "The voyage will do him good, and the consolation of seeing his parents whom he left twelve years ago will, I hope, have the effect of making him a well and strong man again."[24]

Machebeuf received a great boost in his recruitment attempts in 1871 due to the intervention of Colorado's first territorial governor, William Gilpin. In the 1860s Gilpin had purchased part of the Sangre de Cristo land grant in southwestern Colorado from Taos trader and scout Céran St. Vrain. The former governor hoped to promote better relations between the Hispanic population and the territorial government. Gilpin's wife was Catholic, although he was not, and he became convinced that the best way to improve relations between the Hispanic and Anglo cultures was through the efforts of Catholic priests. Gilpin had already communicated his interest to Machebeuf's old friend the Jesuit missionary Peter J. de Smet, but nothing had come of it.

Early in 1871 Gilpin offered to donate a portion of the land to the Jesuits if they would staff and build a school. De Smet forwarded the request to the Reverend Donato Gasparri, the superior of the Neapolitan Jesuits in New Mexico.[25] The request arrived after the Jesuits' 1860 exile from Naples in the turmoil of Italian unification.

In August of the same year, Machebeuf wrote to Gasparri, asking for Jesuits to work in Colorado, offering support for the construction of a college. Machebeuf was eager to have the Jesuits' presence in the valley. At the time he had only two priests in the area, Father Rolly in Conejos, on loan from New Mexico, and Father Munnecom, stationed in Trinidad and complaining of poor health. The timing of the two requests may not have been entirely accidental. Regardless, the Jesuits replied favorably to both offers. On 9 December 1871 Salvatore Persone, S.J., and a Jesuit brother reached Conejos to begin work in Colorado. Two months later they were joined by Fr. Alexander Leone and another brother. Their mission included three thousand Catholics, living in twenty-five different towns and villages, in a territory 120 miles long and 25 miles wide. In their first year the Jesuit fathers heard twenty-five hundred confessions. For the previous twelve years Machebeuf had served the entire area almost singlehandedly.[26]

By June 1872 Machebeuf as usual had developed grand plans for the valley. "In the San Luis Valley, 200 miles southwest of Denver, we have two parishes, and another will be formed as soon as I have a priest for it," he proudly wrote his sister in France. "A rich English company which owns 40,000 acres of land in the valley has offered me ground for a college under the direction of the Jesuit Fathers." Machebeuf told his sister of his plans to meet their superior in a few weeks and confidently predicted, "when the college is built I shall give them charge of the entire valley, which is cut off from the rest of the Territory by high mountains."[27]

In the same exuberant letter, Machebeuf boasted to his sister what a grand city Denver had become. The population had more than doubled in the last two years, he explained, before giving her a summary of the expansion and renovation of his church. Additionally, there were numerous improvements to report. Particularly excited by running water, he described the steam pump that provided pressurization for the water supply. He completed his description explaining, "the lawns, gardens, walks, bordered with shrubs and flowers, are sprinkled by means of rubber tubes which a child can handle, and the force of the water is such that a stream can be sent to any part of the yard by merely directing the nozzle." The water lines were not the only improvement. "The streets are lined with trees, and the houses with their lawns give beauty and healthfulness. . . . You see that our town is putting on the airs of a great city."[28]

Buoyed by his recent successes, Machebeuf had recovered his confidence. Once again he was his optimistic self. Denver was becoming a great city, and a great city needed schools, churches, and hospitals. A great city needed a bishop like Machebeuf — happiest when he could rest in action, at his best when he had too much to do, with a scope and vision as vast as the Rocky Mountains. As the year 1872 drew to a close, Machebeuf reviewed his achievements and the burgeoning growth of the Colorado Territory. The railroad had come. The Indian Wars were all but over. The time of renewal had begun.

EIGHTEEN

Two Steps Forward

✧

While smaller towns in Colorado lacked the few civilized amenities that Machebeuf boasted of, Machebeuf had even greater plans for his "great city" of Denver. "We have also a beautiful plan (on paper) of a hospital at Denver under the direction of the Sisters of Charity," he wrote his sister. "Of the five railroad companies three have offered to help us, and Protestant and Catholic alike will assist us in putting up the first wing of the building."[1]

Machebeuf wanted to call the hospital the "Hotel Dieu." He was confident it would attract patients from all over the world, drawn by Colorado's healthful climate. When the sisters arrived in Denver in 1873, they took one look at Machebeuf's "beautiful plan" and abandoned it as "unsuitable and beyond their means." One of the sisters recorded her views of Machebeuf's plan. "The Hospital," she remembered, "was to be five stories high and was to contain fifty rooms, many of them larger than most parish churches. The Bishop seemed infatuated with the plan. Whenever Sister Joanna went to see him on business, it mattered not of what nature, he would, in a few minutes, try to divert her attention to the plan, which he kept near him in his office." Machebeuf was never one to conceal his enthusiasm for a project. "He would unfold it, and, in his quick, abrupt way, would from time to time, while expatiating on the size, height, breadth, and depth, exclaim, 'Here, now, see! see!' pointing out every turn and twist of the fifty imaginary rooms, and the rooms remained imaginary, for higher than the foundation the building never went." The sisters may not have approved of Machebeuf's grand plan, but they did stay in Denver and eventually built the hospital that became St. Joseph's Hospital at the corner of Eighteenth and Humboldt.[2]

The money to finance Machebeuf's plans continued to drain his capital, and his debts created continual pressure. By the beginning of 1873 he decided to send Raverdy on an extended trip to Europe. In addition to visiting his family, Raverdy was entrusted with the mission of raising additional capital. He would solicit funds in cities both on the East Coast and in Europe and make another request for funding to the Society for the Propagation of the Faith in Paris.

Machebeuf scarcely realized how much he had come to depend on the quiet, loyal Raverdy. His initial hesitation in making Raverdy his vicar general had been due to Raverdy's extreme shyness, which made it difficult for him to preach or speak in public, but no one was more deserving of the title. In spite of his quiet manner, Raverdy proved himself extremely loyal, steady, and hardworking, quietly attending to the matters Machebeuf left half-finished, tying up the dozens of loose ends Machebeuf left behind him as he rushed on to something new. During Raverdy's long absence, Machebeuf realized how much he missed his patient vicar general. "I thank God a thousand times for having given me such a co-laborer," he wrote while Raverdy was away. "What a comfort he has been to me in my loneliness and troubles! What a void in the house and in the parish, and how painfully I feel his absence!"[3]

With the judicious, methodical Raverdy away in Europe, Machebeuf appointed Fr. Honoratus Bourion to the parish at Central City, the second largest in the territory. Bourion, a native of France, had moved to Colorado from Marquette, Michigan, hoping the dry climate of the West would improve his health. A driving, ambitious man, Bourion lost little time in developing expansive plans for an academy, a hospital, and an elaborate new church in Central City. Local residents encouraged him in his ideas, hoping that Central City might one day be named the capitol when Colorado became a state.[4]

Soon the foundations of the cathedral-size church had been laid, and the people of Central City then began construction of the Select Academy, which would be staffed by Sisters of Charity from Leavenworth. The cost of the school alone was estimated to be about $30,000, the church another $75,000. To finance the school, and the rest of Bourion's grand plans, a $500,000 lottery was organized, the grand prize being the Teller House, a hotel valued at $100,000. The money raised would build a "Home for Invalids," cover the construction of the school, and underwrite the completion of the church.[5]

The date for the grand prize drawing was set for 3 July 1873, and promotional leaflets soon circulated throughout the area. Listed as trustees on the project were Fr. Bourion, Pastor of Notre Dame des Neiges, Thomas Mullen, mayor of Central City, and William H. Bush of the Teller House. On 31 March Machebeuf approved the project, and his endorsement appeared on the bottom of the leaflets. "I heartily approve of the charitable object and shall give it all the assistance, and encouragement in my power," read the reference in part. Ticket sales went well and money began to pour in. Then the unthinkable happened; "Unfortunately, the treasurer proved to be a rogue and decamped with the funds."[6]

Disaster followed embarrassment. On 23 May 1873 a fire swept through Central City. The majority of the buildings, flimsy wooden structures perched on steep hillsides, were destroyed. The old church, the priest's residence, and the temporary convent of the sisters were all leveled. Debts piled up and creditors turned to Bourion and Machebeuf for payment. At the same time, the mines in Central City began to play out and the national economy plunged into recession.[7]

The foundations of the church were hastily enclosed to serve as a temporary church, and Father Bourion took responsibility for the majority of the debts. But Bourion's magnanimous gesture was not without contingent demands. He tried to force Machebeuf to sign the church property over to him, so that he might use it either for security or to guarantee his position as resident pastor of Central City. A long, drawn-out battle of wills began between Machebeuf and Bourion, one that would stretch over several years.

The year 1874 brought Machebeuf financial challenges from almost every quarter. Pressed, he traveled to St. Louis, hoping to find financial support from business interests there. Little came of the effort in terms of investors, but Machebeuf took the opportunity to strengthen himself spiritually by making an eight-day retreat in the Jesuit novitiate at Florissant.[8]

He returned to Denver to find the city in an uproar about his financial situation. Many of the parishioners of Central City, upset by the loss of the raffle money, organized a protest and drafted a letter of complaint to the Holy See. Chief among them was General Hughes, the same General Hughes who had given the welcoming address at Machebeuf's reception after his consecration.[9] News of the fiasco circulated among the Catholic community in Denver, and rumors spread that Machebeuf was going bankrupt. An unidentified member of the Central City parish, or possibly a disgruntled Father Quigley, took it upon himself to write to Eugene Kelly in New York, the only sound financial supporter Machebeuf had found.

In September 1874 Kelly hit the panic button. The previous year Machebeuf had failed to make a $500 interest payment on Kelly's loan. In September Kelly received the alarming letter from Denver. "In this letter," Kelly wrote to Machebeuf, "the writer says that you are on 'the verge of bankruptcy' and 'some believe that you are insane,' that you owe $75,000 and are paying 2½% interest (per month) on call for the sum. That there is imminent danger of my losing the money you owe me." Kelly soundly chastised Machebeuf for his "policy of holding on to property and paying such exorbitant interest," then concluded, "It will be hard that after my friendship and charitable regard I am in danger of losing from faults or bad judgment of you."[10]

Machebeuf managed to calm Kelly down. Later in the month Kelly wrote to Machebeuf, apologizing for taking the "villainous letter from the scoundrel" so seriously. After an exchange of several letters, Kelly agreed to refinance the original 1868 loan. He issued a new loan in the amount of $25,000 at 12 percent, allowing Machebeuf to pay off other loans with higher rates. Even so, Kelly chided Machebeuf, telling him "you had better let your people live and pray in shanties than borrow money at such ruinous rates." Machebeuf was not as bad a businessman as Kelly thought. He promptly paid off $10,000 of Kelly's new loan, by borrowing from another source at 10 percent, lowering his interest payments by $200 a year.[11]

Regardless of his sometimes unorthodox approach to finance, Machebeuf was succeeding in underwriting the development of the church in the area. "I cannot give you an idea of the growth of the Church in Colorado that would be equal to the fact," he wrote his sister in May 1875. "At the time of my last voyage to France we had but three parishes in the south and two in the north. Today there are five in the north and material for ten in the south." He had accomplished a great deal in the midst of all his financial turmoil. "Our boarding school of Loretto has a good number of pupils, and we opened our College of St. Joseph last September under the direction of a very experienced French priest. . . . Our hospital is going up slowly but surely, and while waiting for it the Sisters occupy a rented house."[12]

Machebeuf also bragged of the preponderance of French priests in New Mexico, Colorado, and Arizona. "You have no doubt learned that Santa Fe has been made an Archbishopric, and our Province is a little Auvergne, for the Archbishop, his two suffragans [Machebeuf and Salpointe] and three-fourths of the priests are Auvergnats." Machebeuf would attend Lamy's confirmation as archbishop of Santa Fe, then begin another round of missionary travels. "Immediately after the confirmation here in June I shall begin again my long pastoral visits towards the west and south," He certainly had not slowed down. He closed. "Last year on one of these trips I traveled over 800 miles and crossed thirteen counties."

In June Machebeuf set out for Santa Fe to take part in Lamy's investiture as archbishop of Santa Fe, traveling part of the way by train, and part by "wretched coach."[13] It was a moving pilgrimage for the aging bishop, a chance to visit with old friends, to stay again in the city that had been his base of operations for ten years. Most of all, it was a chance to honor the efforts of his oldest and dearest friend.

The morning of 16 June 1875 broke clear and calm. At daybreak nine cannon shots roared out over the City of Santa Fe as the soldiers at Fort Marcy loudly proclaimed the official beginning of the day's events. Music wafted over the plaza from Lamy's garden where the band of St. Michael's College gratefully serenaded him on his last morning as a bishop. The Christian Brothers Lamy first brought to Santa Fe had opened their school on 15 December 1859. But it was not until 1874 that the Territory of New Mexico granted a charter for the College of the Christian Brothers of New Mexico. Named for the Mission of San Miguel, St. Michael's College celebrated Lamy's investiture and its first year of fully authorized operation as a college.[14]

The streets of Santa Fe were dressed for the occasion. Church sodalities, Catholic social organizations, had hung colored banners from porches and posts. Small evergreen trees had been brought in and planted, lining the streets of the city. Just off the plaza, a grand new cathedral of golden stone rose around the old adobe structure of St. Francis Church and promised to be a fitting seat for an archbishop. The cathedral still under construction, the older church too small for the anticipated crowd, the investiture was held in the courtyard of the college, surrounded by the welcoming shade of the porticos, next to the centuries-old chapel of San Miguel.

By nine o'clock dignitaries began to gather for the procession. Priests in colored silken vestments gathered in front of the cathedral. Bishops Machebeuf and Salpointe arrived with their retinues, followed by the new archbishop. In Cathedral Place the procession took shape, then headed slowly down San Francisco Street.

First came the Eighth Cavalry Band, their boots shiny black against the dusty streets, their buttons like polished gold against the dark fabric of their uniforms. They were followed by the sodalities — not only adults, but little girls in white dresses, little boys sporting bright red ribbons. Behind the children came their familiar teachers, the Christian Brothers in their robes and the sisters in immaculate habits.

Twenty priests, who had come to assist at the pontifical mass and give their warmest congratulations to their new archbishop, made up the next part of the procession. Then came Machebeuf, hobbling along on his bad leg, in full bishop's regalia. Salpointe followed with the pallium hand-carried from Rome, which, on behalf of Pope Pius IX, he would drape over the shoulders of Bishop Lamy. Finally, came Lamy himself, under a "magnificent" purple canopy sent from France expressly for the purpose, the fabric glowing in the sun, rippling in the calm spring air. The procession wove down San Francisco Street, across the Santa Fe River, and back up College Street to the courtyard.[15]

At ten o'clock the ceremonies began. Five thousand people filled the courtyard, where the colonnades of the patio were draped with garlands of fresh pine and a newly constructed altar stood backed by U.S. flags. As the choir of St. Michael's completed the opening hymn, Machebeuf, assisted by Fathers Eguillon and Gasparri, began the pontifical high mass. Following the reading of the Gospel, Eguillon, Lamy's new vicar general, gave a homily in Spanish. Salpointe gave another in English. At the moment of investiture, Lamy knelt before Salpointe. The bishop of Arizona slowly read the papal decree in Latin, Spanish, and English, then lowered the pallium over Lamy's shoulders. Lamy responded in Latin, giving the oath of his new estate. At the end of the mass, Machebeuf spoke, highlighting the thirty-seven years of friendship he had shared with Lamy, sharing reminiscences of their work, side by side, over the years. Finally, Lamy's slender figure turned to the crowd, and in a clear voice he offered his thanks "that the universal Father of the faithful has deigned to cast his eye upon our poor town of Santa Fe, lost in deserts and unknown to the whole world," praising the "free republican institutions of the country" that came with the U.S. government.[16]

The mass concluded with the Te Deum, and the procession reformed and made its way to the archbishop's garden. There a hundred prominent guests lunched under the trees, the Eighth Calvary Band playing softly in the background. Acting-governor of the New Mexico Territory William G. Ritch addressed the group, crediting Lamy with "the reforms, the general elevation of the moral tone, and the general progress that has been effected."[17]

The party broke up in midafternoon, but the day's celebrations were far from complete. The people of Santa Fe lit bonfires in the streets at dusk, and the Fort Marcy musicians entertained in the plaza, illuminated by farolitos and luminarias. Leading citizens made speeches from the bandstand, followed by a display of fireworks and a balloon ascension. Beyond the crowded plaza, on the walls of the new cathedral, transparencies were projected of Pope Pius IX, Lamy, Machebeuf, and Salpointe. The evening concluded with a torchlight procession, the flames flickering against the ancient adobe walls in the streets of Santa Fe.[18]

Later, writing his report to Rome, Lamy diplomatically remarked that everyone contributing to the event had been "equally brilliant." He reported that the investiture had been accomplished "with all the solemnity which our poor capital allowed us." A few days later, Machebeuf sadly packed his valise and returned to the challenges of his own poor territory.[19]

His financial wolves in Denver temporarily at bay, Machebeuf turned his attention to the ongoing crisis in Central City. A beautiful new convent and school for the Sisters of Charity had been built, but the contractors had yet to be paid. One of them, William Newell, filed a lien on the property for $1,400. Banks were pressing Bourion for payment and security on loans they had already issued. In April he had written to Machebeuf, outlining debts totaling over $20,000 for the church and the school. In the interim the mayor of Central City reissued titles for the properties, in the names of Machebeuf and the Sister Superior of the Academy. "You have the buildings, I have the debts," Bourion wailed. "Do something about it."[20]

Machebeuf was far from happy with Bourion. He was still taking potshots from Denver parishioners for the raffle fiasco. He considered Bourion's building plans extravagant in terms of the resources available. The status of the titles to the church and school in Central City was a further complication. The Mother Superior suffered a nervous breakdown; two of the other nuns left the convent; and the sisters in Leavenworth decided the debts were too great. Withdrawing, the remaining sisters left the new academy, "so big, so beautiful, and so empty."[21] Another group of sisters would have to be recruited to run the school. Machebeuf was not eager to further entangle himself financially. Last but not least, he had little faith in Bourion's financial judgment.

Superficially his opposition to Bourion is difficult to understand; their approaches toward finance seem much the same. But Machebeuf's debts were almost all the result of land purchases. He was determined to secure as much land as possible for the church before the rise in land values made it prohibitively expensive. With the exception of his unrealized Hotel Dieu, none of his structures could be considered extravagant. He and Raverdy had spent their first ten years in Denver residing in a seventy-five-dollar wooden shack. By comparison, Bourion was constructing expensive, elegant structures. Machebeuf also discounted Bourion's claims of imminent foreclosure. Machebeuf knew through other sources how the banks were most likely to respond.[22] From May to August Machebeuf negotiated with both the banks and Bourion.

The result was a highly unusual arrangement. Bourion borrowed money from his family to pay off $12,089 of the debts. He had already reduced the total debts somewhat, having raised $12,475 through fairs and other charitable events. Machebeuf temporarily assumed financial responsibility for the parish, but ultimately the parish itself would have to pay for costs incurred. Bourion would rebate all interest due as long as he remained pastor of Central City. If he were removed, $1,400 in interest would be due annually. The property, the church and the academy, was put in trust to Bourion, and he met the interest payments on the remaining debts. Temporarily, at least, Bourion remained pastor in Central City, and the banks and other creditors were quieted. Machebeuf turned his attention to other concerns.

The Sisters of Loretto had been successful with St. Mary's Academy in Denver, so they decided to expand their efforts. They sent three sisters to Pueblo to open another school. Within a few months they secured a four-room brick house and successfully began the Loretto Academy.[23]

Machebeuf continued roaming the territory in his buggy, checking on smaller communities, urging the construction of churches and chapels, organizing committees to raise funds or oversee construction. In the spring of 1876 he wrote his brother, Marius, trying to give him an idea of how his time was spent. "When I was at Sandusky," he told Marius, "Bishop Rappe said to me: 'My dear sir, on Saturday and Sunday I am priest and bishop to confess, preach, officiate, etc.; on Monday and the rest of the week I am banker, contractor, architect, mason, collector, in a word, a little of everything.'" At the time he did not fully appreciate the remark from Rappe, but after eight years as a missionary bishop, Machebeuf now confessed, "it exactly describes my position in Colorado, where everything must be built up from the bottom. I wonder I am not sick, but I have not the time. A real American has no time to be sick, no time to eat or sleep, no time for anything except the 'go ahead.'"[24]

As he explained to his brother, the previous year had been a hard one for the aging bishop. "There were many failures of banks and business houses, and the grasshoppers destroyed our crops. These misfortunes have brought on a stagnation in business, and consequent hard times." He detailed to Marius how he had consolidated his loans, reducing his interest payments to 10 and 12 percent. He also reported winning a suit in the supreme court for the title to a block of ground he was reserving for a cathedral, but financial problems continued to plague him — often two steps forward marked another step back. "Our College of St. Joseph is closed," he noted, "leaving a deficit of $500 or $600 which I must pay."

The spring of 1876 found Machebeuf planning yet another fund-raising trip. That year Archbishop Purcell of Cincinnati, who first recruited Machebeuf in France, was celebrating his golden jubilee, fifty years in the priesthood. Lamy was unable to attend the event, so Machebeuf served as the official representative of the Province of Santa Fe. Machebeuf extended the trip, traveling once again to Baltimore, Philadelphia, New York, and Cleveland.

In Maryland, one member of the Jesuit Community at Woodstock College recorded his impressions of Machebeuf's visit. "The lame Vicar Apostolic of Colorado and Utah . . . the Right Reverend James P. Macheboeuf, was introduced to the community on June 8, 1876, by the then Bishop of Richmond, Cardinal Gibbons. He was attracted by the presence here of his fellow missionary, Father Miège." Despite getting Machebeuf's first name wrong and misspelling his surname, the writer was impressed with the bishop. "During his all too short stay he was a very welcome addition to our recreations. His fertile imagination, rich vocabulary and wide experience furnished no end of pious and inspiring entertainment." As usual, Machebeuf regaled the Jesuits with stories from the wild, wild West. "[He] had some kind of roving commission under Bishop Lamy from the banks of the Rio Grande over Texas, New Mexico, Arizona, Colorado and Utah, bringing spiritual aid to the few scattered Catholic families in that vast region, and offering his ministrations to miners, cow-boys[,] gamblers and the froth of border settlements, if they would listen to him. . . . His adventures and escapes were innumerable."[25]

Machebeuf also made stops in Milwaukee, Chicago, and St. Louis, trying to recruit more priests and seminarians, begging anything that might help his diocese spiritually or materially. In Chicago he made arrangements for the Jesuits to come and give missions in Colorado. In St. Louis he convinced the Sisters of St. Joseph to send a colony of sisters to Central City to occupy the convent and academy abandoned by the Sisters of Charity.[26]

The agreeable sisters must not have been suffragettes. Had they been, they certainly would have withheld their services, for in February 1877, Machebeuf made his views on women's suffrage clear. Delivering a series of lectures on the subject, Machebeuf had little patience with women impatient with their station. What kind of women did Machebeuf consider supporters of suffrage? "Battalions of old maids, disappointed in getting husbands of any sort; women separated from their husbands or divorced by men of sacred obligations imposed by God himself. . . . Women who, although married, are discontented and wish to improve their condition by holding the reins of the family government." There were also "women without any family, who scorn to be tied down to the sacred duty of what they call the drudgery of mothers; women who, too often, manage (God knows by what means, by what unnatural crimes) to be relieved from the cares of a family." As far as Machebeuf was concerned, women's rights should be limited to "a right to the love, affection, assistance and protection of a devoted husband . . . a right to the respect, esteem and veneration of an impartial public, as long as they deserve it, by their modesty, self-respect and dignity."²⁷ Overall, Machebeuf's observations on women, as delivered in his lectures on suffrage, are remarkable only in terms of their lack of imagination. They are a shopping list of some of the rationalizations men have relied upon for centuries to prevent women from achieving an equitable position in society. Nothing in Machebeuf's background would lead one to expect anything else. Machebeuf had never really known a woman. His own mother died when he was fairly young; his sister entered the convent; and propriety and the essential deportment of the priesthood forbade any direct or private contact with women.

Machebeuf's observations on suffrage reflect, in part, the conservatism of his rural French Catholic background. What, according to Machebeuf, was the origin of the scandalous promotion of suffrage? "There is a class of liberal christians who talk very loudly about the Bible, and pretend to follow the Bible." He also demonstrated a strictly dualistic interpretation of sex roles, completely in keeping with the Jansenistic influences of his past. The only appropriate model for women was that of the Virgin Mary. "The infinite wisdom of God," Machebeuf explained, "has resolved the difficulty of uniting virginity and fecundity in His virgin-mother, and thus qualified her to be the worthy model of woman in every state of life." Machebeuf issued the gravest of warnings to women who rejected that model. In fact, he attributed the excesses of the French Revolution to such emancipated women. "In times of public excitement or revolution, women are more fierce than men. . . . What frightful examples of this sad truth were given during the days of terror of the French revolution of 1793, brought on by infidelity!" Only liberated women could have perpetrated such unspeakable acts. "The most horrid crimes and massacres," Machebeuf asserted, "were committed at the instigation of women's clubs, and the same horrors of 1793 were repeated in 1871, during the short days of the Commune." Pulling out all the stops to prevent the societal disaster of women getting the vote, Machebeuf continued, "In the cruel execution of the hostages, women were more conspicuous than men in exciting the infuriate mob; no religious or human consideration could restrain them in their madness. Victims from every state and rank of society were to be immolated before peace could be restored." This held an important lesson for the people of Colorado, he concluded. "If the people of Colorado have at heart the success and prosperity of their new State, they will not be foolish enough to try this fatal experiment over again." Colorado did grant women the vote, without the dire consequences Machebeuf predicted.[28]

After completing his successful lectures, Machebeuf set out on another pastoral visit. By 3 September he was in Trinidad, giving confirmation to 260 new Catholics. The next morning brought tragic news. Fr. Louis Merle, the pastor of Walsenberg, had been killed on his way to meet Machebeuf in Trinidad. The buggy Merle was riding in hit a washout and both Merle and the driver were thrown out of the vehicle. Merle broke his neck. Machebeuf and several of the Jesuits from Trinidad made their way to Walsenberg for the funeral.

Machebeuf left the Walsenberg parish temporarily in the hands of the Jesuits and left immediately for Santa Fe, hoping to persuade Lamy to part with one of his priests. Upon hearing the news, Lamy agreed to give Machebeuf Gabriel Ussel, the young priest who served in Arroyo Hondo and later Taos and whom Machebeuf had liked so much. Ussel came north with Machebeuf, traveling by way of Conejos so that Machebeuf could complete his pastoral visit. On Sunday, 15 October 1876, he installed Father Ussel as the pastor of Walsenberg. Machebeuf had added an old friend to the ranks of his men in Colorado. For the next thirty years Ussel remained in the post.[29]

In August 1877 the frustrated Father Bourion left his post in Central City, leaving the parish more than fourteen thousand dollars in debt. Machebeuf replaced him with Fr. Joseph Finotti, a scholarly Jesuit and former professor at Georgetown University, who had come west for his health. Finotti did his best to urge the parishioners of Central City to pay off the debts, but they were largely unsympathetic toward their former pastor and his legacy. In 1878 Bourion's brother, Edward, arrived on the scene, claiming possession of his brother's loans to the Central City Parish. Insistent and petulant, Edward began to harass Machebeuf and Finotti for "his" money. "I am the man to settle with about the debts of the Church here," he announced. "What are you going to do about it?" He threatened to publish notices that both the academy and the church were in default of payment, to advertise them for sale through a bank in Golden. "I bought all these notes from my brother," he wrote to Finotti in less than diplomatic fashion. "I am going to Denver tomorrow to let the Bishop know that you did nothing towards the debt of the Church and let him know my intention. Remember I mean business."[30]

Machebeuf quieted Edward with a payment of a thousand dollars in cash, borrowing the money to do so. He also tried to negotiate a reduction of the debt by four thousand dollars, if the parishioners of Central City paid the rest. Edward refused to accept the offer, but he never carried through with the threatened foreclosure. Another of the Central City creditors, Maxine Dagenais, did file suit, which frightened Machebeuf. If it sparked enough similar court actions, it would bankrupt the parish. Given the over-extended state of his financial situation, bankruptcy in Central City might result in bankruptcy for the whole diocese. He could never meet all his debts if they were presented simultaneously. His worst-case scenario never came to pass, but the complicated finances of Central City would not be fully resolved for another eight years.[31]

Central City was but one of the parishes draining Machebeuf's resources. Few of the missions could support a priest or his residence, much less finance the construction of a church. Often the priests assigned would begin projects then find themselves unable to complete them. Biographer W. J. Howlett notes, "In their difficulties they always turned to Bishop Machebeuf for assistance, and his diaries show that he was constantly helping one or another of them by donations to the priest or church — or by signing notes which in many cases he had to pay." By the end of 1878 Machebeuf had doubled his debt to Kelly in New York. The charitable banker issued another loan for fifteen thousand dollars bringing the total amount to thirty thousand. Once again, Machebeuf had, in effect, robbed Peter to pay Paul.[32]

It was also in 1878 that Machebeuf made official his commitment to the nation that had been his home for almost forty years. On 23 February 1878 Machebeuf was issued his final certificate of naturalization and formally became a citizen of the United States of America. Machebeuf had met the requirements of the court. Although some might challenge him on his financial judgment, few would challenge him on the requirement that he "has sustained good moral character, and appeared to be attached to the principles contained in the Constitution of the United States, and well disposed to the good order, well being and happiness of the same."[33]

Before being granted citizenship, Machebeuf had spent the last three months of 1877 on pastoral visits. Undeterred by his financial problems, his optimism rings through his letters to his sister. He had spent the previous three months "traveling 1,500 miles — over mountains and through valleys and plains — in sunshine, in rain and in snow."[34]

Once again, in his usual style, Machebeuf dodged lightning on the trip. In many of the southern communities, "the smallpox was raging, especially among the children of the Mexicans, and my boy-driver and I had often to eat and sleep in the very room where three or four were sick, and it might be one or two dead, but we never had the slightest symptoms of the disease." Exposure to smallpox was not the only close brush on this particular trip. "Coming down a little incline . . . the buggy ran into the horses, crowding them to the edge of the precipice and pitching us over upon the rocks. I was on the lower side, and in falling Father [Thomas Aquinas] Hayes came down upon me," Machebeuf blithely reported. "He was greatly alarmed and asked me if I was hurt. I answered that I would tell him if he would get up and give me a chance to find out."[35]

As always, the irrepressible Machebeuf seemed undaunted by his latest encounters with death. He had deceived the Grim Reaper too many times before; his faith was unshakable. Calmly concluding the long letter to his sister, he reassured her, "Thus you see the life of a missionary, and how Providence protects him in all sorts of dangers. Why should we fear sickness and death?"[36]

NINETEEN

Silver to Lead

✦

On 30 July 1878 the *Rocky Mountain News* announced "the great event of the century in Colorado." A long article explained the wonders of the solar eclipse the city had witnessed the day before. A group of three Jesuit professors from Woodstock College, remembering Machebeuf's visit two years earlier, decided to travel to Denver to formally observe the event. "We arrived in Denver about eight o'clock, when it was quite dark, and betook ourselves immediately to the residence of Bishop Macheboeuf [*sic*], where we were most hospitably received," one of the visiting Jesuits recorded. "Three days remained before the eclipse, and during the two following we were shown the city and vicinity through the kindness of the Bishop and his priests."

The visiting Jesuits were impressed by the city of Denver, describing it as a "bright, lively, elegant little city of 20,000 inhabitants, with some fine business streets and many handsome residences." On 29 June Machebeuf joined the men viewing the eclipse. "It was certainly a solemn as well as a beautiful spectacle — the sudden conversion of day into night, the subduing effect upon animals, the beautiful appearances of the clouds in the mountains, and the exquisite halo surrounding the dark moon." As the shadow of the moon was cast over Colorado the temperature dropped. "Although the day had been very warm, it became so cool during the totality, that Fr. Degni, who wore his duster while using the telescope, called for another coat, to the amusement of the Bishop, who had joined us for the beginning of the eclipse."[1] Machebeuf, hardened by years of winter travel in the Rockies, had a hard time understanding Father Degni's delicacy. Gracious

host that he was, he saw his three distinguished, delicate visitors off in three
different directions, then left Denver on another pastoral visit.

In the fall of 1878 Machebeuf returned to Denver. "I have just returned
from a second trip of six weeks among the highest mountains that I have
visited in Colorado," he wrote his sister, "in the southwestern part of the
state near the borders of New Mexico." Machebeuf had begun a tour of the
communities in April, but heavy snow prevented him from reaching many
of the smaller towns and isolated mining camps. "I then turned in another
direction", he explained, "and went to the new town of Leadville, which
now has 25,000 inhabitants."[2]

The sudden growth of Leadville was nothing short of spectacular. In May
1878 a few miners sold their claims in the area for $250,000. News of the
sale spread rapidly, and soon a silver rush had begun. By the following
spring, silver fever had become pandemic, and thousands were flooding into
Leadville and neighboring communities. The flood of immigrants and
prospectors meant new demands on the church, demands that kept Machebeuf in Denver. In February he wrote, "It is my fixed determination to go to
Europe this year if I can possibly get away. But you cannot form an idea of
the manner in which my work comes up to demand my attention and
occupy my time." Trying to give a better picture of what he was up against,
he continued, "Just now it is the enthusiasm, the fever, and I might almost
say, the madness of the crowds coming from all parts of the United States, of
every nationality, and every shade of religious belief, and of no belief at all
except in money, all bound for Leadville, the new silver mining camp, which
rivals, at least on paper, the richest mines of California and Nevada."[3]

Machebeuf had one priest assigned to Leadville, but he was badly in need
of an assistant, and Machebeuf had no one to send him. The church there
was so overcrowded "that one-half of the people strive to hear mass kneel-
ing in the cold and snow outside the church in the street."[4] Five of the
Sisters of Charity moved to Leadville and opened a hospital in the town,
but they were "overburdened with work," and although several new priests
had come to Colorado for their health, the supply could not keep up with
the ever-increasing demand.

Delayed by the new demands on his time, Machebeuf finally left for
Europe months after his proposed departure. He planned the trip to make a
report of his first ten years as a bishop, and to offer his "homages" to his
new pontiff, Pope Leo XIII. Gone was the gentle, aristocratic humor and
affection Pius IX had shown Machebeuf when he excused him from the
Vatican Council. The new pope was considered the candidate of the mod-
erates, and in the conclave following Pius IX's death, he had received forty-

four of the sixty-one votes. Thin, with a high-domed forehead and gold-rimmed glasses, Leo XIII was expected to have a brief and transitional pontificate. Instead, it lasted more than twenty-five years, marked by his patience, strong will, and calm energy.[5] Given the as-yet-unknown personality of the new pope, Machebeuf could not be sure just how he would be received in Rome.

Machebeuf's reception in Rome was not what he expected. Rumors of his financial instability continued to circulate through Denver and throughout the church hierarchy in the rest of the country. The rumors had reached Rome ahead of him, and he found himself before a Roman court of inquiry convened to evaluate the status of his financial affairs. Any evaluation of Machebeuf's complicated monetary involvements would take time. Hurt by the misunderstanding and distrust he found in Rome, he retired to Clermont while investigations slowly continued.[6]

Waiting uneasily in Clermont, wondering what the Roman court would determine, Machebeuf turned to friends for advice about his financial concerns. It was in Clermont that he struck upon the idea of issuing bonds. If bonds were issued on the holdings of the church in Colorado, as well as on his personal holdings, then sold on the French market, he could generate thousands of dollars and pay off his more-pressing creditors at home. The bonds would allow him to pay off the holders at lower interest rates, over a longer period of time, cutting the costs of his borrowing and allowing time for property values to rise. He could then redeem the bonds with money that would result from property sales and other diocesan revenues. In his usual impulsive fashion, Machebeuf traveled to Paris and issued the bonds, leaving the management of the bond issue in the hands of Parisian financial agents.[7]

After months of waiting he received word from Rome. The Roman authorities asked him for further information regarding his finances and explanations of some of the more complicated arrangements. Sorely wounded by their apparent lack of faith in his abilities, Machebeuf offered his resignation. It was refused. If he could not resign, he suggested, they should appoint a coadjutor, another priest to oversee the financial activities of the diocese.

Years later, writing to Cardinal Gibbons in Baltimore, Machebeuf explained the refusal of his 1880 request for a coadjutor, "His Eminence had refused to take any step without the approbation of the Archbishop of the Province. . . . [A]s Archbishop Lamy and Bishop Salpointe had not approved it, the project had been abandoned or put off for an indefinite period of time."[8]

This was by far the most disappointing of his visits to Rome. In spite of all his effort, in spite of all the small economic miracles he had wrought over years, his judgment and ability to effectively serve as a bishop had been questioned. The church in Colorado had made substantial progress under his direction. On his arrival in 1860, the church consisted of just Raverdy and himself. At the time of his consecration as a bishop, in 1868, he still had only three priests to cover all of Colorado and Utah. By 1878 he had built up his staff to twenty-three priests, not to mention the sisters working in Denver, Central City, Pueblo, Trinidad, and Leadville. Machebeuf had secured thousands of acres of land throughout the territory, constructed numerous churches and countless chapels, begun schools and hospitals. The rumors, focused on his liabilities, almost never took note of the assets he had secured and developed in the process. Most of all, the distrust in Rome reopened his own doubts, the doubts that had plagued him prior to accepting his elevation to the episcopacy. Now, questioning his ability to manage the affairs of the diocese, the Roman authorities were unwilling to accept his resignation or provide him with an appropriate counselor and aide. Discouraged, the aging bishop returned to Denver, confidence undermined, still seeking elusive answers to his unceasing financial worries.

Machebeuf had seen financial success in two projects in his Denver parish. In 1878 a number of his parishioners had formed the Denver Catholic School Building Association. A Catholic community setting up a corporation was unusual and innovative at the time. The corporation helped finance the construction of a number of schools in the Denver area. In December 1880 another group of parishioners established the Denver Catholic Cathedral Association. Raverdy and four men from the parish would sell stock to finance construction of a building at Fifteenth and Stout. The structure would provide rental space for stores, a public hall, and additional room for classes. The rent would offset dividend payments, and when completely paid for, the building would be turned over to the Cathedral parish. While Machebeuf was not directly involved in either of these initial corporations, he seems to have paid some attention to the concept and the resulting success, because in the years ahead he would use a variation of the same to resolve his personal financial situation.[9]

In 1882 and 1883 Machebeuf saw relative success in the sale of some of the properties he had bought earlier. The sales brought enough profit to temporarily ease his economic situation and give credence to his long-term strategy in terms of land acquisition. One sale in 1882 grossed $25,000, and others, in 1883, $42,000. Just as Machebeuf began to feel more hopeful, the general financial condition throughout the country took a downturn and the land market went sour. Stubbornly, Machebeuf held onto his property holdings, refusing to sell any land except in a favorable market, struggling to make interest and capital payments.

One of the greatest sources of support for the embattled bishop during this period was the Jesuits. From the five men Lamy recruited in 1867, the Jesuits had slowly increased the manpower assigned to the American Southwest. By 1872 they had fourteen men assigned to the New Mexico Mission, and by 1879 the number had grown to fifty. Increasingly Machebeuf had come to depend on them in the southernmost areas of Colorado, the areas with the largest Hispanic population. They were firmly established in Conejos and Pueblo, and by 1875 in the city of Trinidad. He convinced three of the Jesuits to come to Denver. On 12 September 1878 they opened a temporary chapel in the parlor of their own recently purchased residence, in the east end of the city.[10]

Hardship was well known to every resident of nineteenth-century Colorado, and the Jesuits were no exception. Pueblo had grown so much that by 1882 Machebeuf found it necessary to establish a second parish in the town. Named St. Patrick's, it, too, was placed under the direction of the Jesuits. But on 18 October 1882, fire destroyed the first Jesuit residence and church in Pueblo. As Francis Tomassini, an assistant priest in the Pueblo parish, later recalled, "Thousands of people were looking at the conflagration, but they could not give any help on account of the strong wind. The two hose companies of the place failed to master the fire, as the water supply was very scanty, and the wind scattered the stream from the hose. . . . In two hours both buildings were destroyed by the fire, only the brick walls remaining." The Jesuits in Pueblo suffered a real setback, "the loss was estimated at $15,000, nothing being insured." Less than a year later they succeeded in building a new church, closer to the center of town and twice as large as the previous one. In August 1883 Machebeuf traveled to Pueblo to inaugurate the new St. Ignatius Church. "The Right Rev. Bishop Machbeuf [sic] was surely gladdened at having this favorable opportunity to give a new mark of his fatherly feelings toward his Catholic children of this city," Tomassini recorded, and the ceremony "was of an imposing and impressive character." Likely Machebeuf was just as "gladdened" at having the church rebuilt by the Jesuits and the people of Pueblo themselves, without burdening him with additional debts.[11]

If there was good news in Pueblo in 1883, bad news came from Europe. The Parisian agents Machebeuf had engaged to administer the sale of the bonds in France failed to make any return. The bonds sold quite well, but the Parisian agents, rather than relaying the proceeds of the sale to Machebeuf in Denver, were pocketing them. Machebeuf sent Raverdy to Paris to investigate the matter, but when Raverdy confronted the men, they still refused to make payment. He had little recourse but to take the matter to the courts. Sale of further bonds was brought to an abrupt halt, and Raverdy began an effort to locate the owners of bonds that had already been purchased. Machebeuf had the embarrassment of another complicated financial affair to unravel, legal expenses, and the expenses of Raverdy's trip, but he never saw any profit from the sale of the bonds.[12]

Still, improvements in transportation brought some consolation to Machebeuf. With railroads completed between Santa Fe and Denver, he could occasionally slip away to Santa Fe, to spend a few days visiting with Lamy, seeking his advice on various problems, enjoying the comfortable understanding shared after decades of friendship. In the spring of 1884 Machebeuf traveled to Santa Fe for one such visit with Lamy, then accompanied him to Albuquerque. Machebeuf remembered Sister Blandina Segale, one of the Sisters of Charity teaching there. He had first met her in Trinidad and entertained the group by describing her efforts plastering the school there, carrying the hod buckets for the plasterer.

"Now Bishop, that you have brought on the conversation about me," Blandina queried, "give us the pleasure of knowing how you became lame."

"My horse got frightened and threw me with my foot in the stirrup and in this posture the animal dragged me. When the horse stopped my leg was broken. Of course I was doing mission work when this happened. My broken leg has not impeded my work."

Machebeuf's injury had actually been the result of the carriage accident in 1863. Either Machebeuf's memory faltered or Blandina's accuracy is suspect. Regardless, Lamy, sensing Machebeuf was in the mood to spin stories, egged him on. "What about the time you dined at one of Harvey's restaurants and the waiter told you you occupied two seats, and for that reason you would have to pay for two persons?"

"Well, it happened at a period when you could board a train and take advantage of 'thirty minutes for dinner.' All who wanted to dine filed into Harvey's dining hall. Some good man took compassion on my lameness and carried my valise. He looked to see where there were vacant places, spying a table where two chairs were not occupied, he placed my valise on one and helped me to seat myself in the other. The gentlemen at the table were congenial. A few minutes after we were seated, the conductor announced: 'Owing to some obstruction a few miles ahead of us, we will be delayed possibly one hour.' We ate our dinner leisurely. When the waiter came to collect, he said to me, 'You occupied two seats — your charge is double.'

The gentlemen at the table looked quizzically at me and I good-humoredly said: 'Justice is one of the prime factors of our Constitution, hence I will follow its dictates.'

"Opening my valise, I said to the waiter, 'Bring dinner for one more — this guest does not want anything damp. Bring equivalents in dry edibles. The men at my table let loose their voice as though a mountain cat were making ready for a spring — the others in the hall joined in the fun, so none of us had any reason to bemoan our delay."[13]

Blandina, writing to another sister of the event, gave a touching portrait of the aging Machebeuf. "I have often noticed his very kind eyes — eyes full of sympathy which show at a glance his thought is for others. His lower lip has the expression of a good grandmother who fears she never does enough for all who belong to her. His whole makeup is: 'You may take advantage of me, but I remain, poor, lame, Bishop Machebeuf, one of the first modern frontier missionaries of the Southwest.' "[14]

The previous year, spring of 1883, the poor, lame Bishop Machebeuf attended the closing exercises of Las Vegas College, which the Jesuits had been operating since 1877. Impressed by the work of the Jesuits, Machebeuf approached the Superior of the Mission, Aloysius M. Gentile, and asked him to send enough Jesuits to establish a college in Denver. The Christian Brothers in Santa Fe, he reasoned, could well meet the educational needs of New Mexico, but the growing city of Denver had no college whatsoever. Dominic Pantanella, the president of Las Vegas College, seconded Machebeuf's suggestion and began to make formal inquiries. He traveled to Europe to obtain approval and support for the establishment of a college in Colorado. He personally presented the case for the proposed college to the general of the society and his advisers. Pantanella's arguments must have been persuasive, for he won the general's approval. On 10 August 1884 he was appointed vice-rector of the college to be opened in the town of Morrison, Colorado, sixteen miles southwest of Denver. Before returning to America, Pantanella began recruiting additional Jesuits for the faculty.[15]

Morrison, Colorado, near the Red Rocks area at the mouth of Bear Creek Canyon, was originally a mining community. Founder George M. Morrison had come in search of gold. He settled for the huge deposits of gypsum in the area, constructed a mill, and began delivering the stone to nearby Denver. An enterprising businessman from Denver, second territorial governor John Evans, who had been involved in gypsum mining and bringing the railroad to Denver, decided the area was perfect for the development of a first-class resort hotel. Evans built his hotel. When completed, the Evergreen Hotel "boasted a stone two-story structure with 42 rooms, parlors, a billiard room, a dancing pavilion, and fine grounds." The hotel never became the successful resort Evans envisioned, but Machebeuf, constantly on the lookout for properties for the church, recognized it would be ideal for a school. He purchased the building and grounds, then deeded the property fee simple to the Jesuits in 1884. Pantanella arrived, with his newly recruited faculty, and prepared the structure for classes, and Machebeuf's dream finally became a reality — he had a Jesuit college in Colorado. On 15 September 1884 the College of the Sacred Heart officially opened its doors.[16]

P. J. Arthuis, one of the French Jesuits staying at Sacred Heart in 1885, could not resist sending a portrait of his curious new bishop to friends back home: "Mgr. Machebeuf, [A]uvergnat, arrived in America almost 25 years ago. This zealous priest was missionary successively in Ohio, New Mexico and then in Colorado. Almost all the churches in Colorado were built since his arrival in that land, and a great number under his direction." Not willing simply to recount Machebeuf's accomplishments, he continued, "On one of his apostolic trips, he took a fall and broke his leg. Upon that new development one of his friends cried 'Well, now at least he'll be obliged to take care of himself and not always going over mountains and valleys in pursuit of his friends.'" Arthuis was beginning to know Machebeuf, for he continued, "Far from it, it seems the lame bishop has become more active since the accident. . . . He said of himself in regard to his episcopacy, 'I am the only priest in Denver, and it doesn't have a choice. For want of better, I was named bishop.'" Arthuis also recognized Machebeuf's support for the Jesuits' work in Colorado. "Mgr. Machebeuf is a sincere and devout friend of the Society," he explained. "He has so much wanted a college directed by us in his diocese, that he has refused other religious [orders] permission to open an establishment of that type, and has bought for us a Swiss-Cottage hotel, that he will donate to us on the condition that we always have a college in Colorado."[17]

The Plenary Council of Bishops of the United States had convened in Baltimore in November 1884. With Cardinal Gibbons presiding, Machebeuf gave the bishops an optimistic report on the development of the church in Colorado. His private correspondence with Raverdy paints a darker picture. Writing to Machebeuf in Baltimore, the vicar general's letters are peppered with ominous reports.

Machebeuf had commissioned a Canadian priest, Percy Phillips, to solicit a loan from Canadian sources, while he sought funding in Baltimore and New York. Raverdy's uneasiness is clear. Writing early in November he noted "[a]s usual a great deal of bother about heavy notes, but I put them off on the grounds of your absence." By the end of the month Raverdy reported, "I had news this week from Fr. Phillips: he meets with disappointment after disappointment. It seems to me very dubious if he can accomplish this loan." And two days later he predicted, "If you or Father Phillips do not succeed in raising a big loan, you will fare pretty badly this winter." One creditor in Silverton was "calling very loud" for interest payments; another advertised sale of mortgaged property because his payments were past due. Raverdy was particularly frightened by the second action, fearing it would create a panic among the creditors.[18]

When Machebeuf returned from the Baltimore Council, his financial situation had reached near-crisis proportions. He gathered together the businessmen of the cathedral parish and most of the priests in his council, seeking a means of easing his burden. "After many propositions and plans, we were advised by a Catholic lawyer who attended all the meetings to form an association to be called the 'Colorado Catholic Loan and Trust Association,'" he later explained. The purpose of the association would be "to issue some shares . . . till I would be able to sell my property as I had done before the failures." In order to evaluate Machebeuf's real estate, "I gave them a list of my property well known to them. The business men, the lawyer, and the clergymen made an estimation of the Denver property and the market price of land in other parts of Colorado."[19]

The unnamed lawyer and the businessmen declined the opportunity to formally take part in the association, but five of Machebeuf's priests agreed; Raverdy; John Quinn, the rector at the Cathedral; M. J. Carmody, the pastor of St. Anne's in Denver; Nicholas Matz; and W. J. Howlett. On 23 March 1885 the five priests entered into an agreement to form a corporation, presenting the papers to the secretary of state the following day.[20] The purpose of the corporation was to acquire all the real estate owned by Machebeuf, pay off the debts, and cover any unsecured debts, so as not to have to sacrifice any of the property.

The members of the association estimated Machebeuf's debts that were secured by trust deeds at $57,220 and his unsecured debts at another $24,500. They evaluated his property at $135,900, although Machebeuf thought that was low, later indicating he considered it worth $172,000. On 31 March 1885 Machebeuf turned over to the association all his personal real estate and mortgages. They included land in the towns of Pueblo, Canon City, Gunnison, Buena Vista, and Golden; in the counties of San

Juan, Clear Creek, and Rio Grande; his vast ranch in Jefferson County; dozens of lots in the Denver area, and entire sections of St. Vincent's addition in Denver.

W. J. Howlett, a member of the association and later Machebeuf's biographer, explained, "Interest bearing bonds were issued and sold to large and small investors, and the money used to pay the most importunate of the creditors, and pieces of property were sold for the same purpose as fast as a fair price could be got for them." The numerous transactions took time, but eventually they worked to the benefit of the church. Howlett concludes, "when it was done there remained a considerable balance to the credit of the diocese."[21]

The sale of the bonds forever resolved the looming threat of Machebeuf's personal bankruptcy. For the first time in twenty years, the aging bishop no longer had to worry about his personal creditors. But the resolution of his relationships with his creditors sadly meant a worsening of his relationships with the U.S. hierarchy and Rome.

In the summer of 1885 Machebeuf received official visits from two of his fellow bishops, inquiring about his financial situation. Salpointe, visiting from Arizona, heard an explanation of the association and promised to write to Rome on Machebeuf's behalf. Bishop O'Connor from Omaha, Nebraska, however, was decidedly cold and unfriendly toward Machebeuf. O'Connor seemed to be under the impression that Machebeuf had sold or negotiated church property without proper authority to do so. He failed to realize that the property assumed by the association was Machebeuf's personal property and not that of any church in Colorado.

Apparently O'Connor communicated his misinterpretation to Rome. By September 1885 Cardinal Simeoni of Propaganda wrote to Machebeuf asking for an explanation of his finances, particularly details of the association. In the same month Machebeuf began a series of letters to Cardinal Gibbons in Baltimore, trying to explain his complicated finances, to clarify that the properties and debts involved were his personally, not those of the church. He had been hurt by the attitude O'Connor demonstrated toward him during his visit and questioned the sources from which O'Connor solicited his information. "He had conversations with a wealthy and most eccentric and proud lady who I am sure did not fail to complain," Machebeuf told Gibbons. "Everytime [sic] I went to see her she reproached me that they [the people of Denver] should have a new Cathedral and that the present pro-Cathedral was not good enough for Denver. . . . Whatever may be the case, I replied to her that schools and new parishes in Denver were more urgent." Based on such questionable sources, O'Connor had formed his opinions and failed to give Machebeuf an opportunity to explain, snubbing him at the end of his visit. "I felt hurt and offended," Machebeuf told Gibbons, "that after having taken dinner alone in that family, he had to pass within one block of my house to go to his hotel and did not come to see me before going to the train which left [that] night."[22]

Perhaps most disturbing to Machebeuf, in the wake of O'Connor's departure, rumors flew around Denver that Rome would have to appoint a coadjutor to take over Machebeuf's financial responsibilities. A coadjutor, a second bishop officially assigned by the Vatican to assist the principal bishop of a diocese, was sometimes assigned when an older bishop was no longer capable of meeting the demands of the episcopacy. Machebeuf, vital, strong, and alert, seemed to take the possible appointment as an insult and was crushed by the prospect of the appointment. He asked Gibbons to write Simeoni in Rome "to rectify this misunderstanding." Additionally, a coadjutor had never been appointed to a vicar apostolic. If it were true they were to appoint a coadjutor, he argued, they should elevate Denver to a diocese rather than set a precedent. Finally, the appointment should at least be a man of his own choosing. He pleaded with Gibbons not "to impose upon me a coadjutor who may be unknown to me and who may not be acquainted with our mode of life and sacrifice in the West, [and] to use your influence to avoid this great humiliation, I would almost say degradation."[23] Machebeuf's words are a haunting echo of Taos's Padre Martinez's request years earlier to Lamy — to appoint a successor if need be, but let it be one of his own choosing, one who knew the people and the land. Now a Frenchman was threatened with the imposition of an outsider.

Once again, too, Machebeuf was haunted by the doubts that prevented his immediate acceptance of the role of bishop. With more than twenty years of hard work behind him, having laid the foundation of the church in Colorado almost single-handedly and having finally resolved all his financial difficulties, he found himself misunderstood, mistrusted, and unappreciated. "If I am not worthy to be appointed the 1st Bishop of Denver, although I have built the 1st Church, I am satisfied to remain Vicar Apostolic, but, for God's sake, spare me the humiliation of a Coadjutor under such circumstance." Crushed, Machebeuf reminded Gibbons of the commitment he had made, of the years of service he had given to the church. Closing the letter, he wrote, "Being now 49 years a priest, my friends were preparing for a golden jubilee, but if a coadjutor were appointed by force for me it would be a lead jubilee."[24]

TWENTY

Twilight

✣

Machebeuf and Lamy's lives ran parallel in so many ways, from their early years in seminary, through ten years on the Ohio frontier, through three decades in the Southwest. Now, once more, transitions in the two friends' lives mirrored one another. In January 1885 Lamy had written to Cardinal Simeoni at the Propaganda requesting approval for his retirement and the appointment of a coadjutor. Lamy urged Simeoni to use his influence with Pope Leo XIII to secure official sanction for the two requests.[1]

Lamy suggested Jean Baptiste Salpointe as coadjutor with the right of succession. Salpointe had spent nineteen years in Arizona continuing the work Machebeuf had begun. Learning of Lamy's plans, Salpointe wrote to Machebeuf, inviting him to Santa Fe to attend his consecration. "Do not forget to bring your mitre, crozier, and pontifical vestments," Salpointe reminded him. "You know we aren't rich here, and have only what we need in terms of rituals." Archbishop Lamy, Salpointe told Machebeuf, was well enough, but now that he had been appointed a coadjutor wanted to do as little as possible. Though it meant additional work for Salpointe, he understood. "I can't blame him — he worked long enough for the right to rest."[2]

Machebeuf traveled to Santa Fe by train, assisting Lamy in the 1 May mass marking the transition. In a four-hour ceremony, Fr. Peter Bourgade of Silver City was consecrated as bishop, replacing Salpointe as vicar apostolic of Arizona. Salpointe was formally recognized as coadjutor to the archbishop of Santa Fe. A full day of festivities followed: a grand dinner, fireworks, and artillery salutes, as the people of Santa Fe celebrated the presence of the four bishops and the consecration of Bourgade.

The following month Pope Leo XIII officially accepted Lamy's resignation, and on 18 July the Vatican wrote informing him of the news. "Certainly, it seems right and just that Y[our] E[xcellency], after all those years of such great and excellent labors in the vineyard of our Lord, should deserve to spend the rest of your life in peace and tranquility." The same day, Cardinal Simeoni sent Salpointe a directive to succeed Lamy immediately, instructing him to make suitable financial arrangements to assure Lamy a "decent living." By the end of August Lamy composed his formal farewell to the clergy and faithful of the archdiocese, the letter to be read in all the churches on Sunday, 6 September. At seventy-two, Lamy was two years younger than Machebeuf, but seemed older. "What has prompted this determination is our advanced age," he explained in the long and moving letter to the people of his archdiocese, "that often deprives us of the necessary strength in the fulfillment of our sacred ministry, though our health may apparently look robust. We shall profit by the days left to prepare ourselves the better to appear before the tribunal of God, in tranquility and solitude."[3]

Such tranquility still eluded Machebeuf. In October 1885 he journeyed from Denver to New York with Salpointe to attend Cardinal John McCloskey's funeral. Extending his trip, he took the opportunity to go Baltimore to meet personally with Cardinal Gibbons for consultation. Both Gibbons and Salpointe recommended that Machebeuf write to Rome and request a coadjutor, giving him the opportunity to recommend preferred candidates, rather than wait and have one assigned he had not chosen. The decision was an important one — not only would Machebeuf be working closely with the man chosen for the remainder of his life, but whoever was chosen would probably succeed him as the next bishop.

By the new year Machebeuf accepted the inevitable, that a coadjutor would be appointed, the only remaining questions being who and when. In January 1886 Machebeuf wrote to Gibbons, telling him that he had made the formal request to Rome. He reminded the Roman officials of his earlier request, in 1880, and explained "having spent five years longer in the same work of the missions, being now over 74 years of age, new settlements being formed and some of them I cannot visit in my crippled condition, I felt the necessity of renewing my application hoping that it would be granted."[4] Along with the formal request Machebeuf submitted a list of his preferred candidates.

Nearly two years elapsed from Machebeuf's request for a coadjutor and the telegram from Rome that informed him of the appointment. During that time six men would be considered for the post, among them John Raverdy, William Howlett, Daniel Riordan, and Nicolas Matz. The remaining two were the vicar general of Fort Wayne and another priest whose identity is not known.

The unknown priest was the first to be eliminated from consideration. He was a member of a religious order which was considered at that time incompatible with the demands of the episcopacy. This was probably one of the Jesuit fathers: John Guida, a member of the faculty at Sacred Heart, Dominic Pantanella, the president of the college who, according to one historian, would have been a true heir to Machebeuf in terms of finances, or Joseph Marra, superior of the Jesuit mission at Las Vegas, New Mexico.

Within a few months rumors began to fly around Denver that Raverdy would be appointed to the post. Machebeuf heard that the pastor of the cathedral in Denver advocated Raverdy and that another bishop had also recommended him. For years Machebeuf had resisted appointing Raverdy to the post of vicar general. He had spent much of his 1868 trip back east, prior to his consecration, searching for another candidate. Raverdy's ultimate appointment had been largely been one of necessity, for although loyal and hardworking, Machebeuf never thought Raverdy demonstrated particular leadership potential. Upset by the rumors of Raverdy's possible appointment as coadjutor, Machebeuf wrote frankly to Cardinal Gibbons, reminding him that he had included Raverdy's name on the list of candidates, but without recommendation.

"Although Father Raverdy who came with me to Colorado in 1860 has always been good, pious and faithful," Machebeuf had previously explained to Gibbons, "he has become extremely unpopular with the majority of the priests by imprudent remarks and harsh ways." Machebeuf had two primary reasons for opposing Raverdy's appointment. The first was Raverdy's inability to work successfully with the Jesuits. "An ex-religious himself, he has the most bitter feelings against all the Fathers of the Society of Jesus," Machebeuf told Gibbons, "whom he accuses and condemns under the most trifling pretexts." Machebeuf was extremely grateful for the work of the Jesuits in Colorado over the years. "For these 15 years past the Jesuit Fathers have worked hard and with success, suffered the greatest hardships and privations to bring back to the practice of their duties from 10,000 to 12,000 Mexicans of the South — In one of the three parishes three fathers, besides the parish church have 18 chapels to visit regularly. By their zeal and spirit of sacrifice they have kept the Faith among the Mexicans. But Fr. Raverdy is blind to all these facts." Raverdy, Machebeuf assured Gibbons, did not share Machebeuf's appreciation for the Jesuits' efforts. His appointment would be disastrous; "the object of this letter is to beg your Grace to use on the contrary all your influence to prevent as a calamity for priests and people the appointment of Fr. Raverdy if his name had ever been sent to Rome."[5]

The second reason that prevented him from recommending Raverdy as a candidate reflected Machebeuf's loyalty to the Hispanic populations in the southern part of the state. One of the Jesuits, Father Brucker, later wrote of that affection. "There can be no doubt that Bishop Machebeuf had a very warm spot in his heart for the Mexicans," the paternalistic Father Brucker wrote. "The reason of this was not only because he had first worked among them in New Mexico as vicar general of Bishop Lamy, but particularly on account of their lively Catholic faith, and, we may add, on account of the childlike manifestations of their love for their Bishop." Writing of Machebeuf's numerous visits in the largely Hispanic communities of southern Colorado Brucker recalled, "he enjoyed as much as they did themselves their hearty and generally very noisy display for his reception, when he encountered from 80 to 100 men on horseback riding out two or three miles to meet him, then nearer to the town the various church societies in procession with banners flying, and all this to the accompaniment of song, music and fireworks."[6]

On these trips Machebeuf would forgo staying in a hotel, in order to stay in the home of one of the Hispanic parishioners. "He would never pass a night at a hotel if there was any sort of a passable Mexican house in the place where he could get accommodations," Brucker recorded. "I well remember one occasion at Del Norte — I wished to take him to the Windsor Hotel, as we had no pastoral residence in the place at that time, but the good Bishop exclaimed: 'Ah, let me alone with your Windsor Hotel! I will stay over night with my old friend Don Nereo Montoya.' . . . So we went to his house, where he gave us the best room he had, but as he had but one room to spare and only one bed in it, we divided the bedding and I slept at the Bishop's feet."[7]

If Raverdy did not appreciate the work of the Jesuits in southern Colorado, Machebeuf felt certain that ministries to those communities would be neglected under his leadership. He was not about to allow a coadjutor to be appointed who valued neither the work of the Jesuits nor the Hispanic population to whom they ministered.

Another candidate for appointment to the position of coadjutor was William J. Howlett, later Machebeuf's biographer. Howlett had grown up in Colorado, been educated at the seminary of St. Sulpice in Paris, and been very successful in Central City, succeeding Joseph Finotti as pastor there in 1880. But when Howlett was transferred to the cathedral in Denver in 1886, he quickly clashed with Machebeuf and Raverdy on parish matters.

Machebeuf advised Gibbons against the selection of Howlett. "I have every reason to form the highest opinion of him," Machebeuf admitted, "but his great success has proved to be a stumbling block for him and an occasion of vanity and self-esteem." Accepting the possibility that Howlett might be appointed coadjutor, Machebeuf had transferred him to Denver, hoping to allow him a period of preparation, time to familiarize himself with person-alities and activities there. "It did not take us long to perceive that he was not the same man he was when he was assistant," Machebeuf explained to Gibbons, "he had been partly spoiled by the mountains, and by degrees had taken the uncouth manners and language of the miners. — Too full of confidence in himself."[8]

The replies to Machebeuf's letters from Cardinal Gibbons suggested that Daniel Riordan, a pastor in Chicago, was the most likely candidate for the position. The man seemed acceptable to Machebeuf, but his own per-sonal favorite was Nicolas Matz, and Machebeuf continued to drop sugges-tions, and not very subtle ones, to that effect. "It is a great consolation to me to be able to say that Fr. Matz, who has also a parish in Denver, justifies entirely our expectations. He is studious and pious. (Some call him a saint) zealous, talented, provident, and a good manager."[9]

Matz was a good choice for the position. Thirty-seven years old, Matz was tall and imposing. Portraits from the period show a thoughtful man with blue-gray eyes, an aquiline nose, and a high forehead. His light brown hair would later turn a stately iron-gray. He was powerful and forceful, sometimes aloof, but was seen to melt into gentleness on occasion, espe-cially when working with children or Hispanics. An Alsatian, Matz was born in Muenster in the Alsace-Lorraine on 6 April 1850. In 1868, when he was eighteen, he had immigrated with his family to Ohio. While attending the Mount St. Mary Seminary of the West in Cincinnati, he first met Machebeuf in 1869, when Machebeuf came to recruit for his Colorado missions. Matz volunteered on the spot. He completed his seminary train-ing and was ordained at Denver's St. Mary's Cathedral in 1874, on his first visit to the West.[10]

Some months before the official decision was made, Machebeuf learned from private sources in Rome that Matz was to be named coadjutor. Greatly pleased, he discussed Matz with his old friend Gabriel Ussel, who continued to serve as pastor of Walsenberg. "I know now who it will be," Machebeuf told Ussel, "and I know of no one more worthy of the position." Matz had a great deal to recommend him. "Born in Europe, but identified with America since his early years, he will understand how to deal with the French, the Italian and other European priests in the common land of their adoption, and he has the advantage of knowing English, French, German, and Italian, and sufficient Spanish to treat with the Mexicans. My poor Mexicans will have a father in Father Matz." The future treatment of the Hispanic population was a most important consideration for Machebeuf, as he explained to Ussel. "With all their defects — or rather their simplicity — they have the ardent faith that moves mountains. During all my years in Colorado, New Mexico and Arizona, I have felt so much at home among these good people, and were it in my power to select I would choose my place as bishop among them. . . . Father Matz has a good heart, I know him well, and I am sure he will show himself the friend and father of my faithful Mexicans."[11]

While Machebeuf was promoting Matz as his preferred candidate for coadjutor, to ultimately succeed him as bishop, he was also pushing for Denver to be raised to a diocese. When Omaha was raised to the status of a bishopric in 1885, Machebeuf became indignant and intensified his efforts. His insistence was due, in part, to the growth of the church in Denver, which seemed to justify the change in classification from vicariate apostolic to diocese. But there were also personal factors involved. The newly appointed Bishop O'Connor of Omaha was the same man who had misunderstood Machebeuf's financial dealings with the Colorado Catholic Loan and Trust Association. Machebeuf still felt hurt by O'Connor's snub on his visit to Denver and suspected that O'Connor had played no small part in Machebeuf's ongoing troubles with Rome.

"When Mgr. J. O'Connor went to Omaha," Machebeuf wrote to Gibbons, in his less-than-objective argument, "he found a good Cathedral built and provided with everything necessary, a large brick house for residence, two parishes, an academy and a hospital. He found in the bank $35,000 deposited by his predecessor and better yet, he found a legacy of $200,000." O'Connor's work in Omaha could hardly be compared to Machebeuf's work in Denver, and Machebeuf was determined that Cardinal Gibbons should be aware of the differences. "What did I find when I went to Denver? No Church or Chapel in the whole territory, obliged to camp out on the 2 bare lots donated in Denver by the Express Co. and worth then about $10 or $15; having no other neighbors but ground squirrels and rattlesnakes which were found in the Sacristy after the 1st Church was built."[12]

Machebeuf detailed an impressive list of his accomplishments in the Denver area; a pro-cathedral, 4 other parishes developed, 5 parish schools and a sixth about to open, a Jesuit college, an academy with 75 boarders and 125 day scholars, 951 students under Catholic education in Denver, an orphan asylum, two hospitals, and a house of refuge. He acknowledged that the Catholic population of Nebraska was larger than Colorado's but attributed this to the fact that the state of Nebraska was older and assured Gibbons that Denver was progressing at a faster rate than Omaha. "Having under our eyes this wonderful progress in material and financial affairs . . . the general feeling [exists] that we have been rather slighted in the striking exception or distinction which was made at Rome between the 2 Vicariates and surely our poor but generous miners, farmers, etc., and our zealous missionaries deserve to be encouraged and to have their efforts better appreciated." In a final, moving, plea, Machebeuf concluded his letter to Gibbons, saying that if Denver were not erected into a diocese it must be because of unknown charges made against him personally in Rome. "Most likely this discrimination is a consequence of that kind of cloud which is floating over my head—and that mysterious reticence with me no doubt is the result of that unfortunate misunderstanding about the security given for our Colorado Catholic Loan and Trust Association." But Machebeuf had no scruples about exposing the very personal interest behind his public request. Concluding his letter, he wrote, "according to every rule of justice, no man can be accused, condemned and punished without a trial. . . . It is surely hard for poor human nature after 47 years of hard missionary life in Ohio, New Mexico, and Colorado, in my old age of 74, to be under such a cloud without knowing the cause or pretext and that, after having sacrificed myself and all I have for the church."[13]

It was another year before Machebeuf's requests were granted. Finally, on 13 June 1887 he received a telegram from Rome informing him that Denver had been elevated to a diocese, that he was now the first bishop of Denver, and that just as he had wished, Nicolas Matz had been appointed his coadjutor. As historian Thomas Feely comments, "Which facet of this double-barrelled good news bulletin more delighted the Bishop is hard to say."[14]

The assistance of the younger energetic Matz assured, easing the burdens of the new diocese, Machebeuf felt free to take a short trip. Ever since his work in Arizona in 1860, Machebeuf had hoped to travel to California. But Lamy had recalled him to Santa Fe and subsequently posted him to Pike's Peak. Now, a change in the status of the Utah Territory provided the aging bishop with an opportunity to venture to the West Coast.

Machebeuf had transferred the administration of Utah to the Archdiocese of San Francisco in 1871. In September 1886 Utah had been elevated to the status of a vicariate apostolic. Lawrence Scanlan, sent by Archbishop Alemany as a missionary to the region in 1873, had his work cut out for him. His 1874 annual report to the Society for the Propagation of the

Faith in Paris records Utah's population as "780 Catholics, 93,360 Heretics, and 5,860 Infidels." Scanlan struggled heroically, building the foundations of the Catholic church in Utah, and ultimately spending forty-two years there. Scanlan worked in the San Francisco-area prior to his assignment to Salt Lake City, Utah, having been under the jurisdiction of the archbishop of San Francisco for sixteen years. Accordingly it was fitting that Scanlan's consecration be held in that city, giving Machebeuf a perfect excuse to finally make the journey he had contemplated over a quarter of a century before.[15]

Machebeuf had an easy trip by railroad from Denver to San Francisco. In late June he arrived in the city by the bay. He first paid his official respects to Archbishop Riordan of San Francisco, who had succeeded his old friend Archbishop Alemany. Given his long association with the Jesuits, it was natural for Machebeuf to stop and pay his respects to the San Francisco Jesuit Community at St. Ignatius College. Unfortunately, records of that visit were destroyed in the 1906 fire and earthquake.[16]

On 29 June 1887 Machebeuf attended Scanlan's consecration in St. Mary's Cathedral. One San Francisco newspaper recorded the event. "Long before the ceremonies began, the edifice was filled to the doors, and hundreds went away unable to obtain entrance." Archbishop Riordan presiding, the bishops of Grass Valley and Sacramento assisting, and Machebeuf in attendance, meant the people of San Francisco could witness a gathering of four bishops and an archbishop — auspicious in any city, but particularly in Catholic-dominated San Francisco.[17]

At seventy-five Machebeuf showed little sign of slowing down, and the San Francisco Catholic *Monitor* printed a copy of his itinerary on the trip. From San Francisco he traveled to Santa Clara to see friends in the Jesuit Community, made stops in San Jose, Salinas, and Santa Cruz, then returned to San Francisco. He left San Francisco again, going to Stockton to visit two priests formerly connected with Colorado, Fathers Van Schie and Maguire. From Stockton he headed to Sacramento, where Bishop Manogue served as his host, and on 10 July he accompanied the new Bishop Scanlan on his return to Salt Lake City. By 17 July he was back in Denver, giving confirmations in two parishes.[18]

Back in Colorado, Machebeuf turned his attention to the work of the Jesuits at the College of the Sacred Heart. Earlier that year, the Jesuits had considered relocating their college once again, this time to Colorado Springs. When Machebeuf learned of the plans, he let it be known that he would never approve the move. In early June a tense conference had taken place between Machebeuf and Joseph Marra, the Superior of the Jesuit

Mission. By 22 June the Jesuits announced that two colleges, would be relocated, not to Colorado Springs, but to Denver. The college in Las Vegas, founded in 1877, and the college in Morrison, founded in 1884, would be combined in the "Old Main" in northwest Denver. Francis Kowald, one of the Jesuits at the college, later remembered that as soon as Machebeuf became aware of the proposed move, "he insisted that any contemplated new College Building must be placed in Denver, the Metropolis of his Diocese, according to plans and stipulations agreed and decided upon from the beginning when he purchased and donated the Morrison College-Building, which was intended only as a temporary location for the future and chief educational institution of his Diocese, to be erected in Denver." A local entrepreneur, John Brisben Walker, came to Machebeuf's aid. He donated forty acres of land to the Jesuits with the stipulation that the land be used to "erect and maintain a College" and that the Jesuits "begin said construction within fifty days from the date hereof (July 22, 1887)." On 13 September 1887 ground was broken for the new Jesuit college in Denver, an impressive four-story stone structure and the beginnings of the school known today as Regis University. The Jesuits kept the Morrison property Machebeuf had given them for another twenty years, using it as a villa, a place of rest and recreation for members of the Jesuit Community in Denver — and Machebeuf got his college in Denver.[19]

Spring comes late in the high altitudes of the Rocky Mountains. Before the arrival of spring 1888, Machebeuf received chilling news from the south. Lamy was dead. Lamy had seemed fine, if tired and a bit frail, when Machebeuf had last seen him. On 7 February 1888 Lamy sent word from his retirement residence outside of Santa Fe that he had a cold. Could a carriage be sent so that he might be brought into town? He had been promptly brought to his old high-ceilinged room in the archbishop's house. Doctors were called in. They diagnosed pneumonia.

Over the next few days, the frail archbishop seemed to drift away, his strength slowly ebbing out of him. On the night of the twelfth he sank into a deep sleep, while his niece Marie, now Mother Francesca, watched over him. In the hours just before dawn he seemed restless, and Mother Francesca called in Louis Mora, the gardener, to help her try to make him more comfortable. By seven o'clock, Mora suggested that they send for a priest. Salpointe had left to attend business in Las Vegas, but another priest came. Taking in the situation in a glance, he began to recite the prayer for the dying. Within half an hour Lamy awoke, Mother Francesca remembered, and "smiled as though he saw a heavenly sight," then silently died "without pain or distress." On the morning of 13 February, bells throughout the city of Santa Fe tolled for Archbishop Lamy.[20]

Machebeuf came as soon as he heard the news, hurrying to Santa Fe by train. On 15 February, Ash Wednesday, he sang the mass for his lifelong friend. He sent up his prayers for the soul of Jean Baptiste Lamy, lying in state in the cathedral he had built, the cathedral that would serve as both his monument and his tomb. The following morning, together with Salpointe and Lamy's vicar general, Pierre Eguillon, Machebeuf sang a solemn pontifical mass. The Office of the Dead was chanted by one hundred priests, and the Collect intoned. "Grant us, Lord, that the soul of thy servant Bishop Juan whom Thou hast withdrawn from earthly toil and strife, may be admitted into the company of thy saints."[21]

Howlett, who traveled with Machebeuf from Denver, remembered the service and Machebeuf's emotional response. "At the funeral he spoke, if speaking it could be called, through tears and sobs, as only he could speak of the dear dead friend." But it was as if Lamy's spirit, rising, took a part of Machebeuf with him. Machebeuf's old weather-beaten face was wet with a steady stream of tears, and he made no attempt to compose himself. He spoke of the years they had shared, the silent halls of seminary, the forests of Ohio, the mountains and deserts of New Mexico. And speaking over the corpse of his best friend, two years younger and now irrevocably snatched away from him, "he uttered the unconscious prophecy that, as he had now seen the angel come to announce the term of that long life, which was even shorter than his, his own call would come next."[22]

If Machebeuf truly believed his own death was growing nearer, he showed no outward sign of it. Throughout the remainder of 1888 he threw himself into his work; his visits to churches, schools, and hospitals seemed to increase. He brought Benedictine and Dominican priests and brothers, and Benedictine and Franciscan sisters to Colorado, increasing the staff of his diocese. He gave retreats, encouraging the younger men and women in their work for the church. Ever the wanderer, he journeyed to Washington, D.C., in 1888 so that he could be present for the laying of the cornerstone of Catholic University. Much to his surprise, he found himself tired after the long journey and exhausting ceremony, needing to lean on something for support, being forced to ask for help to steady himself walking. He began to have occasional spells of dizziness but stubbornly refused to attribute them to his age. At seventy-six he still believed himself as young as he felt in his heart.[23]

Palm Sunday, 14 April 1889, brought Machebeuf one last chance to deceive his old adversary, Death. Returning from the dedication of the new St. Leo's Church, his driver swerved to avoid an oncoming streetcar. The wheel of his buggy caught in the rail of the streetcar track and snapped. The carriage flipped over, and both Machebeuf and his companion, Bishop Borgess of Detroit, were unceremoniously thrown from the vehicle. When help arrived, they found him badly bruised, bleeding heavily from cuts on his head and his arm.[24]

Machebeuf refused to allow the incident to slow him down. After a short period of recovery, he continued his mission trips throughout his diocese. On one of these trips, in Canon City, a stubborn Irish priest, Father Culkin, greeted him with a clenched fist and a pistol. That was hardly a challenge for the man who had walked through the rifles of the ranchers years before, who counseled condemned murderers and shook hands with raiding Apache warriors, the man Lamy always sent to "whip the cats."[25]

On 3 July 1889 he returned from yet another of his pastoral visits. For some time Machebeuf had kept a little room at St. Vincent's Orphanage for his personal use. When his own residence was overrun with visitors, when he had too many pressing business concerns, he would retire to the little room at the orphanage. There he could relax, write letters, or just sit and smile, amused by the innocence of the children at the orphanage. Returning from the pastoral visit, he retired to his little hideaway.

When Death finally came for Machebeuf, the Reaper had to creep in silently, to catch him unaware. Too many times Machebeuf had met Death in open conflict, in accident or life-threatening illness. If Death were to capture Machebeuf, it would have to do so quietly, before he could once again escape. Machebeuf and Death knew each other too well, had met too many times. Death did come quietly for Machebeuf. Lying in his little room in the orphanage, his body just seemed to give up.

Machebeuf lay in bed, drifting between two worlds, and one wonders what thoughts came to him as he looked back over his life. Perhaps he saw the vistas, the wide expanses of the lands he had known: the rugged countryside of Auvergne that bred toughness and wildness into his soul, the thick green forests of Ohio, the muted golds and pastels of the deserts in southern New Mexico, Arizona, and Mexico, or the rugged majesty of the Rockies, their gray granite walls and thick carpets of pine. Perhaps he saw, once again, the oceans: the choppy, gray of the cold Atlantic he had crossed nine times, the stormy waters of Lake Ontario that almost claimed him in shipwreck, the brilliant blue of the Pacific when he first saw it from the coast of Mexico, or the shorelines of ragged bluffs, beautiful redwoods, and gnarled cypress that lined the coasts of northern California. Perhaps he saw once again the sweeping majesty of thousands of antelope and buffalo swarming across the snow-covered plains, the snow of the ice-bound St. Lawrence, or the white peaks of the Sangre de Cristos. Maybe he saw once more the people he had known — bishops and buffalo hunters, miners and Mexicans, everyone from the impoverished immigrants to the French royal family and the three popes he had known. And perhaps he heard once again the music of a lifetime: the music of the mass, the timeless Litany of the Saints, the choirs of countless churches, the Papagos singing in San Xavier del Bac, the Mexican bands who had welcomed him in small towns, the thousands of faceless voices whispering their confessions as softly as the wind in the pines.

Perhaps, once again, he saw Lamy's smile, heard Lamy's voice telling him, "You are the very man for Pike's Peak." In his twenty-nine years in Colorado Machebeuf had accomplished a great deal. Lying in the tiny room in the orphanage was the bishop to some 50,000 Catholics in Colorado. In 1860 he and Raverdy had been the only Catholic priests in Colorado; by 1889 there were 64 priests. Once a land with only a few mission churches, Colorado now had 54 churches, 53 chapels, and 85 mission stations. From the first sisters he had recruited, there were now 168, caring for the sick in 11 Catholic hospitals, teaching in 9 academies for young ladies and 16 parish schools, as well as administering the orphanage and a protective home. The Jesuits he had courted and supported now had their fine four-story stone college and a high school for the young men of Denver. In all, 4,028 students were receiving formal education in Catholic schools. Perhaps Machebeuf just knew that his work was finally complete.[26]

While the sisters wept and prayed around his bed, Machebeuf calmly gave instructions for Bishop Matz to be summoned. From the hands of the handsome young bishop, the man he himself had selected to succeed him, Machebeuf received the last sacraments "with piety and resignation."[27] On the morning of 10 July 1889, Machebeuf, quietly smiling and at peace, willingly slipped into death. Perhaps Lamy came to fetch him, impatient of waiting, eager to continue their friendship in the beyond. If not, it must have been the Angel of Death that came for the soul of Joseph Machebeuf, the angel he had recognized at Lamy's funeral. For Machebeuf, Trompe-la-Mort, deceiver of death and adventurer that he was, would never have gone peacefully into death were he not in the company of angels.

Epilogue

The news of Machebeuf's death shocked the city of Denver. He had so often escaped death, many expressed outright disbelief, while others looked dumbfounded and incredulous. The Sisters of Loretto took Machebeuf's body to their chapel, the same chapel where he had so often sung the morning mass. On 15 July his body was transferred to his humble pro-cathedral to lie in state.

On the morning of 16 July, with Archbishop Salpointe beside him, Bishop Matz sang the pontifical high mass and one hundred priests chanted the Office of the Dead. The people of Denver filled the church to overflowing and crowded the streets outside. Thousands of people trailed into the city from nearby towns and mission stations to attend his final farewell. Priests and sisters, businessmen and miners, Irish, German, and Italian immigrants, Hispanics and Anglos, all came to pay their last respects. No church in the city was vast enough to hold them all.

William Howlett, who first met Machebeuf in 1865, remembered that occasion. "The special impression made then, and which has never been forgotten, was that he was a man of very advanced age. In reality he had not yet completed his fifty-third year, but his hair was turning grey and his face was thin and wrinkled as that of a man of eighty." Over the years Howlett's impression of Machebeuf changed. "The twenty-five years of such missionary life he had lived seemed to have left him a weather-beaten wreck near the limit of its power to hold longer together. Strange as it may appear," Howlett mused, "that impression could never afterwards be felt and even when Bishop Machebeuf lay in his coffin the writer could see nothing of the worn-out, decrepit features of his first impression, but a strong, rugged face that might have braved many more years of storm and sunshine."[1]

Howlett was not alone in his affection for Machebeuf. Everyone who comes into contact with his character becomes enchanted by Machebeuf. One acquaintance referred to Machebeuf as "the ugliest little man I ever saw . . . with the most heavenly smile." Historian Thomas Feely notes, "Bankers and ecclesiastical authorities were eventually conquered by his generous spirit when he described the benefits for the Church that would come from the growing West. Though they may not have concurred in his judgments on financial matters, they loved the man." Summarizing Machebeuf's work in Colorado, Feely writes, "the remarkable fact is that this wisp of a man overcame the odds of a dour temperament and ill-health, of turbulent financial crises and an unestablished, frightfully poor Catholic population, and of cultural conflicts and inadequate personnel, to erect an institutionalized edifice that would have made a more efficient administrator proud." Or more succinctly, "when all is added up Machebeuf comes within inches of greatness. He had the color and the character of the West. His love of his fellow man was divinely impetuous in the reckless, wholehearted fashion of the frontier."[2]

Throughout his life, as even after his death, Machebeuf inspired tremendous affection and loyalty. Raverdy, who first accompanied Machebeuf to Colorado in 1860, who served him faithfully for twenty-nine years, was in Chicago when he heard of Machebeuf's death, on his way back from a trip to Europe. Although seriously ill himself, when Raverdy heard the news, he got up out his sickbed and took the first train to Denver. At the end of Machebeuf's funeral mass the ghostly form of Raverdy appeared, supported by two assistants, the crowd parting silently to let him pass. Someone placed a chair beside Machebeuf's coffin, and Raverdy, as if oblivious to the ceremony in progress around him, sat silently on the chair, gazing at the face of his friend, while a continual stream of tears coursed down his face. After the mass, Raverdy was helped back into bed. A few weeks later, still following Machebeuf, he died.

Raverdy's body was laid beside the body of Joseph Machebeuf in a vault at the Sisters of Loretto's chapel. Machebeuf never built a great cathedral — construction of parish churches and schools took precedence. He carried his preference for the humble even into death — along with his wanderlust. The ranch Machebeuf once planned to use for his own retirement was consecrated by his successor, Bishop Matz, and became Mount Olivet Cemetery. Three years after his death, Machebeuf's remains were removed from the vault in the sisters' chapel and transferred to a receiving vault in the new cemetery. On 12 July 1939 Machebeuf made one final move, from the receiving vault to his niche in the cool timeless stone of Gallagher Chapel. There he remains.

The *Annales de la Propagation de la Foi,* the journal of the pious society that had so long supported both Lamy and Machebeuf's missionary work, ran Machebeuf's obituary in the fall of 1889. At the time of his death, they noted, the wanderer had one more journey planned, another trip to Europe to attend his sister's fiftieth anniversary as one of the Sisters of the Visitation. Summing up Machebeuf's life, the unknown writers for the Society commented, "Fifty-three years in the priesthood, fifty years in the apostolate, twenty-one years in the episcopacy: hence to summarize his life, it was no more than one long sacrifice for the salvation of souls."[3] It is difficult to reconcile that solemn description with the mischief, optimism, and unwavering sense of humor that Machebeuf demonstrated throughout his life. Apparently, after all those years, the writers of the *Annales* didn't know Machebeuf very well.

Notes

In citing works in the notes, short titles have been used. Collections have been identified by the following abbreviations:

AASF   Archdiocesan Archives of Santa Fe
BCA   Baltimore Chancery Archives
CIN/ND   Cincinnati Archdiocesan Archives in the University of Notre Dame Archives
DAA   Denver Archdiocesan Archives
L/SPF/ND   Lyon Archives of the Societé pour la Propagation de la Foi in University of Notre Dame Archives
ND   University of Notre Dame Archives
RA   Riom Archives of the Monastère de la Vistation, Riom, France
SF/ND   Santa Fe Archdiocesan Archives in the University of Notre Dame Archives
VPF   Vatican Archives of the Sacred Congregation for the Propagation of the Faith

INTRODUCTION

1. Cather, *Death Comes for the Archbishop*, 38.

CHAPTER I

1. Ussel, "Memoires," 85–100; Steele, "The View From the Rectory," 99 n. 3.
2. Ussel, "Memories," 85–100; Steele, "The View From the Rectory," 92.
3. Ussel, "Memories," 85–100; Steele, "The View From the Rectory," 99 n. 3.
4. Gougaud and Gouvion, *France Observed*, 60.

CHAPTER 2

1. Howlett, *Life of the Right Reverend Joseph P. Machebeuf,* 20–21.
2. Butler, *Butler's Lives of the Saints,* 166.
3. Howlett, *Life of the Right Reverend Joseph P. Machebeuf,* 22.
4. Ibid.
5. Horgan, *Lamy of Santa Fe,* 16.
6. Canu, *Religious Orders of Men,* 115.
7. Ibid., 121; Howlett, *Life of the Right Reverend Joseph P. Machebeuf,* 23.
8. Howlett, *Life of the Right Reverend Joseph P. Machebeuf,* 24.
9. Daniel-Rops, *The Church in an Age of Revolution,* 150.
10. Ibid., 183.
11. Howlett, *Life of the Right Reverend Joseph P. Machebeuf,* 28.
12. Daniel-Rops, *The Church in an Age of Revolution,* 183.

CHAPTER 3

1. White, *The Diocesan Seminary in the United States,* 14–16.
2. Boisard, *La Campagnie de Saint Sulpice,* 38–44.
3. Canu, *Religious Orders of Men,* 114.
4. Gibson, *A Social History,* 82.
5. Ibid., 88.
6. Howlett, *Life of the Right Reverend Joseph P. Machebeuf,* 29.
7. Ibid.
8. Gibson, *A Social History,* 69.
9. Ibid., 70, 71.
10. Ibid., 88; the quotation is from Beaudoin, *Le Grand Séminaire de Marseille,* 70.
11. Horgan, *Lamy of Santa Fe,* 12, 15; Warner, *Archbishop Lamy,* 34.
12. de Dalmases, *Ignatius of Loyola,* 215–17.
13. Horgan, *Lamy of Santa Fe,* 15; Warner, *Archbishop Lamy,* 34.
14. Warner, *Archbishop Lamy,* 22.
15. Horgan, *Lamy of Santa Fe,* 17–18.
16. Machebeuf, "Reminiscences," 31 January 1889.
17. Howlett, *Life of the Right Reverend Joseph P. Machebeuf,* 30.

CHAPTER 4

1. Machebeuf, "Reminiscences," 31 January 1889.
2. Howlett, *Life of the Right Reverend Joseph P. Machebeuf,* 35.
3. Machebeuf, "Reminiscences," 31 January 1889.
4. Howlett, *Life of the Right Reverend Joseph P. Machebeuf,* 25.
5. Gibson, *A Social History,* 69.
6. Ibid., 145.
7. St. John, *The Blessed Virgin,* 2, 44.

8. Howlett, *Life of the Right Reverend Joseph P. Machebeuf,* 34.

9. Howlett, *Life of Bishop Machebeuf,* 422 n. for pp. 32–33.

10. Howlett, *Life of the Right Reverend Joseph P. Machebeuf,* 35.

11. White, *The Diocesan Seminary in the United States,* 41–42.

12. Machebeuf, "Reminiscences," 31 January 1889.

13. Howlett, *Life of the Right Reverend Joseph P. Machebeuf,* 39; DAA, Machebeuf Diaries, Clermont, 28 September 1838.

14. Machebeuf, "Reminiscences," 31 January 1889.

15. Howlett, *Life of the Right Reverend Joseph P. Machebeuf,* 34.

16. *Le Semaine Religieuse de Clermont,* 13 September 1869.

17. Howlett, *Life of the Right Reverend Joseph P. Machebeuf,* 43–44.

CHAPTER 5

1. Howlett, *Life of the Right Reverend Joseph P. Machebeuf,* 45.

2. Horgan, *Lamy of Santa Fe,* 19.

3. Howlett, *Life of the Right Reverend Joseph P. Machebeuf,* 46–48; RA, Machebeuf to father, Paris, 24 May 1839.

4. Howlett, *Life of the Right Reverend Joseph P. Machebeuf,* 49; RA, Purcell to Machebeuf's father, Paris, 26 May 1839.

5. Howlett, *Life of the Right Reverend Joseph P. Machebeuf,* 51; RA, Machebeuf to father, Havre, 7 July 1839.

6. Howlett, *Life of the Right Reverend Joseph P. Machebeuf,* 51; RA, Machebeuf to father, Havre, 7 July 1839.

7. Horgan, *Lamy of Santa Fe,* 20; Howlett, *Life of the Right Reverend Joseph P. Machebeuf,* 53.

8. Horgan, *Lamy of Santa Fe,* 21, 23; RA, Machebeuf to father, Havre, 7 July 1839.

9. Howlett, *Life of the Right Reverend Joseph P. Machebeuf,* 57; RA, Machebeuf to father, on board *Silvie de Grasse,* 8 August 1839.

10. Howlett, *Life of the Right Reverend Joseph P. Machebeuf,* 57; RA, Machebeuf to father, on board *Silvie de Grasse,* 8 August 1839.

11. Howlett, *Life of the Right Reverend Joseph P. Machebeuf,* 59; RA, Machebeuf to father, on board *Silvie de Grasse,* 8 August 1839; quotation is from Horgan, *Lamy of Santa Fe,* 23.

12. Howlett, *Life of the Right Reverend Joseph P. Machebeuf,* 59; RA, Machebeuf to father, on board *Silvie de Grasse,* 8 August 1839.

13. Howlett, *Life of the Right Reverend Joseph P. Machebeuf,* 60.

14. U. S. Department of the Interior, *Chesapeake and Ohio Canal,* 105, 54; Dickens, *Pictures from Italy,* 332.

15. Trollope, *Domestic Manners,* 194–95.

16. Horgan, *Lamy of Santa Fe,* 25; Dickens, 341, 342.

17. Dickens, *Pictures from Italy,* 347; Wade, *The Urban Frontier,* 314, 55.

18. Horgan, *Lamy of Santa Fe,* 25.

19. Billington, *The Protestant Crusade*, 57, 75.

20. Ibid., 65, 184.

21. Howlett, *Life of the Right Reverend Joseph P. Machebeuf*, 64; RA, Machebeuf to father, Tiffin, Ohio, 24 January 1840.

22. Machebeuf, "Reminiscences," 18 October 1889.

23. Howlett, *Life of the Right Reverend Joseph P. Machebeuf*, 67; RA, Machebeuf to father, Tiffin, Ohio, 24 January 1840.

24. Howlett, *Life of the Right Reverend Joseph P. Machebeuf*, 65; RA, Machebeuf to father, Tiffin, Ohio, 24 January 1840.

25. Howlett, *Life of the Right Reverend Joseph P. Machebeuf*, 73; RA, Machebeuf to sister, Tiffin, Ohio, 14 February 1840.

26. Howlett, *Life of the Right Reverend Joseph P. Machebeuf*, 74; RA, Machebeuf to sister, Tiffin, Ohio, 14 February 1840.

27. Howlett, *Life of the Right Reverend Joseph P. Machebeuf*, 75; RA, Machebeuf to sister, Tiffin, Ohio, 14 February 1840.

28. Machebeuf, "Reminiscences," 18 October 1889.

29. Ibid.

30. Howlett, *Life of the Right Reverend Joseph P. Machebeuf*, 77

CHAPTER 6

1. Ohio State Archeological and Historical Society, *The Ohio Guide*, 308–9.

2. Hennepin, *A New Discovery*, 108–9.

3. Ohio State Archeological and Historical Society, *The Ohio Guide*, 308–9.

4. Dickens, *Pictures from Italy*, 381.

5. Howlett, *Life of the Right Reverend Joseph P. Machebeuf*, 91, 85.

6. Ibid., 105, 85; RA, Machebeuf to brother, Upper Sandusky, 30 June 1842.

7. Howlett, *Life of the Right Reverend Joseph P. Machebeuf*, 86; RA, Machebeuf to sister, Lower Sandusky, 10 March 1841.

8. Howlett, *Life of the Right Reverend Joseph P. Machebeuf*, 91; RA, Machebeuf to father, Lower Sandusky, 26 March 1841.

9. Howlett, *Life of the Right Reverend Joseph P. Machebeuf*, 91; RA, Machebeuf to father, Lower Sandusky, 26 March 1841.

10. Billington, *The Protestant Crusade*, 22.

11. Howlett, *Life of the Right Reverend Joseph P. Machebeuf*, 90; RA, Machebeuf to father, Lower Sandusky, 26 March 1841.

12. Howlett, *Life of the Right Reverend Joseph P. Machebeuf*, 95; RA, Machebeuf to sister, Norwalk, 26 May 1841.

13. Ohio State Archeological and Historical Society, *The Ohio Guide*, 308–9; Dickens, *Pictures from Italy*, 382.

14. Howlett, *Life of the Right Reverend Joseph P. Machebeuf*, 94, 95–96; RA, Machebeuf to sister, Norwalk, 26 May 1841.

15. Howlett, *Life of the Right Reverend Joseph P. Machebeuf*, 105, 102; RA, Machebeuf to brother, Upper Sandusky, 30 June 1842; RA, Machebeuf to sister, Monroeville, 28 February 1842.

16. Howlett, *Life of the Right Reverend Joseph P. Machebeuf*, 91.

17. Ibid., 101; Ohio State Archeological and Historical Society, *The Ohio Guide*, 308–9.

18. Howlett, *Life of the Right Reverend Joseph P. Machebeuf*, 99–100.

19. Taylor, *The Transportation Revolution*, vol. 4, *Economic History of the United States*, 344–45.

20. Howlett, *Life of the Right Reverend Joseph P. Machebeuf*, 105–6; RA, Machebeuf to brother, Upper Sandusky, 30 June 1842; Taylor, *The Transportation Revolution*, vol. 4, *Economic History of the United States*, 345.

21. Howlett, *Life of the Right Reverend Joseph P. Machebeuf*, 108; RA, Machebeuf to father, St. Alphonsus, Peru, Ohio, 4 October 1842.

22. Howlett, *Life of the Right Reverend Joseph P. Machebeuf*, 113.

23. Billington, *The Protestant Crusade*, 34.

24. Horgan, *Lamy of Santa Fe*, 41; Howlett, *Life of the Right Reverend Joseph P. Machebeuf*, 113.

CHAPTER 7

1. Howlett, *Life of the Right Reverend Joseph P. Machebeuf*, 112; RA, Machebeuf to father, Montreal, 12 January 1843.

2. Howlett, *Life of the Right Reverend Joseph P. Machebeuf*, 112; RA, Machebeuf to father, Montreal, 12 January 1843.

3. Howlett, *Life of the Right Reverend Joseph P. Machebeuf*, 114; RA, Machebeuf to sister, Sandusky City, 26 July 1843.

4. Howlett, *Life of the Right Reverend Joseph P. Machebeuf*, 114; RA, Machebeuf to sister, Sandusky City, 26 July 1843.

5. Howlett, *Life of the Right Reverend Joseph P. Machebeuf*, 118; RA, Machebeuf to sister, Sandusky City, 23 October 1843.

6. Howlett, *Life of the Right Reverend Joseph P. Machebeuf*, 119; RA, Machebeuf to sister, Sandusky City, 23 October 1843.

7. Aron, *The Ursulines*, 45, 75.

8. Dickens, *Pictures from Italy*, 14–15.

9. Howlett, *Life of the Right Reverend Joseph P. Machebeuf*, 129.

10. Chandlery, *Pilgrim-Walks in Rome*, 344.

11. Dickens, *Pictures from Italy*, 112; Eliot quoted in Chandlery, *Pilgrim-Walks in Rome*, 344; Howlett, *Life of the Right Reverend Joseph P. Machebeuf*, 128.

12. Chandlery, *Pilgrim-Walks in Rome*, 14, 344.

13. Dickens, *Pictures from Italy*, 112.

14. Ibid., 113; Horgan, *Lamy of Santa Fe*, 51.

15. *New Catholic Encyclopedia*, 6:787, 14:638.

16. Howlett, *Life of the Right Reverend Joseph P. Machebeuf*, 128–29; Horgan, *Lamy of Santa Fe*, 50.

17. *New Catholic Encyclopedia*, 8:993–94.

18. Howlett, *Life of the Right Reverend Joseph P. Machebeuf*, 128.

19. Ibid., 132.

20. Horgan, *Lamy of Santa Fe*, 51; Howlett, *Life of the Right Reverend Joseph P. Machebeuf*, 128; ND, Machebeuf to Purcell, Paris, 10 April 1845.

21. Howlett, *Life of the Right Reverend Joseph P. Machebeuf*, 137.

CHAPTER 8

1. Howlett, *Life of the Right Reverend Joseph P. Machebeuf*, 136; Horgan, *Lamy of Santa Fe*, 53.

2. Howlett, *Life of the Right Reverend Joseph P. Machebeuf*, 136–37.

3. Horgan, *Lamy of Santa Fe*, 55.

4. Ibid; Howlett, *Life of the Right Reverend Joseph P. Machebeuf*, 143.

5. Howlett, *Life of the Right Reverend Joseph P. Machebeuf*, 141.

6. Ibid., 145.

7. Ibid., 148–49.

8. Howlett, *Life of Bishop Machebeuf*, 149; Horgan, 75; RA, Machebeuf to sister, on board *Peytona*, 17 January 1851.

9. *New Catholic Encyclopedia*, 14:638.

10. Horgan, *Lamy of Santa Fe*, 55; VPF, "Beatissime pater" Baltimore Council to Pius IX, Baltimore, 13 May 1849.

11. Horgan, *Lamy of Santa Fe*, 73.

12. Ibid., 74; Howlett, *Life of the Right Reverend Joseph P. Machebeuf*, 153, 154; RA, Machebeuf to sister, on board *Peytona*, 20 January 1851.

13. *New Catholic Encyclopedia*, 14:639–40.

14. Howlett, *Life of the Right Reverend Joseph P. Machebeuf*, 154; RA, Machebeuf to sister, on board *Peytona*, 20 January 1851.

15. Howlett, *Life of the Right Reverend Joseph P. Machebeuf*, 155; RA, Machebeuf to sister, on board *Peytona*, 20 January 1851.

16. Howlett, *Life of the Right Reverend Joseph P. Machebeuf*, 153; RA, Machebeuf to sister, on board *Peytona*, 20 January 1851.

17. Steele, "A Lady Writer Reports Some Incidents," 75; Howlett, *Life of the Right Reverend Joseph P. Machebeuf*, 153; RA, Machebeuf to sister, on board *Peytona*, 20 January 1851.

18. Howlett, *Life of the Right Reverend Joseph P. Machebeuf*, 153; RA, Machebeuf to sister, on board *Peytona*, 20 January 1851.

19. Banvard, "Description of Banvard's Panorama," 136; Lyell, "Carnival in New Orleans," 148.

20. Howlett, *Life of the Right Reverend Joseph P. Machebeuf,* 156; RA, Machebeuf to sister, on board *Peytona,* 20 January 1851.

CHAPTER 9

1. Horgan, *Lamy of Santa Fe,* 99; RA, Machebeuf to sister, New Orleans, 23 January 1851.

2. Howlett, *Life of the Right Reverend Joseph P. Machebeuf,* 156, 157; RA, Machebeuf to sister New Orleans, 25 January 1851.

3. Howlett, *Life of the Right Reverend Joseph P. Machebeuf,* 159.

4. Chavez, *But Time and Chance,* 96.

5. Howlett, *Life of the Right Reverend Joseph P. Machebeuf,* 159, 160; RA, Machebeuf to sister, Santa Fe, 29 September 1851.

6. Howlett, *Life of the Right Reverend Joseph P. Machebeuf,* 160; Howlett, *Life of Bishop Machebeuf,* 428; RA, Machebeuf to sister, Santa Fe, 29 September 1851.

7. Howlett, *Life of the Right Reverend Joseph P. Machebeuf,* 160; RA, Machebeuf to sister, Santa Fe, 29 September 1851.

8. Horgan, *Lamy of Santa Fe,* 104.

9. Ibid.

10. Ibid., 105; Howlett, *Life of the Right Reverend Joseph P. Machebeuf,* 161; RA, Machebeuf to sister, Santa Fe, 29 September 1851.

11. *New Catholic Encyclopedia,* 4:682–83, 659–60.

12. Simmons, *New Mexico,* 107.

13. Chavez, *But Time and Chance,* 42.

14. Ibid., 92.

15. Horgan, *Lamy of Santa Fe,* 107; L/SPF/ND, Lamy to L/SPF, Santa Fe, 28 August 1851.

16. Horgan, *Lamy of Santa Fe,* 108; L/SPF/ND, Lamy to L/SPF, Santa Fe, 28 August 1851.

17. Howlett, *Life of the Right Reverend Joseph P. Machebeuf,* 165–66; RA, Machebeuf to sister, Santa Fe, 29 September 1851; Horgan, *Lamy of Santa Fe,* 109; L/SPF/ND, Lamy to L/SPF, Santa Fe, 28 August 1851.

18. Albert, *Western America in 1846–57,* 40; Horgan, *Lamy of Santa Fe,* 109.

19. Howlett, *Life of the Right Reverend Joseph P. Machebeuf,* 166; RA, Machebeuf to sister, Santa Fe, 29 September 1851; Horgan, *Lamy of Santa Fe,* 110.

20. Horgan, *Lamy of Santa Fe,* 115, 116; RA, Machebeuf to sister, Peña Blanca, N.Mex., 31 May 1852; CIN/ND, Lamy to Purcell, Santa Fe, 2 September 1851.

21. Horgan, *Lamy of Santa Fe,* 113; Howlett, *Life of the Right Reverend Joseph P. Machebeuf,* 30; Chavez, *But Time and Chance,* 93.

22. Horgan, *Lamy of Santa Fe,* 132–39.

23. Chavez, *My Penitente Land,* 232.

24. Horgan, *Lamy of Santa Fe,* 140.

25. Ibid., 141.
26. Ibid., 148; RA, Machebeuf to sister, Santa Fe, 29 September 1851.

CHAPTER 10

1. Fuentes, Carlos, *The Buried Mirror,* 130–31, 132, 134.
2. Chavez, *My Penitente Land,* 208, 209; Horgan, *Lamy of Santa Fe,* 73.
3. Horgan, *Lamy of Santa Fe,* 192, 128.
4. Chavez, *Très Macho — He Said,* 18–19; Emory, *Notes of a Military Reconnaissance,* 465.
5. Chavez, *Très Macho — He Said,* 22–23; Danielson Papers, L. Smith, journal no. 2, April 1852.
6. Chavez, *My Penitente Land,* 259.
7. Horgan, *Lamy of Santa Fe,* 128; VPF, Machebeuf to VPF, Rome, 1856.
8. Chavez, *But Time and Chance,* 16.
9. Ibid., 14, 17, 21, 44.
10. Horgan, *Lamy of Santa Fe,* 130.
11. Chavez, *But Time and Chance,* 90.
12. Mares, "Padre Martínez: New Perspectives from Taos," 32; Danielson Papers, H. W. Read, *Home Mission Record,* May 1851, letter, 11 January 1851.
13. Mares, "Padre Martínez: New Perspectives from Taos," 33; Danielson Papers, H. W. Read, *Home Mission Record,* May 1851, letter, 12 January 1851.
14. Danielson Papers, L. Smith, *Home Mission Record,* April 1852, letter, 5 September 1851.
15. Chavez, *But Time and Chance,* 90, 98, 100; Horgan, *Lamy of Santa Fe,* 148.
16. Horgan, *Lamy of Santa Fe,* 153.
17. Howlett, *Life of the Right Reverend Joseph P. Machebeuf,* 180, 181, 182; RA, Machebeuf to sister, Peña Blanca, 31 May 1852.
18. Howlett, *Life of the Right Reverend Joseph P. Machebeuf,* 181; RA, Machebeuf to sister, Peña Blanca, 31 May 1852.
19. Howlett, *Life of the Right Reverend Joseph P. Machebeuf,* 189.
20. Horgan, *Lamy of Santa Fe,* 162.
21. Ibid., 165.
22. Ibid., 190; Chavez, *Très Macho — He Said,* 43.
23. Chavez, *Très Macho — He Said,* 45; Baptismal book, Albuquerque, September–November 1852.
24. Chavez, *But Time and Chance,* 102; Horgan, *Lamy of Santa Fe,* 175.
25. Horgan, *Lamy of Santa Fe,* 169.
26. Ibid., 174.
27. Ibid., 174.
28. Ibid., 175.
29. Ibid., 176; Chavez, *But Time and Chance,* 103.
30. Chavez, *Très Macho — He Said,* 33.

31. Mares, "Padre Martínez: New Perspectives from Taos," 44.

32. Chavez, *Très Macho — He Said*, 35.

33. Horgan, *Lamy of Santa Fe*, 16

34. Chavez, *Très Macho — He Said*, 36–37.

35. Ignatius of Loyola, *The Spiritual Exercises of St. Ignatius*, 137.

36. Chavez, *Très Macho — He Said*, 36–37.

37. Steele, "The View from the Rectory," 84.

38. Ibid.

39. Chavez, *Très Macho — He Said*, 75.

40. Steele, "The View from the Rectory," 84–85.

CHAPTER 11

1. Chavez, *But Time and Chance*, 105.

2. Ibid., 106.

3. Ibid., 106–7.

4. Ibid., 108.

5. Ibid., 110; AASF, Horgan Collection, Machebeuf to Martínez, 3 February 1853, no. 3.

6. Chavez, *But Time and Chance*, 111; AASF, Martínez to Lamy, 24 February 1853, no. 4.

7. Chavez, *But Time and Chance*, 112; AASF, C. de Baca to Lamy, 28 January 1853, no. 2.

8. Chavez, *But Time and Chance*, 112; AASF, Lamy to C. de Baca, 22 February 1853, no. 2.

9. Horgan, *Lamy of Santa Fe*, 191.

10. Ibid.; VPF, Lamy to Armijo, 17 March 1853.

11. Howlett, *Life of the Right Reverend Joseph P. Machebeuf*, 192–93; RA, Machebeuf to sister, Santa Fe or Albuquerque, 1854.

12. Howlett, *Life of the Right Reverend Joseph P. Machebeuf*, 192–93; RA, Machebeuf to sister, Santa Fe or Albuquerque, 1854.

13. Howlett, *Life of the Right Reverend Joseph P. Machebeuf*, 192–93; RA, Machebeuf to sister, Santa Fe or Albuquerque, 1854.

14. Howlett, *Life of the Right Reverend Joseph P. Machebeuf*, 194; RA, Machebeuf to sister, Santa Fe or Albuquerque, 1854.

15. Chavez, *But Time and Chance*, 117; AASF, Martínez, Ortiz, Lujan, and Chávez to Lamy, Santa Fe, Horgan Collection, VPF, 2 April 1853, no. 2a.

16. Chavez, *But Time and Chance*, 119; AASF, Lamy to Purcell, Santa Fe, Lamy File, 10 April 1853, no. 6.

17. Howlett, *Life of the Right Reverend Joseph P. Machebeuf*, 195.

18. Steele, "Padre Gallegos, Père Machebeuf, and the Albuquerque Rectory," 63, 64.

19. Ibid., 66; Machebeuf to Zubiría, Albuquerque, 11 May 1854; RA, Machebeuf to sister, Santa Fe, 30 November 1854.

20. Steele, "Padre Gallegos, Père Machebeuf, and the Albuquerque Rectory," 67.

21. Ibid., 68, 69.

22. Howlett, *Life of the Right Reverend Joseph P. Machebeuf*, 198; RA, Machebeuf to sister, 30 November 1854.

23. Howlett, *Life of the Right Reverend Joseph P. Machebeuf*, 206.

24. Ibid., 196–97.

25. Horgan, *Lamy of Santa Fe*, 208–9.

26. Ibid., 201–9.

27. Howlett, *Life of the Right Reverend Joseph P. Machebeuf*, 200.

28. Ibid., 201.

29. Horgan, *Lamy of Santa Fe*, 211; VPF, Lamy to VPF, Santa Fe, 1 February 1856.

30. Horgan, *Lamy of Santa Fe*, 213; CIN/ND, Lamy to Purcell, Santa Fe, 30 December 1856.

31. Horgan, *Lamy of Santa Fe*, 221.

32. Ibid., 222; RA, Machebeuf to sister, on board *Sultana*, 12 April 1856.

33. Horgan, *Lamy of Santa Fe*, 222.

34. Ibid., 226, 227; VPF, Gallegos to Pius IX, Washington, D.C., 24 April 1856; VPF, N.Mex. legislators to Pius IX, Santa Fe, 31 January 1856.

35. Horgan, *Lamy of Santa Fe*, 228; VPF, Machebeuf to VPF, Rome, 1856.

36. Horgan, *Lamy of Santa Fe*, 228; VPF, Machebeuf to VPF, Rome, 1856

37. Chavez, *But Time and Chance*, 128; VPF, 1856, no. 12a.

38. Chavez, *Très Macho — He Said*, 89–103.

39. Horgan, *Lamy of Santa Fe*, 237; RA, Machebeuf to sister, on board *Alma*, 20 August 1856.

40. Horgan, *Lamy of Santa Fe*, 238; Howlett, *Life of the Right Reverend Joseph P. Machebeuf*, 212–18.

41. Horgan, *Lamy of Santa Fe*, 238; Howlett, *Life of the Right Reverend Joseph P. Machebeuf*, 212–18.

42. Horgan, *Lamy of Santa Fe*, 238; Howlett, *Life of the Right Reverend Joseph P. Machebeuf*, 212–18.

43. Horgan, *Lamy of Santa Fe*, 238; Howlett, *Life of the Right Reverend Joseph P. Machebeuf*, 212–18.

44. Horgan, *Lamy of Santa Fe*, 238; Howlett, *Life of the Right Reverend Joseph P. Machebeuf*, 212–18.

45. Horgan, *Lamy of Santa Fe*, 239; RA, Machebeuf to brother, camp near New Mexico, 3 November 1856.

CHAPTER 12

1. Chavez, *But Time and Chance*, 129; AASF, Martínez to Lamy (translated by Chavez), Lamy File, 22 April 1856, no. 21, Horgan Collection, 1856, no. 2.

2. Chavez, *But Time and Chance*, 131; *Santa Fe Gazette*, 24 May 1856, reprinted 31 May.

3. AASF, Lamy to Martínez, Lamy File, 5 May 1856, no. 22, duplicate in Horgan Collection.

4. Horgan, *Lamy of Santa Fe*, 231; McCall, *New Mexico in 1850*, 135.

5. Darley, *The Passionists of the Southwest*, 9.

6. Chavez, *But Time and Chance*, 36.

7. Ibid., 36; Ahlborn, "The Penitente Moradas of Abiquiú," 126.

8. Chavez, *My Penitente Land*, 238.

9. Horgan, *Lamy of Santa Fe*, 231; SF/ND, Martínez to Lamy, Taos, 1 October 1856.

10. Ussel, "Memoires"; Howlett, *Life of Bishop Machebeuf*, 434–35 n. for p. 229.

11. Steele, "Kit Carson and Padre Martínez," 77; Horgan, *Lamy of Santa Fe*, 242.

12. Horgan, *Lamy of Santa Fe*, 231; SF/ND, Martínez to Lamy, Taos, 1 October 1856.

13. Chavez, *But Time and Chance*, 137; AASF, Martínez to Lamy, Horgan Collection, 12 November 1856, no. 10.

14. Horgan, *Lamy of Santa Fe*, 242.

15. Mares, "Many Faces of Padre Antonio José Martínez," 23.

16. Chavez, *But Time and Chance*, 136; AASF, Taladrid to Lamy, Lamy File, 23 October 1856, no. 12.

17. Steele, Thomas J., S.J., personal correspondence with the author; Howlett, *Life of Bishop Machebeuf*, 434 n. for p. 229.

18. Steele, "Kit Carson and Padre Martínez," 73.

19. Guild and Carter, *Kit Carson*, 96, 165–66; Horgan, *Lamy of Santa Fe*, 130.

20. Steele, "Kit Carson and Padre Martínez," 73–74.

21. Ibid., 74.

22. Ibid., 74, 75.

23. Ibid., 75–76.

24. Steele, "The View From the Rectory," 99 n. 2.

25. Chavez, *But Time and Chance*, 149.

26. Mares, "Many Faces of Padre Antonio José Martínez," 31; McGavran [Dr. Harry G.] Papers, Charles Beaubien to Manuel Alvarez, 5 June 1856, New Mexico State Archives.

27. Howlett, *Life of the Right Reverend Joseph P. Machebeuf*, 231; Steele, "The View from the Rectory," 93; Ussel, "Memoires," 85–100.

28. Horgan, *Lamy of Santa Fe*, 243; Howlett, *Life of the Right Reverend Joseph P. Machebeuf*, 232; Steele, "The View from the Rectory," 93; Ussel, "Memoires," 85–100.

29. Steele, "The View from the Rectory," 92; Ussel, "Memoires," 85–100.

30. *New Catholic Encyclopedia*, 5:706.

31. Howlett, *Life of the Right Reverend Joseph P. Machebeuf*, 232; Steele, "The View from the Rectory," 93; Ussel, "Memoires," 85–100.

32. Howlett, *Life of the Right Reverend Joseph P. Machebeuf,* 233.

33. Chavez, *But Time and Chance,* 150; AASF, Burial book 42, Taos.

34. Chavez, *But Time and Chance,* 142; AASF, J. E. Ortiz to Lamy, J. E. Ortiz File, 23 July 1857, no. 1.

35. Chavez, *But Time and Chance,* 157.

36. Daniel-Rops, *The Church in an Age of Revolution,* 37.

37. Mares, "Many Faces of Padre Antonio José Martínez," 25.

38. Ibid., 34–35; Minge Collection, Antonio José Martínez, "Proclamation regarding Archbishop Lamy."

39. Mares, "Many Faces of Padre Antonio José Martínez," 35; Danielson Papers, *Home Mission Record,* vol. 9, no. 12, December 1860.

40. Chavez, *But Time and Chance,* 158.

41. Steele, *Works and Days,* 132 n. 32; Steele, "The View From the Rectory," 73.

42. Steele, "The View From the Rectory," 79.

43. Howlett, *Life of the Right Reverend Joseph P. Machebeuf,* 234.

44. Ibid., 237.

45. Ibid., 238.

46. Ibid., 239.

47. Horgan, *Lamy of Santa Fe,* 185, 257, 258; RA, Machebeuf to brother, Santa Fe, 16 July 1858.

48. Howlett, *Life of the Right Reverend Joseph P. Machebeuf,* 246; RA, Machebeuf to sister, Santa Fe, 28 April 1859.

49. Howlett, *Life of the Right Reverend Joseph P. Machebeuf,* 246; RA, Machebeuf to sister, Santa Fe, 28 April 1859.

50. Howlett, *Life of the Right Reverend Joseph P. Machebeuf,* 246; RA, Machebeuf to sister, Santa Fe, 28 April 1859.

51. Salpointe, *Soldiers of the Cross,* 227.

52. Ibid., 227, 224–25.

53. Horgan, *Lamy of Santa Fe,* 264.

54. "Bishops and Holy Men Galore," 82; Horgan, *Lamy of Santa Fe,* 265.

55. Horgan, 265–66.

56. Tucson Diocesan Archives, Loza Authorization, 16 January 1859.

57. Horgan, *Lamy of Santa Fe,* 268.

58. Salpointe, *Soldiers of the Cross,* 226, 227; Horgan, *Lamy of Santa Fe,* 269.

59. Horgan, *Lamy of Santa Fe,* 269; Defouri, *Historical Sketch of the Catholic Church,* 73–74.

60. Duell, *Mission Architecture as Exemplified in San Xavier del Bac,* 70; Pyne, "Rescue Mission," *Phoenix Gazette,* 13 June 1990.

61. Duell, *Mission Architecture as Exemplified in San Xavier del Bac,* 70; Ashenburg, "Mission Masterpiece: San Xavier del Bac."

62. Howlett, *Life of the Right Reverend Joseph P. Machebeuf,* 257–58.

CHAPTER 13

1. Howlett, *Life of the Right Reverend Joseph P. Machebeuf*, 287; Horgan, *Lamy of Santa Fe*, 277.

2. Horgan, *Lamy of Santa Fe*, 278.

3. Howlett, *Life of the Right Reverend Joseph P. Machebeuf*, 287.

4. Horgan, *Lamy of Santa Fe*, 277.

5. Ibid., 276; VPF, Lamy to VPF, Santa Fe, 14 June 1860.

6. Howlett, *Life of the Right Reverend Joseph P. Machebeuf*, 289.

7. Dorset, *The New Eldorado*, 6; Hafen, *Pikes Peak Gold Rush Guidebooks of 1859*, 35.

8. Dorset, *The New Eldorado*, 9; Howlett, *Life of the Right Reverend Joseph P. Machebeuf*, 274, 275.

9. Hafen, *Pikes Peak Gold Rush Guidebooks of 1859*, 30.

10. Howlett, *Life of the Right Reverend Joseph P. Machebeuf*, 274; Howlett, *Life of Bishop Machebeuf*, 439 n. for p. 284.

11. Feely, "Leadership in the Early Colorado Catholic Church," 31; *Le Semaine Religieuse*, 24 August 1889.

12. Feely, "Leadership in the Early Colorado Catholic Church," 32; Horgan, *Lamy of Santa Fe*, 278–79.

13. Horgan, *Lamy of Santa Fe*, 279; Noel, *Colorado Catholicism*, 13–14; quotation is from Feely, "Leadership in the Early Colorado Catholic Church," 31–32.

14. Dorsett, *The Queen City*, 28, 29.

15. Horgan, *Lamy of Santa Fe*, 279; Dorsett, *The Queen City*, 30.

16. Howlett, *Life of the Right Reverend Joseph P. Machebeuf*, 295–96.

17. Feely, "Leadership in the Early Colorado Catholic Church," 33.

18. Dorset, *The New Eldorado*, 78; Feely, "Leadership in the Early Colorado Catholic Church," 33; Howlett, *Life of the Right Reverend Joseph P. Machebeuf*, 295.

19. Horgan, *Lamy of Santa Fe*, 281; RA, Machebeuf to brother, Denver, 7 September 1861.

20. Howlett, *Life of the Right Reverend Joseph P. Machebeuf*, 298; RA, Machebeuf to brother, San Miguel, N.Mex., 14 January 1862.

CHAPTER 14

1. Howlett, *Life of the Right Reverend Joseph P. Machebeuf*, 299.

2. Ibid., 272.

3. Ibid., 279.

4. Ibid., 299.

5. Horgan, *Lamy of Santa Fe*, 297; Howlett, *Life of the Right Reverend Joseph P. Machebeuf*, 301.

6. Howlett, *Life of the Right Reverend Joseph P. Machebeuf*, 301.

7. Ibid., 307.

8. Ibid.

9. Ibid., 309.

10. Horgan, *Lamy of Santa Fe*, 297–98.

11. Howlett, *Life of the Right Reverend Joseph P. Machebeuf,* 310.

12. Horgan, *Lamy of Santa Fe*, 298.

13. Ibid.

CHAPTER 15

1. Feely, "Leadership in the Early Colorado Catholic Church," 31.

2. The quotation is from Dorset, *The New Eldorado*, 37; Howlett, *Life of the Right Reverend Joseph P. Machebeuf,* 316.

3. Ibid., 312.

4. Ibid., 313; RA, Machebeuf to sister, Denver, 22 July 1864.

5. Howlett, *Life of the Right Reverend Joseph P. Machebeuf,* 317.

6. Dorset, *The New Eldorado*, 158.

7. Hansen, *Colorado: A Guide to the Highest State*, 285.

8. Dorset, *The New Eldorado*, 159.

9. Ibid., 161–62.

10. Ibid., 162.

11. Fritz, *Colorado: The Centennial State*, 208.

12. Howlett, *Life of the Right Reverend Joseph P. Machebeuf,* 329.

13. Ibid., 318.

14. Ibid., 316.

15. Ibid., 317.

16. Ibid., 322–23.

17. Segale, *At the End of the Santa Fe Trail*, 84, 288n.

18. Howlett, *Life of the Right Reverend Joseph P. Machebeuf,* 324.

19. Ibid., 325.

CHAPTER 16

1. McCartney, "The Church and Fenianism," 14–15.

2. Vaughan, *A New History of Ireland*, 418; quotation is from D'Arcy, *The Fenian Movement in the United States*, 112.

3. D'Arcy, *The Fenian Movement in the United States*, 49n.

4. Feely, "Leadership in the Early Colorado Catholic Church," 34–35; DAA, Kenrick to Machebeuf, St. Louis, 19 February 1866.

5. Horgan, *Lamy of Santa Fe*, 326.

6. Howlett, *Life of the Right Reverend Joseph P. Machebeuf,* 326; Feely, "Leadership in the Early Colorado Catholic Church," 35.

7. Horgan, *Lamy of Santa Fe*, 335.

8. Ibid., 334–36.

9. Ibid., 337–38.

10. Ibid., 341.

11. Ibid., 343.

12. Ibid., 347, 348, 349.

13. Ibid., 350.

14. Howlett, *Life of the Right Reverend Joseph P. Machebeuf*, 330–31.

15. Ibid., 329; RA, Machebeuf to brother, Denver, 15 April 1867.

16. Howlett, *Life of the Right Reverend Joseph P. Machebeuf*, 335; RA, Machebeuf to sister, Denver, 13 September 1867.

17. Howlett, *Life of the Right Reverend Joseph P. Machebeuf*, 336; RA, Machebeuf to sister, Denver, 13 September 1867.

18. Horgan, *Lamy of Santa Fe*, 55; CIN/ND, Machebeuf to Purcell, Denver, 26 March 1868.

19. Horgan, *Lamy of Santa Fe*, 55; CIN/ND, Machebeuf to Purcell, Denver, 26 March 1868; Feely, "Leadership in the Early Colorado Catholic Church," 82.

20. Howlett, *Life of the Right Reverend Joseph P. Machebeuf*, 337–39; RA, Machebeuf to sister, Denver, 14 April 1868.

21. Howlett, *Life of the Right Reverend Joseph P. Machebeuf*, 340.

22. Ibid.; RA, Machebeuf to brother, New York, 8 July 1868.

23. Feely, "Leadership in the Early Colorado Catholic Church," 93; DAA, entry in Machebeuf's diary for 1869.

24. Howlett, *Life of the Right Reverend Joseph P. Machebeuf*, 341; RA, Machebeuf to brother, New York, 8 July 1868.

25. Feely, "Leadership in the Early Colorado Catholic Church," 94, 95; DAA, Kelly to Machebeuf, New York, 18 September 1874.

26. Feely, "Leadership in the Early Colorado Catholic Church," 94; DAA, Machebeuf to brother, New York, 8 July 1868.

27. Howlett, *Life of the Right Reverend Joseph P. Machebeuf*, 342; RA, Machebeuf to sister, Cleveland, 29 July 1868.

28. Howlett, *Life of the Right Reverend Joseph P. Machebeuf*, 343.

29. Ibid.

30. Merton, *The Waters of Siloe*, 120.

31. Ibid., 121–22.

CHAPTER 17

1. *New Catholic Encyclopedia*, 5:480–81.

2. Howlett, *Life of the Right Reverend Joseph P. Machebeuf*, 343.

3. Horgan, *Lamy of Santa Fe*, 355; CIN/ND, Lamy to Purcell, Santa Fe, 18 July 1868.

4. Howlett, *Life of the Right Reverend Joseph P. Machebeuf*, 344; Horgan, *Lamy of Santa Fe*, 355.

5. Howlett, *Life of the Right Reverend Joseph P. Machebeuf*, 344.

6. Ibid., 345–46.

7. Ibid., 347–48.

8. Horgan, *Lamy of Santa Fe*, 355; DAA, Lamy to whom it may concern, Santa Fe, 21 September 1868.

9. Howlett, *Life of the Right Reverend Joseph P. Machebeuf*, 349–50.

10. Ibid., 351.

11. Machebeuf, "Report on the State of Catholicism in Utah," 320–22.

12. Howlett, *Life of the Right Reverend Joseph P. Machebeuf*, 352, 344.

13. Ibid., 354.

14. Ibid., 356–57; Horgan, *Lamy of Santa Fe*, 361.

15. Howlett, *Life of the Right Reverend Joseph P. Machebeuf*, 357; DAA, Machebeuf to Raverdy, Clermont, 20 August 1869.

16. Horgan, *Lamy of Santa Fe*, 361; CIN/ND, Machebeuf to Purcell, Paris, 21 September 1869.

17. Howlett, *Life of the Right Reverend Joseph P. Machebeuf*, 357–58; DAA, Machebeuf to Raverdy, Clermont, 20 August 1869.

18. Howlett, *Life of the Right Reverend Joseph P. Machebeuf*, 358; DAA, Machebeuf to Raverdy, Clermont, 20 August 1869.

19. Joyce, *Ulysses*, 117.

20. Horgan, *Lamy of Santa Fe*, 361–62.

21. Howlett, *Life of the Right Reverend Joseph P. Machebeuf*, 364.

22. Ibid.; RA, Machebeuf to brother, Denver, 20 April 1870.

23. Howlett, *Life of the Right Reverend Joseph P. Machebeuf*, 365; RA, Machebeuf to sister, Denver, 2 July 1870.

24. Howlett, *Life of the Right Reverend Joseph P. Machebeuf*, 369.

25. Troy, "Historia Societatis Jesu in Novo Mexico et Colorado," 47.

26. Feely, "Leadership in the Early Colorado Catholic Church," 44–45; Howlett, *Life of the Right Reverend Joseph P. Machebeuf*, 373; Owens, *Jesuit Studies—Southwest*, 59.

27. Howlett, *Life of the Right Reverend Joseph P. Machebeuf*, 371; RA, Machebeuf to sister, Denver, 22 June 1872.

28. Howlett, *Life of the Right Reverend Joseph P. Machebeuf*, 371; RA, Machebeuf to sister, Denver, 22 June 1872.

CHAPTER 18

1. Howlett, *Life of the Right Reverend Joseph P. Machebeuf*, 371; RA, Machebeuf to sister, Denver, 22 June 1872.

2. Howlett, *Life of the Right Reverend Joseph P. Machebeuf*, 372; Buckner, *The Sisters of Charity of Leavenworth, Kansas*, 243; Feely, "Leadership in the Early Colorado Catholic Church," 71.

3. Howlett, *Life of the Right Reverend Joseph P. Machebeuf*, 374.

4. Feely, "Leadership in the Early Colorado Catholic Church," 53.

5. Ibid., 54.

6. Ibid.; Howlett, *Life of the Right Reverend Joseph P. Machebeuf*, 375.

7. Feely, "Leadership in the Early Colorado Catholic Church," 55.

8. Howlett, *Life of the Right Reverend Joseph P. Machebeuf,* 381.

9. Feely, "Leadership in the Early Colorado Catholic Church," 104.

10. Ibid., 95; DAA, Kelly to Machebeuf, New York, 2 September 1874.

11. Feely, "Leadership in the Early Colorado Catholic Church," 96; DAA, Kelly to Machebeuf, New York, 18 September 1874.

12. Howlett, *Life of the Right Reverend Joseph P. Machebeuf,* 376; RA, Machebeuf to sister, Denver, 14 May 1875.

13. Horgan, *Lamy of Santa Fe,* 379.

14. *College of Santa Fe 1987–89 Bulletin,* "The Past," 12–13.

15. Horgan, *Centuries of Santa Fe,* 262; Horgan, *Lamy of Santa Fe,* 379.

16. Howlett, *Life of the Right Reverend Joseph P. Machebeuf,* 381–82; Defouri, *Historical Sketch of the Catholic Church,* as cited in Howlett, *Life of the Right Reverend Joseph P. Machebeuf,* 381–82; Horgan, *Lamy of Santa Fe,* 380.

17. Horgan, *Centuries of Santa Fe,* 264.

18. Ibid., 265.

19. Horgan, *Lamy of Santa Fe,* 381; VPF, Lamy to VPF, Santa Fe, 30 July 1875, Lamy to Franchi, Santa Fe, 7 July 1875.

20. Feely, "Leadership in the Early Colorado Catholic Church," 110; DAA, Bourion to Machebeuf, Central City, 29 April 1875.

21. Feely, "Leadership in the Early Colorado Catholic Church," 108.

22. Ibid., 111.

23. Howlett, *Life of the Right Reverend Joseph P. Machebeuf,* 384.

24. Ibid., 377; RA, Machebeuf to brother, Denver, 21 April 1876.

25. *Woodstock Letters,* vol. 56, no. 2, June 1927, 215–16.

26. Howlett, *Life of the Right Reverend Joseph P. Machebeuf,* 382.

27. Machebeuf, "Woman's Suffrage," 6, 12.

28. Ibid., 3, 13, 16.

29. Owens, *Jesuit Studies — Southwest,* 64; Howlett, *Life of the Right Reverend Joseph P. Machebeuf,* 383.

30. Feely, "Leadership in the Early Colorado Catholic Church," 46, 116; DAA, Edward Bourion to Finotti, Central City, 3 May 1878.

31. Feely, "Leadership in the Early Colorado Catholic Church," 117–18.

32. Howlett, *Life of the Right Reverend Joseph P. Machebeuf,* 374; Feely, "Leadership in the Early Colorado Catholic Church," 96.

33. DAA, Machebeuf naturalization papers, 23 February 1878

34. Howlett, *Life of the Right Reverend Joseph P. Machebeuf,* 380; RA, Machebeuf to sister, Denver, 29 January 1878.

35. Howlett, *Life of the Right Reverend Joseph P. Machebeuf,* 379; RA, Machebeuf to sister, Denver, 29 January 1878.

36. Howlett, *Life of the Right Reverend Joseph P. Machebeuf,* 379; RA, Machebeuf to sister, Denver, 29 January 1878.

CHAPTER 19

1. *Woodstock Letters*, vol. 8, no. 1, January 1879, 25–32.

2. Howlett, *Life of the Right Reverend Joseph P. Machebeuf*, 389; RA, Machebeuf to sister, Denver, 22 September 1878.

3. Howlett, *Life of the Right Reverend Joseph P. Machebeuf*, 387–88.

4. Ibid.

5. *New Catholic Encyclopedia*, 8:647–48.

6. Howlett, *Life of the Right Reverend Joseph P. Machebeuf*, 390.

7. Ibid., 391.

8. Feely, "Leadership in the Early Colorado Catholic Church," 132; BCA, Machebeuf to Gibbons, Denver, 13 January 1886.

9. Feely, "Leadership in the Early Colorado Catholic Church," 123–24.

10. Owens, *Jesuit Studies — Southwest*, 72.

11. Ibid.; *Woodstock Letters*, vol, 13, no. 1, March 1884, Francis X. Tomassini to C. Piccirillo, Pueblo, Colo., 19 January 1884.

12. Howlett, *Life of the Right Reverend Joseph P. Machebeuf*, 393–94.

13. Segale, *At the End of the Santa Fe Trail*, 210–11; Horgan, *Lamy of Santa Fe*, 417–18.

14. Segale, *At the End of the Santa Fe Trail*, 211–12.

15. Stansell, *Regis: On the Crest of the West*, 25, 20–21; Vollmar, "History of the Jesuit Colleges of New Mexico and Colorado," 63; Troy, "Historia Societatis Jesu in Novo Mexico et Colorado," 129.

16. Arnold, *The View from Mt. Morrison*, 10; Stansell, *Regis: On the Crest of the West*, 27.

17. *Lettres de Jersey*, 254, P. J. Arthuis to P. Le Cain, Morrison, Colo.

18. Feely, "Leadership in the Early Colorado Catholic Church," 122; DAA, Raverdy to Machebeuf, Denver, 7, 28, 30 November 1884.

19. Feely, "Leadership in the Early Colorado Catholic Church," 124; BCA, Machebeuf to Gibbons, Denver, 10 September 1885.

20. Feely, "Leadership in the Early Colorado Catholic Church," 126.

21. Howlett, *Life of the Right Reverend Joseph P. Machebeuf*, 395.

22. Feely, "Leadership in the Early Colorado Catholic Church," 131; BCA, Machebeuf to Gibbons, Denver, 10 September 1885.

23. Feely, "Leadership in the Early Colorado Catholic Church," 131; BCA, Machebeuf to Gibbons, Denver, 10 September 1885.

24. Feely, "Leadership in the Early Colorado Catholic Church," 131; BCA, Machebeuf to Gibbons, Denver, 10 September 1885.

CHAPTER 20

1. *New Catholic Encyclopedia*, 2:592; Horgan, *Lamy of Santa Fe*, 429.

2. Horgan, *Lamy of Santa Fe*, 430; DAA, Salpointe to Machebeuf, Santa Fe, 5 April 1885.

3. Horgan, *Lamy of Santa Fe*, 430, 431; VPF, VPF to Lamy, Rome, 18 July 1885, Simeoni to Salpointe, Rome, 18 July 1885; AASF, Resignation of Archbishop Lamy, Santa Fe, 26 August 1885.

4. Feely, "Leadership in the Early Colorado Catholic Church," 132; BCA, Machebeuf to Gibbons, Denver, 13 January 1886.

5. Feely, "Leadership in the Early Colorado Catholic Church," 134, 135; BCA, Machebeuf to Gibbons, Denver, 13 January 1886.

6. Howlett, *Life of the Right Reverend Joseph P. Machebeuf*, 399.

7. Ibid., 399–400.

8. Feely, "Leadership in the Early Colorado Catholic Church," 137; BCA, Machebeuf to Gibbons, Denver, 28 December 1886.

9. Feely, "Leadership in the Early Colorado Catholic Church," 138; BCA, Machebeuf to Gibbons, Denver, 14 June 1887.

10. Feely, "Leadership in the Early Colorado Catholic Church," 145–46.

11. Howlett, *Life of the Right Reverend Joseph P. Machebeuf*, 400–401.

12. Feely, "Leadership in the Early Colorado Catholic Church," 140; BCA, Machebeuf to Gibbons, Denver, 8 March 1886.

13. Feely, "Leadership in the Early Colorado Catholic Church," 141; BCA, Machebeuf to Gibbons, Denver, 8 March 1886.

14. Feely, "Leadership in the Early Colorado Catholic Church," 139.

15. Gaffey, *Citizen of No Mean City*, 123; Mulhall, "Lawrence Scanlan," 9.

16. Riordan, *The First Half-Century of St. Ignatius Church and College*, 277.

17. *San Francisco Daily Examiner*, 29 June 1887.

18. *San Francisco Catholic Monitor*, "Right Rev. J. P. Machebeuf," 13 July 1887.

19. Stansell, *Regis: On the Crest of the West*, 36–37, 45–46; Kowald, "Sacred Heart College."

20. Horgan, *Lamy of Santa Fe*, 438.

21. Ibid.

22. Howlett, *Life of the Right Reverend Joseph P. Machebeuf*, 404.

23. Ibid., 406.

24. Ibid., 406–7; Feely, "Leadership in the Early Colorado Catholic Church," 171.

25. Feely, "Leadership in the Early Colorado Catholic Church," 171n.

26. Ibid., 540.

27. Howlett, *Life of the Right Reverend Joseph P. Machebeuf*, 408.

EPILOGUE

1. Howlett, *Life of the Right Reverend Joseph P. Machebeuf*, 411–12.

2. Steele, Thomas J., S.J., letter to the author 26 February 1995; Feely, "Leadership in the Early Colorado Catholic Church," 168–70, 539.

3. *Annales de la Propagation de la Foi, Tome Soixante-Unieme*, 462–63.

Note on Sources

The principal source of information about Joseph Machebeuf's life, as well as the life of Jean Baptiste Lamy, are the letters Machebeuf wrote to his sister and to other family members living in France. Machebeuf wrote over one hundred of these letters, from the time of his departure from Clermont until his death. The original French letters are housed in the Riom Archives of the Convent of the Visitation in Riom, France. Around the turn of the century, biographer W. J. Howlett obtained complete handwritten copies of these letters. Those copies are now in the Denver Archdiocesan Archives. In my work at the Denver Archives I secured complete copies in the original French of those handwritten letters. The most readily available English translation of the letters is Howlett's, as published in his biography. His translations are quite good, and for the most part I have followed his lead, referring to the French originals when I felt a passage was unclear or if I wished to use additional material from the same letter. Accordingly, I have cited both Howlett (for the translation), and the original letter (for content and as the primary source). Machebeuf wrote most of his letters in English during his later years (such as materials relating to diocesan decisions or his correspondence with Cardinal Gibbons) and they require no translation. For most of the Spanish-language materials, I have used Fray Angelico Chavez's translations and cited his work accordingly. The Machebeuf letters have served as sources of information not only for W. J. Howlett, but also for Paul Horgan in his biography of Lamy, for Fray Angelico Chavez in his work on Martínez and Gallegos, and for numerous other scholars. As a rule, the first source I cite is the immediate source of the material. Whenever available, however, I cite its location in closely related sources; for example, both Howlett and Horgan, or both Horgan and Chavez. My reason for doing so was to indicate that my interpretation was based on a review of both sources, which often took opposing positions.

Bibliography

Ahlborn, Richard E. "The Penitente Moradas of Abiquiú." *Contributions from the Museum of History and Technology.* Paper 59–64 on History. Washington, D.C.: Smithsonian Institution Press, 1969.

Albert, James W. *Western America in 1846–57, the original travel diary . . . with Illustrations in color from his sketchbook.* San Francisco: J. Howell, 1965.

Annales de la Propagation de la Foi. Paris: Tome Soixante-Unieme, 1889.

Archdiocesan Archives of Santa Fe.

Arnold, Sam. *The View from Mt. Morrison: The Story of a Colorado Town.* Denver: Fur Press, 1974.

Aron, Marguerite. *The Ursulines.* Translated by M. Angela Griffin, O.S.U., New York: Declan X. McMullen Co., 1947.

Ashenburg, Katherine. "Mission Masterpiece: San Xavier del Bac." *New York Times,* 8 November 1992.

Baltimore Chancery Archives.

Banvard, John. "Description of Banvard's Panorama, 1849." In *Before Mark Twain: A Sampler of Old, Old Times on the Mississippi,* edited by John Francis McDermott. Carbondale: Southern Illinois University Press, 1968.

Beaudoin, Y. *Le Grand Séminaire de Marseille (et scolasticat oblat) sous la direction des oblats de Marie immaculatae: 1827–1862, règlements of the Marseilles seminary.* Ottawa: Etudes Oblates, 1966.

Billington, Ray Allen. *The Protestant Crusade, 1800–1860: A Study into the Origins of American Nativism.* New York: MacMillan, 1938.

"Bishops and Holy Men Galore." Compiled by Alice Darton; edited by Fr. Frederick McAninch. Typescript. Tucson Diocesan Archives.

Boisard, P. *La Campagnie de Saint Sulpice: Trois Siecles d'Histoire.* Paris, 1959.

Buckner, Mary. *The Sisters of Charity of Leavenworth, Kansas.* Kansas City: Hudson-Kimberly, 1898.

Butler, A. *Butler's Lives of the Saints.* Vol. 1. New York: P. J. Kennedy and Sons, 1956.

Canu, J. *Religious Orders of Men, The Twentieth-Century Encyclopedia of Catholicism.* New York: Hawthorn Books, 1960.

Cather, Willa. *Death Comes for the Archbishop.* New York: Vintage Books, 1971.

Catholic Encyclopedia. Vol. 4. New York: Encyclopedia Press, 1908.

Chandlery, P. J., S.J. *Pilgrim-Walks in Rome: A Guide to Holy Places in the City and Its Vicinity.* London: Manresa Press, 1908.

Chavez, Fray Angelico. *But Time and Chance: The Story of Padre Martinez of Taos, 1793–1867.* Santa Fe: Sunstone Press, 1981.

——. *My Penitente Land: Reflections on Spanish New Mexico.* Albuquerque: University of New Mexico Press, 1974.

——. *Très Macho — He Said.* Santa Fe: William Gannon, 1985.

Cincinnati Archdiocesan Archives in the University of Notre Dame Archives.

College of Santa Fe 1987–1989 Bulletin. "The Past." Santa Fe: College of Santa Fe, 1987.

Daniel-Rops, H. *The Church in an Age of Revolution, 1789–1800.* London: J. M. Dent and Sons, 1965.

Danielson Papers. Mrs. Betty Danielson. Albuquerque, N.M. The collection includes microfilm copies of *Home Mission Record* and letters of Baptist missionaries in the nineteenth century. Many originals housed in American Baptist Convention Historical Library, Rochester, New York, were destroyed by fire. Copies in the Danielson Papers now serve as primary source materials.

D'Arcy, William, O.F.M. *The Fenian Movement in the United States: 1858–1886.* Washington, D.C.: Catholic University of America Press, 1947.

Darley, Alex M. *The Passionists of the Southwest, or The Holy Brotherhood: A Revelation of the 'Penitentes.'* 1893. Reprint, Glorieta, N.M.: Rio Grande Press, 1968.

de Dalmases, C., S.J. *Ignatius of Loyola, Founder of the Jesuits.* St. Louis: Institute of Jesuit Sources, 1985.

Defouri, V. Rev. James H. *Historical Sketch of the Catholic Church in New Mexico.* San Francisco, 1887.

Denver Archdiocesan Archives.

Dickens, Charles. *Pictures from Italy and American Notes for General Circulation.* Cambridge, Eng.: Houghton, Osgood, Riverside Press, 1879.

Dorset, Phyllis Flanders. *The New Eldorado: The Story of Colorado's Gold and Silver Rushes.* London: Collier-Macmillan, 1970.

Dorsett, Lyle W. *The Queen City: A History of Denver.* Vol. 1 in the Western Urban History Series. Boulder: Pruett Publishing, 1977.

Duell, Prent. *Mission Architecture as Exemplified in San Xavier del Bac.* Tucson: Arizona Archaeological and Historical Society, 1919.

Emory, Lt. W. H. *Notes of a Military Reconnaissance, 1846–1847.* U.S. and Mexican Boundary Survey, 34th Congress, 1st Session, Exec. Doc. No. 135. Washington, D.C. 1857.

Feely, Thomas Francis. "Leadership in the Early Colorado Catholic Church." Ph.D. dissertation, University of Denver, 1973.

Fritz, Percy Stanley. *Colorado: The Centennial State.* New York: Prentice-Hall, 1941.

Fuentes, Carlos. *The Buried Mirror: Reflections on Spain and the New World.* New York: Houghton Mifflin, 1992.

Gaffey, James P. *Citizen of No Mean City: Archbishop Riordan of San Francisco, 1841–1914.* San Francisco: Consortium Books, 1976.

Gibson, R. *A Social History of French Catholicism, 1789–1914.* London: Routledge, 1989.

Gougaud, H., and C. Gouvion. *France Observed.* New York: Oxford University Press, 1977.

Guild, Thelma S., and Harvey L. Carter. *Kit Carson: A Pattern for Heroes.* Lincoln: University of Nebraska Press, 1984.

Hafen, LeRoy R. *Pikes Peak Gold Rush Guidebooks of 1859.* Glendale, Calif.: Arthur Clark, 1941.

Hansen, Harry, ed. *Colorado: A Guide to the Highest State.* American Guide Series. 1941. Revised edition, New York: Hastings House, 1970.

Hennepin, Louis. *A New Discovery of a Vast Country in America.* Vol. 1. Edited by R. G. Thwaites. Chicago: A. C. McClug, 1903.

Horgan, Paul. *The Centuries of Santa Fe.* New York: E. P. Dutton, 1956.

——. *Lamy of Santa Fe: His Life and Times.* New York: Farrar, Straus and Giroux, 1975.

Howlett, W. J., *Life of the Right Reverend Joseph P. Machebeuf, D.D.* Pueblo, Colo.: Franklin Press, 1908.

——. *Life of Bishop Machebeuf.* Edited by Thomas J. Steele, S.J., and Ronald S. Brockway. Denver: Regis College, 1987.

Ignatius of Loyola. *The Spiritual Exercises of St. Ignatius.* Translated by Anthony Mottola. Garden City, N.Y.: Image Books, 1964.

Joyce, James. *Ulysses.* In *James Joyce's Dublin*, edited by Edward Quinn. London: Secker and Warburg, 1974.

Kowald, Francis X., S. J. "Sacred Heart College, Morrison, Colorado, 1884-1888." Manuscript. Regis College Archives, Denver.

Le Semaine Religieuse de Clermont, 13 September 1869.

——. 24 August 1889.

Lettres de Jersey. Vol. 14. Lettre du P. J. Arthuis au P. Le Cain, College du Sacré-Coeur à Morrison, Colorado, 1885. Gleeson Library Collection. University of San Francisco.

Lyell, Charles. "Carnival in New Orleans, 1846." In *Before Mark Twain: A Sampler of Old, Old Times on the Mississippi*, edited by John Francis McDermott. Carbondale: Southern Illinois University Press, 1968.

Lyon Archives of the Societé pour la Propagation de la Foi in University of Notre Dame Archives.

Machebeuf, Joseph P. "Reminiscences." *Catholic Universe,* 31 January 1889.
———. "Reminiscences." *Catholic Universe,* 18 October 1889.
———. "Report on the State of Catholicism in Utah." *Annales de la Propagation de la Foi.* Lyon: Tome Quarante-Unieme, 1869.
———. "Woman's Suffrage, A Lecture Delivered in the Catholic Church of Denver, Colorado, 6 February 1877," Denver: Tribune Steam Print House, 1877.
Mares, E. A. "The Many Faces of Padre Antonio José Martínez." In *Padre Martínez: New Perspectives from Taos,* edited by E. A. Mares. Taos: Millicent Rogers Museum, 1988.
———. "Padre Martínez: New Perspectives from Taos." In *Padre Martínez: New Perspectives from Taos,* edited by E. A. Mares. Taos: Millicent Rogers Museum, 1988.
———, ed. *Padre Martínez: New Perspectives from Taos.* Taos: Millicent Rogers Museum, 1988.
Maurois, A. *A History of France.* New York: Farrar, Straus and Cudahy, 1948.
McCall, Col. George Archibald. *New Mexico in 1850: A Military View.* Edited by Robert W. Frazer. Norman: University of Oklahoma Press, 1968.
McCartney, Donal. "The Church and Fenianism." In *Fenians and Fenianism,* edited by Maurice Harmon. Dublin: Scepter Books, 1968.
McGavran [Dr. Harry G.] Papers. New Mexico State Records Center and Archives, Santa Fe.
Merton, Thomas. *The Waters of Siloe.* New York: Harcourt, Brace, 1949.
Minge Collection. "Proclamation Regarding Archbishop Lamy," by Antonio José Martínez, translated by E. A. Mares. New Mexico State Records Center and Archives, Santa Fe.
Mulhall, M. Peter Damian. "Lawrence Scanlan, 1843–1915: Missionary Builder of Utah's Catholic Church." Master's thesis, University of San Francisco, 1966.
New Catholic Encyclopedia. Vols. 2, 4, 5, 6, 8, 14. New York: McGraw-Hill, 1967.
Noel, Thomas J. *Colorado Catholicism and the Archdiocese of Denver, 1857–1989.* Boulder: University Press of Colorado, 1989.
Ohio State Archeological and Historical Society. *The Ohio Guide.* New York: Oxford University Press, 1962.
Owens, M. Lilliana. *Jesuit Studies — Southwest.* No. 1, Jesuit Beginnings in New Mexico, 1867–1882. El Paso: Revista Católica Press, 1950.
Pyne, Lynn. "Rescue Mission." *Phoenix Gazette,* 13 June 1990.
Riom Archives of the Monastère de la Vistation, Riom, France.
Riordan, Joseph W., S.J. *The First Half-Century of St. Ignatius Church and College.* San Francisco: H. S. Crocker, 1905.
Salpointe, J. B. *Soldiers of the Cross: Notes on the Ecclesiastical History of New Mexico, Arizona, and Colorado.* Banning, Calif.: St. Boniface's Industrial School, 1898.
San Francisco Catholic Monitor, 13 July 1887.
San Francisco Daily Examiner, 29 June 1887.
Santa Fe Archdiocesan Archives in the University of Notre Dame Archives.

Segale, Sister Blandina. *At the End of the Santa Fe Trail.* Milwaukee: Bruce Publishing, 1948.

Simmons, Marc. *New Mexico: An Interpretive History.* 1977. Reprint, Albuquerque: University of New Mexico Press, 1988.

Stansell, Harold L., S.J. *Regis: On the Crest of the West.* Denver: Regis Educational Corp., 1977.

Steele, Eliza. "A Lady Writer Reports Some Incidents of Steamboat Travel, 1841." In *Before Mark Twain: A Sampler of Old, Old Times on the Mississippi*, edited by John Francis McDermott. Carbondale: Southern Illinois University Press, 1968.

Steele, Thomas J., S.J. "Kit Carson and Padre Martínez." In *Folk and Church in Nineteenth-Century New Mexico.* Colorado Springs: Colorado College, Hulbert Center for Southwest Studies, 1993.

———. "Padre Gallegos, Père Machebeuf, and the Albuquerque Rectory." In *Folk and Church in Nineteenth-Century New Mexico.* Colorado Springs: Colorado College, Hulbert Center for Southwest Studies, 1993.

———. "The View from the Rectory." In *Padre Martínez: New Perspectives from Taos*, edited by E. A. Mares. Taos: Millicent Rogers Museum, 1988.

———. *Works and Days.* Albuquerque: Albuquerque Museum, 1983.

St. John, Bernard. *The Blessed Virgin in the Nineteenth Century: Apparitions, Revelations, Graces.* London: Burns and Oates, 1903.

Taylor, George R. *The Transportation Revolution, 1815–1860.* Vol. 4, *The Economic History of the United States.* New York: Rinehart, 1951.

Trollope, Frances. *Domestic Manners of the Americans.* 5th edition. Edited by Donald Smalley. New York: Alfred A. Knopf, 1949.

Troy, Ferdinand M., S.J. "Historia Societatis Jesu in Novo Mexico et Colorado." Manuscript. Regis College Archives, Denver.

Tucson Diocesan Archives.

University of Notre Dame Archives.

U.S. Department of the Interior. *Chesapeake and Ohio Canal.* Washington, D.C.: Division of Publications, National Park Service, 1991.

Ussel, Gabriel. "Memoires." Photostat. Colorado Historical Society. Denver.

Vatican Archives of the Sacred Congregation for the Propagation of the Faith.

Vaughan, W. E., ed. *A New History of Ireland.* Vol. 5, *Ireland under the Union, I, 1801–1870*, Oxford: Clarendon Press, 1989.

Vollmar, Edward R., S. J. "History of the Jesuit Colleges of New Mexico and Colorado, 1867–1919." Master's thesis, St. Louis University, 1938.

Wade, Richard C. *The Urban Frontier: The Rise of Western Cities, 1790–1830.* Cambridge: Harvard University Press, 1967.

Warner, L. H. *Archbishop Lamy: An Epoch Maker.* Santa Fe: Santa Fe New Mexican Publishing, 1936.

White, Joseph Michael. *The Diocesan Seminary in the United States: A History from the 1780s to the Present.* Notre Dame: University of Notre Dame Press, 1989.

Woodstock Letters, The. Volume 8, no. 1, January 1879. Woodstock, Md.: Woodstock College Print, 1879.

——. Volume 13, no. 1, March 1884. Woodstock, Md.: Woodstock College Print, 1884.

——. Volume 56, no. 2, June 1927. Woodstock, Md.: Woodstock College Print, 1927.

Index